Karen Brown
CALIFO...

Golden Gate Bridge
San Francisco

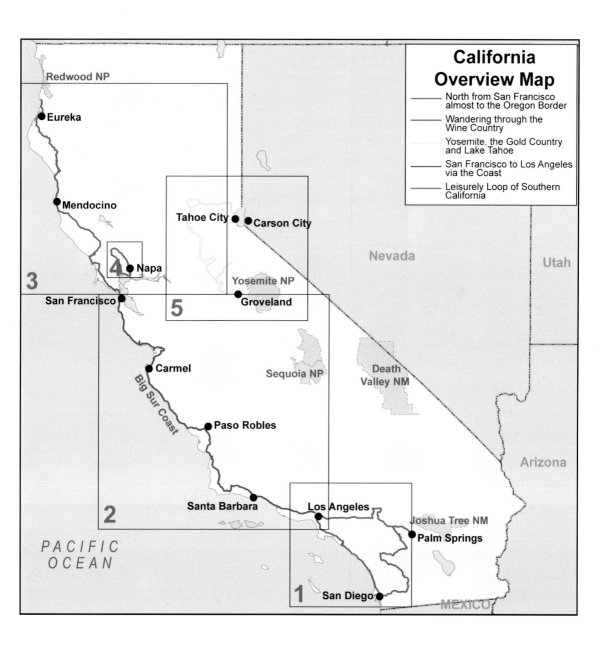

California
Overview Map

North from San Francisco
almost to the Oregon Border

Wandering through the
Wine Country

Yosemite, the Gold Country
and Lake Tahoe

San Francisco to Los Angeles
via the Coast

Leisurely Loop of Southern
California

Redwood NP

Eureka

Mendocino

Tahoe City • • Carson City

Nevada

Utah

3

4 • Napa

Yosemite NP

San Francisco

5 • Groveland

Carmel

Sequoia NP

Death
Valley NM

Big Sur Coast

Paso Robles

Arizona

2

Santa Barbara

Los Angeles

Joshua Tree NM

• Palm Springs

PACIFIC
OCEAN

1

San Diego

MEXICO

California Map 1

- Places to Stay
- Leisurely Loop of Southern California
- Ferry Route

0   10 Miles

0   10 KM

PACIFIC OCEAN

Palmdale

Victorville

Lucerne Valley

Simi Valley

Pasadena

Lake Arrowhead

Big Bear

San Bernardino

Los Angeles

Malibu

Santa Monica

Playa Del Rey

Hermosa Beach

Long Beach

Anaheim Disneyland

Santa Ana

Riverside

Newport Beach

Balboa

San Juan Capistrano

Laguna Beach

Dana Point

Catalina Island

Avalon

Idyllwild

Palm Springs

La Quinta

Mission SanAntonio de Pala

Palomar Observatory

Escondido

Rancho Santa Fe

Solana Beach

Julian

La Jolla

Pacific Beach

San Diego

Coronado

San Francisco
580
Moss
Beach
Livermore
Modesto
Yosemite NP
Mariposa
Half Moon
Bay
280
99
49
Bishop
1
San Jose
Merced
140
395
A?o
Nuevo
S.R.
17
101
Felton
Aptos
Gilroy
152
33
Kings
Canyon NP
Santa Cruz
Capitola
San Juan Bautista
99
Monterey
25
Fresno
Pacific Grove
Sequoia NP
Carmel
Pebble Beach
5
San Joaquin
Carmel Highlands
Carmel
Valley
Pinnacles NM
Soledad
Woodlake
Big Sur
Visalia
Andrew Molera SP
King City
Bixby Creek Bridge
Nepenthe
198
Big
Sur
Coast
Pfeiffer Big Sur SP
101
41
Pixley
Julia Pfeiffer Burns SP
1
San Miguel
San Simeon (Hearst Castle)
Cholame
99
Cambria
Paso Robles
46
PACIFIC
OCEAN
Morro Bay
Bakersfield
San Luis Obispo
58
Pismo Beach
Arroyo Grande
Maricopa
1
Santa Maria
166
Los Olivos
Ballard
Solvang
Lompoc
33
Buellton
5
14
Santa Barbara
101
Simi Valley
Pasadena
Ventura
Los Angeles

California Map 2

• Places to Stay

— San Francisco to Los Angeles
via the Coast

0   20 Miles

0   20 KM

Malibu
Santa
Monica
Playa Del Rey

California Map 3

- Places to Stay
- North from San Francisco almost to the Oregon Border

0 — 20 Miles
0 — 20 KM

Redwood NP
Trinidad
Humboldt Bay
Arcata
Eureka
Ferndale
Scotia
Humboldt Redwoods SP
Garberville
Leggett
Fort Bragg
Skunk RR
Mendocino
Little River
Albion
Elk
Point Arena
Gualala
Fort Ross
Willow Creek
Weaverville
Hayfork
Willits
Ukiah
Clear Lake
Lakeport
Cloverdale
Healdsburg
Forestville
Santa Rosa
Occidental
Inverness
Olema
Point Reyes NS
San Rafael
Muir Beach
Tiburon
Sausalito
Mount Shasta
McCloud
Shasta Lake
Whiskeytown
Shasta-Trinity NRA
Redding
Drakesbad
Lassen Volcanic NP
Red Bluff
Orland
Chico
Quincy
Willows
Oroville
Yuba City
Colfax
Arbuckle
Sacramento R.
Placerville
Sacramento
Fairfield
Angels
Stockton
Vallejo

PACIFIC OCEAN

101   169   299   36   44   32   99   70   89   20   80   49   50   253   128   1   12   29   37   680   505   16   26   4   3

California Map 4

- Places to Stay
- Wandering Through the Wine Country

0   5 Miles
0   5 KM

128

29   Tubbs Ln

18
19

Petrified Forest Road

Dunaweal Ln

Calistoga

17
16

Larkmead Ln

29

14

15

Calistoga Road

Lake Hennessey

Lake Berryessa

13   St Helena

12

11

128   10

Rutherford Cross Rd

Zinfandel Ln

29

9

Rutherford

Sugarloaf State Park

6

Oakville Cross Rd

8

7

12

12

Annadel State Park

Oakville

5

Yountville Cross Rd

20

21

Kenwood

Silverado Trail

22

Yountville

4

Glen Ellen

29

3

Madrone Rd

Oak Knoll Ave

23

121

121

Jack London State Park

Arnold Dr

2

Trancas St

🍇 Napa Valley

1. Hess Collection
2. Jarvis Winery
3. Trefethen Vineyards
4. Domaine Chandon
5. Goosecross Cellars
6. Plumpjack
7. Opus One
8. Robert Mondavi
9. Beaulieu Vineyards
10. Nichelini Winery
11. Rutherford Hill
12. V. Sattui Winery
13. Beringer Vineyards
14. Frank Family
15. Schramsberg
16. Sterling Vineyards
17. Clos Pegase
18. Château Montelena
19. Vincent Arroyo

🍇 Sonoma Valley

20. Landmark Vineyards
21. Château St. Jean
22. Kunde Winery
23. Benziger Winery
24. Buena Vista
25. Gloria Ferrer Winery
26. Viansa Winery

24

Sonoma

12

121

Napa

121

12

12   121

12   29

12

Petaluma

101   116

25

121   26

29

To San Francisco

Cromberg

49

89

80

Malakoff
Diggins

Reno

50

Fallon

20

Truckee

431

NV

20

Nevada
City

Tahoe
City

28

Virginia City

95

Grass
Valley

89

Lake
Tahoe

Carson City

Colfax

49

Sugar Pine
Point SP

Emerald
Bay

CA

Foresthill

Yerington

South Lake Tahoe

Coloma

50

California Map 5

80

Placerville

88

● Places to Stay
  Yosemite, the Gold Country
  and Lake Tahoe

Sacramento

0   15 Miles

16

0   15 KM

Amador City

Volcano

Calaveras
Big Trees SP

Bear Valley

Sutter Creek

26

4

108

395

Jackson

Bridgeport

99

Murphys

5

Angels
Camp

Columbia

Yosemite NP

Mono
Lake

Stockton

Sonora

Twain Harte

4

Jamestown

120

Chinese
Camp

Groveland

120

Yosemite Village

Modesto

132

49

Wawona

Mariposa

Oakhurst

Contents

To Pam and Ann

Cover painting: Golden Gate Bridge, San Francisco

Authors: June Eveleigh Brown, Clare Brown and Karen Brown.

Editors: Anthony Brown, Clare Brown, Karen Brown, June Eveleigh Brown, Debbie Tokumoto.

Illustrations: Vanessa Kale, Barbara Maclurcan Tapp.

Cover painting: Jann Pollard.

Maps & Technical support: Andrew Harris.

Distributed by National Book Network, 15200 NBN Way, Blue Ridge Summit, PA 17214, USA. Tel: 717-794-3800 or 1-800-462-6420, Fax: 1-800-338-4500, Email: custserv@nbnbooks.com

A catalog record for this book is available from the British Library.

ISSN 1535-4032

Introduction

San Francisco, Cable Car

California, the Golden State, is fascinating with its diverse regions, dramatic scenery, exciting places to visit, and appealing places to stay. There is almost too much—it can be confusing to decide the most important sights to see and the where to stay. This book is written to help you through the maze: we have done your homework for you. The first section of the book presents five detailed driving itineraries that spider-web across the state. The second section features our personal recommendations of places to stay, written with the sincere belief that where you lay your head each night makes the difference between a good and a great vacation.

About Itineraries

Five driving itineraries map and describe routes through the various regions of California so that you can choose one that includes the area you have your heart set on visiting. Each routing can easily be tailored to meet your own specific needs by leaving out some sightseeing, or linking several itineraries together.

CAR RENTAL

The itineraries are designed for travel by car. If you are staying in San Francisco at the beginning of your trip, it is not necessary to pick up a rental car until you leave the city since the public transportation system is so convenient and this is a wonderful town for walking. However, if your vacation begins in Los Angeles, you will need a car within the city to get from place to place and should pick it up on arrival at the airport.

DRIVING TIMES

California is a large state, approximately 1,000 miles from tip to toe. If you stay on the freeways, you can quickly cover large areas of territory, but if you choose to savor the beauty of the coast along California's sensational Hwy 1 or dip into the countryside along scenic back roads, plan on traveling about 30 miles in an hour and remember to allow extra time for stopping to enjoy countryside vistas.

MAPS

Itineraries are outlined on maps that precede them and, in the color section, at the front of the book. The colored section also shows all the towns in which we have a recommended place to stay: Map 1 *Leisurely Loop of Southern California*, Map 2 *San Francisco to Los Angeles via the Coast*, Map 3 *North from San Francisco almost to the Oregon border*, Map 4 *Wandering Through the Wine Country*, and Map 5 *Yosemite, The Gold Country and Lake Tahoe*. For detailed trip planning it is essential to supplement our maps with comprehensive maps. Rand McNally maps are available on our website, *www.karenbrown.com*.

PACING

At the beginning of each itinerary we suggest our recommended pacing to help you decide the amount of time to allocate to each one. The suggested time frame reflects how much there is to see and do. Use our recommendation as a guideline only, and choreograph your own itinerary based on how much leisure time you have and whether your preference is to move on to a new destination each day or settle in and use a particular place as a base.

WEATHER

At the beginning of each itinerary a brief note is given on what you can expect to encounter weather-wise in the various regions. In California a whole new climate emerges in just a short distance. The idea that the entire state is sunny and warm year-round can all too quickly be dispelled when the summer fog rolls into San Francisco or 3 feet of winter snow falls in the High Sierras.

About Places to Stay

We include a wide range of accommodation: bed & breakfasts, inns, hotels, sophisticated resorts. Some are great bargains, others very costly; some are in cities or well-trafficked areas, others in remote locations; some are quite sophisticated, others more simple. The common denominator is that each place has some special quality that makes it appealing. Our descriptions are intended to give you an honest appraisal of each property so that you can select an accommodation based on your personal preferences. The following pointers will help you appreciate and understand what to expect when traveling the "Karen Brown way."

BATHROOMS

We do not specify whether the bath is equipped with stall-shower, tub-shower, tub only, or Jacuzzi, so you'll need to ask when you make your reservation.

BREAKFAST

Breakfast is usually included in the room rate, and we make note if it is not. Although properties take great pride in their morning offerings, know that breakfast can range from a gourmet buffet feast to muffins and coffee. Sometimes breakfast is limited to a continental in your room or a hot breakfast with others in the dining room, and sometimes both. Breakfast times vary as well—some innkeepers serve a hot breakfast at a specified time, while others replenish a buffet on a more leisurely schedule. Breakfasts are as unique as the inns themselves.

CANCELLATION POLICIES

Although policies vary, places in this guide are usually more rigorous than large chain hotels about their cancellation policies. Understand their terms when securing a reservation.

CHECK-IN

Often smaller properties are specific about check-in time—generally between 3 and 6 pm. Let the innkeeper know if you are going to arrive late so that they can make special arrangements. Small establishments are frequently staffed only by the owners themselves and that window of time between check-out and check-in is often the one opportunity to shop and run personal errands.

CHILDREN

Many places in this guide do not welcome children. They cannot legally refuse accommodation to children but, as parents, we really want to stay where our children are genuinely welcome, so ask when making reservations. In the descriptions on our website (*www.karenbrown.com*) we have an icon that indicates at what age children are welcome.

Introduction–About Places to Stay

COMFORT

As influential as charm, comfort plays a deciding role in the selection of properties recommended. Firm mattresses, a quiet setting, good lighting, fresh towels, lovely bathrooms—we do our best to remember these things when considering inns. The charming decor and innkeeper will soon be forgotten if you do not enjoy a good night's sleep and comfortable stay.

CREDIT CARDS

Whether or not an establishment accepts credit cards is indicated in the list of icons at the bottom of each description by the symbol [CREDIT]. We have also specified in the accommodation description which cards are accepted as follows: AX–American Express, MC–MasterCard, VS–Visa, or simply, all major.

FOOD

The majority of places featured in this guide do not have restaurants, but staff are always very knowledgeable about and happy to recommend local favorites. Frequently, in addition to breakfast, tea or wine and hors d'oeuvres are served in the afternoon or evening either at a specific time or on a self-serve basis at your leisure. Sometimes, if you request it in advance, a picnic lunch can also be prepared.

If you have any special dietary requirements, most properties will gladly try to accommodate you. Not having the resources a restaurant would have, they usually plan a breakfast menu that features one entrée, making sure to have the necessary ingredients on hand. It is best to mention any special requests at the time you make your reservation, both as a courtesy and from a practical point of view. The innkeeper will want the chance to stock items such as low-fat dairy products, egg substitutes, and sugar-free syrups.

ICONS

Icons allow us to provide additional information about our recommended properties. We have introduced the following icons in this guide to supplement each property's description. For easy reference, an icon key can also be found on the inside back cover flap.

Services:

* Air conditioning in rooms
* Beach nearby
* Breakfast included
* Children welcome
* Cooking classes offered
* Credit cards accepted
* Dinner upon request
* Direct-dial tel. in room
* Dogs by special request
* Elevator
* Exercise room
* Internet for guests
* Mini-refrigerator in rooms
* Some non-smoking rooms
* Parking (free or paid)
* Restaurant
* Spa (massage etc.)
* Swimming pool
* Tennis
* Television with English channels in guestrooms
* Wedding facilities
* Wheelchair friendly
* Wireless for guests

Activities:

* Golf course nearby
* Hiking trails nearby
* Horseback riding nearby
* Skiing nearby
* Water sports nearby
* Wineries nearby

RESERVATIONS

The two best ways to make a reservation are to telephone or, if an inn participates in our website, to connect to them online. Another convenient and efficient way to request a reservation is by fax. When planning your trip, be aware that many inns require a two-night stay on weekends and over holidays.

RESPONSIBILITY

All of the properties featured have been visited and selected solely on their own merits. Our judgments are made based on charm, setting, cleanliness, and, above all, the warmth of welcome. Each property has its own appeal, and we try to present you with a very honest appraisal. However, no matter how careful we are, sometimes we misjudge a places merits, or the ownership changes, or—unfortunately—standards are not maintained. If you find that a property does not meet the standards we promise, please let us know, and accept our sincere apologies.

ROOM RATES

Rates can vary often, between high-season, low-season, midweek, weekend, and holiday pricing. We have quoted high-season rates for 2010, generally a range from the lowest-priced bedroom for two people (singles usually receive a very small discount) to the most expensive suite, including breakfast. The rates given are those quoted to us by the property. Please use these figures as a guideline and be certain to ask at the time of booking what the rates are and what they include. Discounted rates may well be available, so do ask about them.

We have not given prices for "special" rooms such as those that can accommodate three people traveling together. Discuss options when making reservations. We make a note of all exceptions, e.g. when an inn does not include breakfast with the price of your room. The rates we quote do not include tax.

SMOKING

In general it is best to assume that smoking is not appropriate. If you need a place where smoking is allowed, be sure to ask the hotel about the specifics of their policy.

SOCIALIZING

Most properties in this guide offer a conviviality rarely found in a "standard" hotel. The gamut runs from intimate gatherings around the kitchen table to sharing a cocktail hour in the sitting room. Breakfast may be a formal meal served at a set hour when the guests gather around the dining-room table, or it may be served buffet-style over several hours where guests have the option to sit down and eat alone or join other guests at a larger table. Some places will bring a breakfast tray to your room. After check-in, many properties offer afternoon refreshment, such as tea and cakes or wine and hors d'oeuvres, which may be seen as another social opportunity. Choose the property that seems to offer the degree of intimacy or privacy that you desire. It's entirely possible to find places that downplay the social aspect of your visit, if privacy is what you're after.

WEBSITE

Please visit the Karen Brown website (*www.karenbrown.com*) in conjunction with this book. Our website provides trip planning assistance, new discoveries, post-press updates, feedback from you, our readers, the opportunity to purchase goods and services that we recommend (rail tickets, car rental, travel insurance, etc.), and one-stop shopping for our guides, associated maps and watercolor prints. Most of our favorite places to stay are featured with color photos and direct website and email links. Also, we invite you to participate in the Karen Brown's Readers' Choice Awards. Be sure to visit our website and vote so your favorite properties will be honored.

WHEELCHAIR ACCESSIBILITY

If a property has *at least* one guestroom that is accessible by wheelchair, it is noted with the symbol ♿. This is not the same as saying it meets full ADA standards.

San Francisco
to Los Angeles
via the Coast

● Orientation/Sightseeing

✂ Itinerary Route

San Francisco

580

Half Moon
Bay

280

1

San Jose

Año
Nuevo
S.R.

17

101

Felton

Aptos

Gilroy

Santa Cruz

Capitola

San Juan Bautista

Merced

Monterey

Pacific Grove

Carmel

Pebble Beach

5

Fresno

Carmel Highlands

Big Sur

99

Andrew Molera SP

King City

Bixby Creek Bridge

Nepenthe

Big Sur Coast

Pfeiffer Big Sur SP

101

Julia Pfeiffer Burns SP

1

Paso
Robles

San Simeon
(Hearst Castle)

Cambria

Atascadero

Morro Bay

Bakersfield

San Luis Obispo

PACIFIC
OCEAN

Pismo Beach

1

Los Olivos
Ballard

Solvang

5

Santa Barbara

101

Los Angeles

Malibu

San Francisco to Los Angeles via the Coast

Golden Gate Bridge

You can drive between San Francisco and Los Angeles in a day or fly in an hour. But rather than rushing down the freeway or hopping aboard an airplane, drive leisurely along the coast between these two metropolises and enjoy the quaintness of Carmel, the charm of Santa Barbara, the splendor of the Big Sur coastline, the opulence of William Randolph Hearst's hilltop castle, and the fun of experiencing a bit of Denmark in Solvang. Also intertwined in this itinerary are stops to appreciate a piece of California's colorful heritage—her Spanish missions. This routing roughly follows the footsteps of the Spanish padres who, in the 1700s, built a string of missions (about a day's journey apart on horseback) along the coast of California from the Mexican border to just north of San Francisco. Today many of these beautiful adobe churches and their surrounding settlements have been reconstructed and are open as museums, capturing a glimpse of life as it was lived by the Spaniards and the Indians in the early days of colonization.

Recommended Pacing: We recommend a minimum stay of two or three nights in San Francisco, affording two full days for a quick introduction to the city, and definitely more time if your schedule allows. San Francisco is a beautiful city and there is much to explore and enjoy. From San Francisco, if you take the direct route, you can easily drive to Carmel in about three hours. However, located just south of San Francisco is the Año Nuevo Reserve, where you can observe the enormous elephant seals in their natural habitat. It takes several hours to walk around the secluded beaches where the seals congregate, so if you want to visit the reserve en route to Carmel, we recommend an early start from the city. Plan on at least two to three nights (or again, if possible, more) in the Carmel, Pacific Grove, or Monterey area. One day can easily be devoured exploring the Monterey Bay Aquarium, Cannery Row, and the wharf. Another full day is needed to drive the Seventeen-Mile Drive, walk the spectacular Point Lobos State Park, visit the beautiful Carmel Mission—and we have yet to even discuss shopping in downtown Carmel! From Carmel, you can drive the dramatic coastline of Big Sur and on to Santa Barbara in four to five hours, but plan to overnight in Cambria if you want to include even just one of the tours of Hearst Castle and visit the artists' town of Cambria—it's too much to do in one day. From Cambria you can go directly to Santa Barbara or tarry for a couple of days and explore the wine region around Paso Robles. Santa Barbara is a beautiful, charming city with an expanse of lovely beach. You'd be disappointed if you didn't plan at least two nights in the area before continuing on to Los Angeles. **The itinerary route is also outlined on Map 2 at the front of the book.**

Weather Wise: San Francisco and the coast are often foggy during June, July, and August. The farther south you go, the earlier in the day the fog burns off. The northern California coast is cool and rainy during the winter. In southern California the weather is warmer year-round and traditionally less rain falls during the winter.

When you ask travelers around the world, "What is your favorite city?" many times the answer is "San Francisco." And it is no wonder: **San Francisco** really is special, a magical town of unsurpassed beauty—spectacular when glistening in the sunlight, equally enchanting when wrapped in fog. But the beauty is more than skin deep: San Francisco offers a wealth of sightseeing, fabulous restaurants, splendid shopping, and a refreshing climate.

There are many large, super-deluxe hotels in San Francisco and we recommend a marvelous selection of small, intimate inns. Study our various recommendations to see what most fits your personality and pocketbook. Be advised that hotel space is frequently tight, so make reservations as far in advance as possible.

A good way to orient yourself in San Francisco is to take a half-day city sightseeing tour (brochures on these tours should be available at your hotel) and then return to the destinations that most catch your fancy. If you like to study before you arrive, there are entire guidebooks devoted to San Francisco and the Visitors Bureau will send you an information packet on what to see and do (San Francisco Convention and Visitors Bureau, 900 Market Street, San Francisco, CA 94101, *www.sfvisitor.org,* 415-391-2000). To keep you on the right track, the following is an alphabetical listing of some of our favorite sights.

Alcatraz: Wreathed in mystery, the often fog-shrouded island of Alcatraz lies in the heart of San Francisco Bay, a scant mile and a quarter from the sights and sounds of downtown. The site of the first lighthouse on the west coast, in operation since 1854, "The Rock" has since been used as an army fortress and a jail. The latter, supposedly escape proofed by the icy-cold waters and dangerous currents of the Bay, was home to criminals deemed "incorrigible" by the Federal penal system. Numbered among its inmates were Al Capone and Robert Stroud, the infamous "Birdman of Alcatraz." Access is by ferry from the San Francisco waterfront. Trips run daily but are extremely popular and should be booked well in advance (contact TeleSails, 415-705-5555, *www.telesails.com*). The island is now under the control of the National Park Service and ranger-guided and audio-assisted tours provide a fascinating insight into the island's history, as well as affording spectacular views of San Francisco and its bridges. Be sure to wear sturdy, comfortable shoes and warm clothing.

Cable Cars: You cannot leave San Francisco without riding one of the colorful trolleys that make their way up and down the breathtakingly steep city hills. Rather than touring by cab or bus, plan your sightseeing around hopping on and off cable cars. You can travel easily from the shopping district of Union Square past Chinatown and the "crookedest street in the world"—Lombard, and on to the Ghiradelli Square-Fisherman's Wharf area. For a behind-the-scenes look at this charmingly antiquated transit system, visit the Cable Car Museum at the corner of Washington and Mason Streets. Here you can view the huge cables that pull the cars from below the streets and a historical display that includes the very first cable car.

California Palace of the Legion of Honor: has a spectacular setting on a bluff in Lincoln Park overlooking the ocean. One of the original castings of Rodin's famous *Thinker* welcomes you to the San Francisco replica of the Palais de la Légion d'Honneur in Paris where Napoleon first established his new government. A self-guided audio tour is available to steer you through the galleries, which include one devoted to medieval art (there's a ceiling from a 15th-century Spanish palace), a British gallery with paintings by Gainsborough and Constable, and 19th- and 20th-century galleries with their popular works by Monet, Renoir, and Picasso. Located at 34th Avenue and Clement Street. (415-750-3600, *www.thinker.org)*

Chinatown: Just a few short blocks from Union Square you enter beneath the dragon arch (at the corner of Bush Street and Grant Avenue) into another world with street signs in Chinese characters, tiny grocery stores displaying Chinese vegetables and delicacies, apothecary shops selling unusual remedies, spicy aromas drifting from colorful restaurants, older women bustling about, and the surrounding hum of unfamiliar phrases. Of course, the streets are jammed with tourists and locals and there is a plethora of rather tacky, but fun-to-explore souvenir shops. Don't limit your exploration of Chinatown to the main thoroughfare of Grant Avenue: poke down the intriguing little alleys and side streets. Plan a visit to 56 Ross Alley, the Golden Gate Fortune Cookie Factory. Down another alley, at 17 Adler Place, is the Chinese Historical Society of America—a small museum portraying the story of the Chinese immigration. The Chinese Cultural Center (415-986-1822, *www.c-c-c.org*), housed in the Holiday Inn at Kearny and Washington streets, offers fascinating docent-led heritage and culinary walks affording a glimpse of the "real Chinatown." It also has a wonderful small museum offering an ever-changing schedule of exhibits.

Coit Tower: Coit Tower, located at the top of Telegraph Hill, is a relic of old San Francisco and fun to visit—not only because of the great view, but because its story is so very "San Francisco." The money to construct the watch tower, which resembles the nozzle of a fire hose, was willed to the city by the wealthy Lillie Hitchcock Coit, a volunteer fireman (or should we say firewoman) who dearly loved to rush to every blaze wearing her diamond-encrusted fire badge. A mural on the ground floor provides a vivid depiction of early California life.

Fisherman's Wharf to Ghiradelli Square: This portion of the waterfront is very popular with tourists. **Pier 39** is lined with New England-style shops; nothing authentic, but a popular shopping and restaurant arcade complete with street performers and a beautiful two-tier carousel. Pier 39 is also home to a new aquarium and some very boisterous and amusing sea lions (415-981-7437, *www.pier39.com*). Pier 41 is where you purchase tickets for the popular excursion to Alcatraz (see listing). **Fisherman's Wharf**, where fishermen haul in their daily catch, has long been a favorite with tourists. It is difficult to find even the heart of Fisherman's Wharf behind all the trinket-filled souvenir shops and tourist arcades, but look carefully and sure enough, you will see the colorful fishing boats bobbing about in the water at the waterfront between Jones and Taylor Streets. Nearby, Fish Alley, a small pier extending out into the harbor, affords a good view of the fishing fleet and the aroma of fresh fish mingling with the salty air. At the corner of Leavenworth and Jefferson **The Cannery**, formerly a fruit cannery, is today an attractive shopping complex. At the foot of Hyde Street **Hyde Street Pier** is home to the Maritime Museum's fleet of historic ships, several of which can be boarded and explored. Our favorite is the *Balclutha* (1886), a three-masted merchant ship typical of the hundreds that came round the Horn to San Francisco. Inspect the comfortable captain's quarters and cramped crew's quarters and exhibits of nautical gear. Just beyond the **Hyde Street cable car turnaround** lies **Ghiradelli Square**, a lovely brick building that used to house the Ghiradelli chocolate factory, now a complex of attractive stores and restaurants. The ship-shaped building in Aquatic Park (in front of Ghiradelli Square) is the land base of the **Maritime Museum**, full of displays on the history of water transportation from the 1800s to the present, including marvelous photos of old San Francisco. (415-447-5000, *www.nps.gov/safr*)

Golden Gate Bridge and **Fort Point:** San Francisco's symbol is the Golden Gate Bridge with its graceful orange arches. The visitors' viewing area on the San Francisco side offers stunning views (if the fog is not in) and access to the pedestrian walkway across the bridge (2½ miles round trip, wear warm clothing). At the base of the Golden Gate Bridge's south pier, Fort Point, built in 1861 as one of the west coast's principal points of defense, provides a fascinating insight into military life during that period. (415-556-1693, *www.nps.gov/fopo*)

Golden Gate Park: You will need to take a bus or taxi to Golden Gate Park, but don't miss it. The park encompasses over 1,000 acres, so large you really cannot hope to see it all, but many attractions are located near one another. Wander through the traditional **Japanese Tea Garden** and enjoy tea and cookies Japanese-style at the tea house (415-752-1171). Across the road from the Japanese Tea Garden, the **Arboretum** features landscaped gardens of many countries and regions including their indigenous plants and flowers. Art lovers head for the adjacent **De Young Museum** whose copper cover roof rises above the trees. It's modern architecture is as impressive as its splendid collection of paintings by American artists and art of the native Americas, Africa, and the Pacific (415-863-3330). Off John F. Kennedy Drive, you can also visit the **Rose Garden** with hundreds of species of roses in every color and where, for the price of an almond, you'll have bluebirds eating our of your hand. A little further east and open year round is the beautifully renovated **Conservatory of Flowers** housing many tropical flowers including a gorgeous lily pond. The 12,000 square-foot Victorian greenhouse is the oldest existing glass and wood conservatory in the United States. If you are hungry, you might want to consider the **Beach Chalet**, a restaurant on the ocean side of the park near the Dutch Windmill. The menu offers good, modern American fare matched with their list of brewery selections. The building once served as the changing rooms for Ocean Beach. On the first floor are beautifully restored murals of San Francisco in its early days and guests enjoy unobstructed views of the surf from tables by the second-floor expanse of window. (415-386-8439)

Lombard Street

Lombard Street: Lombard is an ordinary city street—except for one lone, brick-paved block between Hyde and Leavenworth where the street goes crazy and makes a series of hairpin turns as it twists down the hill. Pretty houses border each side of the street, and banks of hydrangeas add color. Start at the top and go down what must be the crookedest street in the world: it is lots of fun. The Hyde Street cable car makes a stop at the top of the hill and from here you can easily walk down to Fisherman's Wharf.

Mission San Francisco de Assisi: This mission at Dolores and 16th Streets is frequently referred to as the Mission Dolores. If you are interested in Californian missions, you will find a visit here worthwhile. It was on this spot that San Francisco was born when Father Francisco Palou founded his mission here in 1776. At one time this was a large complex of warehouses, workshops, granaries, a tannery, soap shop, corrals, Indian dwellings, and even an aqueduct. Today, all that is left is the chapel and next to it the garden where gravestones attest to the fragility of life. Although small, the chapel is beautiful in its simplicity with 4-foot-thick adobe walls and massive redwood timbers. (415-621-8203)

Museum of Modern Art (MOMA): A cylindrical, striped turret rising from blocks of red bricks gives a hint of what lies within this futuristic building at 151 Third Street. To help you appreciate the exhibits, an audio-cassette can be rented in the lobby to guide you through the museum's permanent collection of abstract expressionistic paintings and avant-garde photography. Even if you are not a fan of modern art, you will be awed by the building's interior: the space soars upwards from the lobby for five stories to a broad catwalk that runs below the cylindrical glass skylight (415-357-4000, *www.sfmoma.org*). Just across the street from the MOMA lie the **Yerba Buena Gardens and Galleries**. The gardens are an oasis of tranquility where a broad expanse of grass leads to a cascading sheet of water—a perfect place to relax and people watch. The galleries offer changing exhibits that showcase the San Francisco Bay Area's cultural diversity. On the top floor, encircled by windows and a spectacular view of the city skyline, is an ice-skating rink. (Open daily 1 pm to 5 pm and evenings with some limitations. 750 Folsom Street between 3rd and 4th, 415-777-3727, *www.skatebowl.com.*)

Sausalito and **Tiburon:** An enjoyable excursion is to take the ferry from Pier 43½ in San Francisco to Sausalito or Tiburon, small towns just across the bay full of intriguing shops, art galleries, and wonderful restaurants. As a bonus, en route you enjoy gorgeous vistas of San Francisco and the Golden Gate Bridge. For information call the Red and White Fleet at 415-673-2900, or visit their website at *www.redandwhite.com*.

Theater: For theater buffs, San Francisco offers an excellent variety of entertainment. Most theaters are located in the heart of the city within walking distance of Union Square. In addition, San Francisco has fine opera and ballet. The San Francisco Visitors Bureau (415-391-2000, *www.sfvisitor.org*) can send you a packet with information on what is going on. You can also call the "hotline" at 415-391-2001 for a recording of all current events.

Union Square: In the center of the city sits Union Square, hallmarked by a small park around which tower deluxe hotels and fancy department stores. Do not tarry too long at the "biggies" because just beyond the square lies every specialty shop imaginable from department stores to any number of designer boutiques. The Crocker Galleria at 50 Post houses collections from top names in international design and many fine specialty stores and restaurants.

Union Street: Union Street (between Laguna and Steiner), lined with lovely restored Victorian houses, offers a wonderful variety of quaint gift shops, elegant boutiques, beautiful antique stores, small art galleries, excellent restaurants, and a multitude of intriguing little shops hidden down tiny brick-paved lanes.

Housed in the Presidio's former army barracks, with a view of the nearby Golden Gate Bridge, is the **Walt Disney Family Museum**. Through videos and exhibits the museum leads you chronologically through Walt's life with much of the narration being provided by the man himself. His experiments with early cartoons, the breakthrough with Mickey Mouse, the production of early animation films, his move into live movies, TV and the building of

Disneyland. (Closed Tuesdays, open 10am to 6pm, the Presidio, 104 Montgomery Street, 415-345-6800, *www.waltdisney.org.*)

It's a three-hour drive south from San Francisco to Carmel taking the scenic Hwy 280 to San Jose and Hwys 17 and 1 on to Carmel. But rather than head directly to Carmel, we suggest you meander down the coast, following the contours of the spectacular coastline, enjoying a number of sights en route—a journey that will deserve a couple of days.

Leave San Francisco to the south on 19th Avenue and take Hwy 280 south (direction San Jose) for 20 miles to Hwy 92 which you take west to Half Moon Bay. Turn left on **Half Moon Bay's** Main Street. Park just across the bridge and visit **Half Moon Bay Feed and Fuel**, an authentic country store selling saddles, rabbits, chickens, animal feed, and farm implements. Poke your head in the variety of shops, restaurants, and art galleries that line the street. Leaving Half Moon Bay, continue down Main Street and join Hwy 1, the coast road, to the south of town.

If it is anywhere approaching a meal time, 17 miles south of Half Moon Bay, take a detour into **Pescadero** to **Duarte's Tavern** famous for its artichoke dishes and fresh fish. Founded in 1894 it's a local landmark.

Thirty miles south of Half Moon Bay is the **Año Nuevo State Reserve**, home to elephant seals whose huge males with their trunk-like snouts reach a whopping 6,000 pounds. From mid-December to the end of March park docents conduct a 3-mile round-trip hike to the breeding grounds of these car-size mammals. Reservation lines open in October for the following season (800-444-7275). If you are not able to book several months in advance, call the park directly at 650-879-2025 and they may be able to advise you if last-minute tickets are available. We have, in the past, secured tickets by arriving at 8:30 am and queuing at the entrance booth for tickets for tours that day. Outside of the breeding season obtaining permits to view the seals (there are often also a great many sea lions in residence) is not a problem: tickets are issued on arrival and you follow the well-marked path to the distant beach where the seals are found. Outside of the breeding season, the best time to visit is during July and August when the juvenile males return to molt.

Ten miles south of Año Nuevo you come to the cluster of houses that makes up the town of **Davenport**. Fronting Hwy 1 is the **New Davenport Cash Store**, which sells everything from handmade jewelry to local pottery and whose restaurant offers a varied and healthful menu with excellent soups and tasty vegetarian dishes.

Downtown **Santa Cruz**, 11 miles south of Davenport, was badly damaged in the 1989 earthquake, but a newly revived Pacific Avenue exhibits all the laid-back charm the town is noted for, with outdoor cafés, a variety of shops and galleries, and numerous street performers. Years ago this busy seaside town, with its bustling **boardwalk** and amusement park bordering a broad stretch of white-sand beach, was a popular day trip for workers in San Francisco. The rides include a heart-stopping wooden roller coaster and a wonderful old-fashioned carousel.

If you enjoy riding trains, you can take the old-fashioned diesel that departs from the boardwalk twice a day during the summer months for the 60-minute ride to Felton. Here you board an old steam train of the **Roaring Camp Railroad**, a train that winds up into a redwood forest. The train leaves several times a day from its main station in **Felton** (except on Christmas) along narrow-gauge tracks built to carry lumber out of the forest. The conductor tells stories of the old days as the train circles up through the trees, making a brief stop at a beautiful ring of redwoods before heading back to the depot. It is possible to take a picnic with you, alight at the top, and take the next train back. Call for schedules and directions: 831-335-4400.

Leave Santa Cruz heading south on Hwy 1 and travel for about 20 miles to Hwy 129 where you head east. Continue on the 129 for approximately 16 miles through small farms and rolling hills to **San Juan Bautista** and its most attractive **mission**. There is far more to see here than just an old church, for an area of the town has been restored to the way it was 150 years ago with the mission as its focus. Facing the square is the restored

Plaza Hotel, now a museum where tickets are sold for admission to the attractions in the park. The focal point of the sightseeing is, of course, the mission, but do not end your touring there. Directly across from the mission is a most interesting house, nicely restored, and furnished as it must have looked many years ago. Adjacent to this is a blacksmith's shop and stables where there is a colorful display of old coaches. Next door to the Plaza Hotel is another home now open as a museum with period furnishings.

Follow Hwy 156 west for a couple of miles until it merges with Hwy 101 going south to the Monterey Peninsula. As you pass through Prunedale, begin to watch for signs indicating a sharp right-hand turn on Hwy 156 west to the Monterey Peninsula. Along the way, fields of artichokes dominate the landscape as you near Castroville, the artichoke capital of the world. When you begin to smell the sea air, stay in the left lane following signs for Hwy 1 south to the Monterey Peninsula. As you approach Monterey, dunes lining the sweep of the bay come into view.

The main sightseeing attractions in **Monterey** are in two areas: the old town and the marina, and the Monterey Bay Aquarium and Cannery Row. A bayside walking and biking path runs from the Marina beside Cannery Row to the Aquarium and beyond to the adjoining town of Pacific Grove. A fun way to explore Monterey is to rent a side-by-side tricycle near the aquarium and pedal to the Marina.

Kayaking lets you enjoy another perspective of Monterey—looking back at the town and gorgeous beaches from the bay. Open-deck kayaks make the sport easy even for the inexperienced and paddling out amongst the seals and otters is fun. All equipment, loose-fitting rain gear (although plan on getting wet), life jackets, and instruction are included in the rental price. We rented from **A B Seas Kayak.** Readers receive a 20% discount on the three-hour package. Located on the Coastguard pier, 32 Cannery Row, 831-647-0147.

In **Old Town** a 3-mile walking tour links the restored buildings of early Monterey. The old adobe structures are interesting and a sharp contrast to the bustle of nearby

Fisherman's Wharf, a quaint wooden fishing pier lined with shops and restaurants. At the end of the pier huge sea lions vie for the fish cast off the fishing boats.

Cannery Row, once the center of this area's thriving sardine industry (the fish are long gone) and brought vividly to life by John Steinbeck in his novels featuring Doc and the boys, is now filled with small stores and tucked into an old warehouse are some outlet stores. The premier attraction in Monterey is the adjacent **Monterey Bay Aquarium** with over 200 galleries and exhibits. The centerpieces of the Aquarium are the huge glass tanks that showcase the underwater world of the local offshore marine habitat from the diverse tidepools to the multitude of life in the Monterey Bay: one tank is populated by huge sharks and colorful schools of fish while another contains a mature kelp forest teeming with fish. Other exhibits include; playful otters and seahorses. The Outer Bay exhibit, a vast tank of water representative of the outer ocean, brings a new dimension to the Aquarium and leaves the visitor with a memorable impression of just how little is known about this body of water. (*www.montereybayaquarium.org,* 831-648-4888)

Monterey is all hustle and bustle (especially in summer) and it is nice to continue on to the neighboring, much quieter town of **Pacific Grove**. To reach Pacific Grove, follow the road in front of the Aquarium up the hill and make a right turn onto Ocean View Boulevard, a lovely drive lined on one side with gracious Victorian homes and splendid views of the sea on the other. Besides being an affluent residential community, Pacific Grove is famous for the Monarch butterflies that return faithfully each October and cluster in the grove of trees next to Butterfly Grove Inn on Lighthouse Avenue.

Carmel lies just a few miles beyond Pacific Grove and there is no more perfect way to arrive than along the famous Seventeen-Mile Drive, which meanders around the Monterey Peninsula coastline between the two towns. The route is easy to find as the road that leads to the "drive" intersects Lighthouse Avenue and is appropriately called The Seventeen-Mile Drive.

The Seventeen-Mile Drive loops through an exclusive residential area of multimillion-dollar estates and gorgeous golf courses. Because the land is private a toll per car is levied at the entrance gate, where you'll receive a map indicating points of interest along the way. The scenic drive traces the low-lying shore, passes rocky coves where kelp beds are home to sea lions, sea otters, cormorants, and gulls (remember to bring your binoculars), and meanders through woodlands where Monterey pines gnarled by the wind stand sentinel on lonely headlands. Along the drive is the famous **Pebble Beach Golf Course**, site of the National Pro-Am Golf Championship each January.

Carmel—filled with Hansel-and-Gretel-style cottages nestled under pines and surrounded by flower-filled gardens—is one of California's most appealing towns. Tourists throng the streets lined with appetizing candy shops, beckoning bakeries, a wonderful selection of restaurants, enticing boutiques, pretty gift stores, and attractive art galleries. The picturesque combination of fairy-tale cottages and a sparkling blue bay makes Carmel so very special. Its main street slopes gently down the hill to a glorious white-sand beach crested by windswept dunes. Just south of town is the **Carmel Mission**, established in 1770 by Father Junipero Serra. Beautifully restored and fronted by a pretty garden, the mission was Father Serra's headquarters. It is from here that the stalwart little priest set out to expand the chain of missions. A small museum shows the simple cell in which Father Serra slept on a hard wooden bed. The church itself, with its Moorish tower, star-shaped window, and profusion of surrounding flowers, has a most romantic appearance.

Carmel has another very special attribute, it is completely dog friendly. The whole town welcomes them and caters to them in every way. Not only do many hotels accept dogs of all sizes, but some even have a packet of doggie treats tied with ribbons awaiting their canine guests. When you take a walk, you find the beach abounds with dogs happily romping beside their masters. When you go shopping, you discover pet boutiques displaying an unbelievable assortment of items: raincoats, bonnets bedecked with flowers, jeweled collars, booties, umbrellas, goggles, hand made sweaters, and sun visors. Browsing through the shopping arcade, you find a whimsical stone fountain with a dog's head. Cool water cascades into three pools, all set at the perfect height for a thirsty pet. A favorite pet friendly restaurant is **Forge in the Forest** whose dog menu includes mouthwatering items as the Quarter Hounder (for the hound with a hankering for beef), Hen House Chicken Strips (grilled and sliced boneless chicken breast), Hot Diggity Dog (an all beef kosher dog for your dog), and the Good Dog (eight ounces of grilled New York steak for that very, very good dog). If you want a night on the town without your pet, hotels have a list of pet sitters.

Located just south of Carmel on Hwy 1, **Point Lobos State Reserve** is, in our estimation, the premier place to enjoy the California coast. A small admission fee entitles you to day use of the park. Walk along the coastal trails and venture down wooden steps to secluded sandy beaches. Rocky coves are home to sea lions, harbor seals, and sea otters. Between December and May migrating gray whales surface and dive offshore. Bring your binoculars and head for Sea Lion Point and the headland on Cypress Grove Trail, the best places to see the whales. Walking trails and picnic areas are well marked and the times of guided nature walks are posted at the entrance gate. (831-624-4909, *www.ptlobos.org*)

Believe everything you ever read about the beauties of the **Big Sur Coastline**: it is truly sensational. However, hope for clear weather, because on foggy or rainy days an endless picture of stunning seascapes becomes a tortuous drive around precipitous cliff roads. (In poor weather, you may wish to take the inland route to Cambria by following the picturesque Carmel Valley Road east to Hwy 101 where you then head south. When you come to Hwy 46, turn west. The road intersects with coastal Hwy 1 just south of Cambria.) As you drive south on Hwy 1, you have an indication that you are approaching Big Sur when you see the road sign "Hill Curves—63 miles," which is exactly what the road does as it clings precipitously to the edge of the cliff. While the road is quite narrow, there are plenty of turnouts and opportunities for taking photos.

If you have plenty of time, you might want to consider a very scenic 10-mile detour east off Hwy 1 following the **Old Coast Road** through beautiful redwood groves and country ranchland. To access the Old Coast Road, turn left just before crossing the dramatic span of Bixby Creek Bridge. You'll be on your own for most of the journey and the road will deposit you back on Hwy 1, across from the entrance to the wonderful **Andrew Molera State Park**. Allow approximately one hour for the adventure, and be aware that the road is not passable after heavy rains.

If you opt to remain on scenic Hwy 1, you will find its passage dramatic over the much-photographed, long concrete span of **Bixby Creek Bridge**. A few miles later, the rocky volcanic outcrop topped by the Point Sur lighthouse appears. About 40 miles south of Carmel is the **Pfeiffer Big Sur State Park** with its camping facilities and many miles of hiking trails among coastal redwood groves. (831-667-2315)

If you choose only one place to stop along the Big Sur drive, make it **Nepenthe**, about 3 miles south of the entrance to Pfeiffer Big Sur State Park. Nepenthe is a casual restaurant, with a '60s-style decor, perched on a cliff high above the ocean offering unsurpassed views (on a clear day) of the coast to the south (831-667-2345). Below Nepenthe, **The Phoenix Shop** has a wonderful selection of clothes, artwork, books, and gifts. Interestingly, at the heart of the complex is a cottage that Orson Welles bought for his then wife, Rita Hayworth.

Another stop along the way where you can gain a closer view of this magnificent coastline is at the **Julia Pfeiffer Burns State Park**. The parking area is to the left of the road. Leave your car and take the short walk leading under the highway and round the face of the cliff, which overlooks a superb small cove with emerald-green water and a white-sand beach. From the rocky bluff a waterfall drops directly into the ocean and the restless sea beats against a craggy point. After the Ragged Point Inn, the bends become less frequent, and as the cliffs give way to the coastal plain, the driving becomes less arduous.

After the road begins to flatten out, watch for **Hearst Castle** impressively crowning the coastal hills. In 1919, William Randolph Hearst commissioned California's famous architect Julia Morgan to design a simple vacation home atop a hill on his estate overlooking the California coastline. Twenty-eight years and $10,000,000 later, he moved to Los Angeles and left his 100-room retreat, La Cuesta Encantada (the enchanted hill), which has never been completed. Hearst Castle continues to delight its millions of visitors: next to Disneyland, Hearst Castle is the most popular visitor attraction in California.

The number of visitors allowed on the hill during any one day is limited, so it is essential that you make reservations in advance. Hearst Castle is open every day except Thanksgiving, Christmas, and New Year's Day. Several different one-hour and forty-five-minute tours are available. Also from September through December, Hearst Castle offers at weekends a magical evening tour and program with a holiday theme. The castle is decorated for Christmas and the staff, dressed in appropriate and wonderful costumes, play the roles of William Hearst and his entourage of friends as they bring history alive. The evening tours are tremendously popular and must be booked well in advance. If traveling with children, inquire also about the special summer children's programs. Tickets for all tours are available for purchase up to eight weeks in advance. (800-444-4445, *www.hearstcastle.org*)

Plan on arriving at the visitors' center at the foot of the hill at least half an hour before your scheduled departure, as the tours leave with clockwork-like precision and do not wait for stragglers. If you arrive early, you can browse through the small museum located next to the departure depot where groups assemble by number for their turn to be taken up the hill by bus. Here you also find an IMAX Theater which shows a special documentary of Hearst Castle.

Of the daily tour programs, Tour 1, the overview of the castle, is the one recommended for first-time visitors. You walk through the gardens to the main house, La Casa Grande, to tour the rooms on the lower level. The sheer size and elaborate decor of the assembly room where Hearst gathered with his guests before dinner sets the opulent mood of this elegant establishment. In the adjoining refectory Hearst and his guests dined in a re-created medieval banquet hall—the bottles of Hearst's favorite ketchup on the table seem rather out of place. In the theater a short home movie of Hearst and some of his celebrity friends gives you an idea of life at the castle during the 1930s. A feeling for the opulence of the guest accommodation is given as you tour the guesthouse, Casa del Sol.

Tour 2 views suites of bedrooms, the kitchen, and the swimming pools. The indoor Roman pool has over half a million Italian mosaic tiles, vast amounts of gold leaf, and took over five years to complete. Tour 3 visits the guest wing of the castle, a guesthouse, and the pools. Tour 4, offered only in summer, does not go into the main house, but focuses on the estate's gardens.

Hearst Castle

From the Hearst-San Simeon State Historical Monument it is just an 8-mile drive south to Cambria. **Cambria** was once a whaling station and a dairy town that shipped butter and cheese to San Francisco. Now the main town lies away from the coast and encompasses two streets of art galleries, gift shops, antique stores, and restaurants.

Leave Cambria and the coast traveling east on 46 through the Santa Lucia coastal mountain range. We have always considered that Hwy 46 affords one of California's most beautiful drives through gorgeous stretches of farmland and lush, gently rolling, golden hills covered with oak trees and vineyards, and it is now the best route to explore the burgeoning **Paso Robles Wine Region**. Once known for cattle ranches and grain fields and historically as a mineral springs resort area, the Paso Robles region has a rich history of winemaking and grape growing—the first grapes were introduced to the region by Spanish conquistadors and the Franciscan missionaries and wine was produced in 1797 at the historic Mission San Miguel Arcángel. Approximately 13 miles inland from Cambria you begin to see farmland give way to row-upon-row and acre-after-acre of vineyards.

(Note: If you have the luxury of time, detour off Hwy 46 west on two separate roads to discover some of California's most beautiful scenery. Santa Rosa Creek Road offers a lovely ramble through pristine countryside to the back side of Cambria (approximately a 35-minute drive) and Old Creek Road is another charming drive (about a 20-minute trip), taking you by Whale Rock Reservoir to the beach city of Cayucos.)

Spend a few days here and you will enjoy not only drives along scenic, rural, uncrowded roads—most of the wineries are open for tasting (most are free) and a few offer self-guided tours. Clustered just off the 46, still on the outskirts of Paso Robles, are several wineries: **Summerwood** is beautiful and **Castoro** is a must for tasting. Castoro Winery also hosts concerts throughout the year. Other wineries not to miss are **Dover Canyon**, **Grey Wolf**, **Midnight Cellars**, **Dark Star**, and **Fratelli Perata**. **Lone Madrone Herb Farm** is also a delightful stop to pick up herbs and gifts for house and garden.

To combine wine tasting with a drive through stunningly scenic countryside, take Vineyard Drive from the 46, traveling to the north, winding through the hills that were once home to Mennonite dairy farms, grain and nut farms, and cattle ranches. Venture on to two of the most picturesque wineries, Justin and Carmody McKnight. Stroll through Justin's lovely gardens and sample their award-winning wines. From **Justin Winery** head over to **Carmody McKnight**, an 1800s farmhouse with a pond in front, and enjoy your wine tasting while overlooking their gardens. A number of signs will tempt you off the main road down local roads to many family-run wineries. Follow Adelaida Road back to the heart of downtown Paso Robles.

Before continuing over to the east side of town to visit a number of the region's larger wineries, take some time to explore historic **Paso Robles**. The **Carnegie Library** in the center of the town park is home to a wonderful collection of local history and a Western Art Gallery. Not far away is the **Pioneer Museum** and there is also the **Estrella Warbird Museum**, which houses a collection of WWI and WWII military fighter planes. You will be thrilled to discover the many antique shops and winery tasting rooms. History is being embraced with the opening of mineral spas. **River Oaks Hot Spring and Spa** (located 3 miles east of town off Hwy 46 east) offers massage, facials, and therapeutic mineral baths in a serene lakeside setting.

To continue wine tasting, head out from Paso Robles on Hwy 46 east to many of the area's larger wineries. **Martin-Weyrich** has a feel of Tuscany and a wonderful gift shop and tasting room. **Eberle Winery** offers picnic baskets made to order with advance notice. Enjoy your picnic on their deck, sample award-winning wines, and take time to tour the Eberle caves. **Meridian Vineyards** has lovely gardens, a great tasting room, and a gift shop. Don't leave out **Tobin James,** with its real western-flavor tasting room, great hospitality, and award-winning wines. Follow your wine map, but don't miss **Wild Horse Vineyards** in Templeton and be sure to explore country roads like Neal Springs in this "El Pomar" area. The Paso Robles Wine Country Alliance have a brochure, tel: 805-239-8463, or visit their website at *www.pasowine.com*.

From Paso Robles travel south on Hwy 101 the short distance on to **San Luis Obispo.** If you want to visit every mission en route, when you reach San Luis Obispo take the Broad Street exit and follow signs to the **mission**, which lies at the heart of this bustling, charming college town.

About 10 miles south of San Luis Obispo, Hwy 101 returns to the coast where you take the exit for Hwy 1 and **Pismo Beach**, a 12-mile arc of white-sand beach backed in part by dunes. This is the home of the famous Pismo clam, which has unfortunately in recent years become rather scarce. As you travel south on Hwy 1, views of the beach are blocked by apartments and motels, but do not despair: 2 miles south of town, leave the freeway by turning right into **Pismo Beach State Park**. After paying the entrance fee, pass quickly over the soft sand. Once your tires hit the well-packed, damp sand, your way feels more secure as you drive along the beach, paralleling the crashing waves. From this vantage point you can really appreciate the beautiful sweep of this white-sand bay. While it is possible to drive about 5 miles south on the beach, the auto exit ramp lies 1 mile to the south.

Leaving Pismo Beach, follow Hwy 1 south passing flat, wide fields of vegetables and eucalyptus groves through Guadalupe, a rather poor agricultural town. The road becomes a divided two-lane road as Hwys 135 and 1 merge. After passing the gates of Vandenburg Air Force Base (on the approach to Lompoc), take a left turn onto Mission Purisma Road, which leads to **Mission La Purisma Concepcion**, founded in 1787 and now carefully restored and maintained by the state park system. A self-guided tour offers you the opportunity to see how the Indians practiced mission crafts such as leather working, candlemaking, and building. The simply decorated church with its sparse furnishings, rough floors, and stenciled walls is typical of Spanish and Mexican churches of the period. One of the nicest aspects of La Purisma Concepcion Mission is its lovely setting—deep in the countryside amidst rolling hills and flower-filled meadows.

Leaving the mission, follow signs for **Buelleton**, which has the redoubtable fame of being the home of split-pea soup—you come to **Andersen's Pea Soup Restaurant** just before Hwy 246 crosses Hwy 101. The menu has more to offer than soup, but it is still possible to sample a bowl of the food that put this little community on the map.

From Buelleton it is just a short drive into **Solvang,** a town settled originally by Danish immigrants, which has now become a rather Disneyfied version of how the perfect Danish village should look—a profusion of thatch-like roofs, painted towers, gaily colored windmills, and cobblestoned courtyards. The shops house a plethora of calorific bakeries and fudge and candy stores interspersed with lots of nifty-gifty Scandinavian-theme craft shops. Interestingly, a large portion of the town's residents truly are of Danish descent. Even if you are not a shopper, Solvang warrants a bakery stop.

Leave Solvang and rejoin Hwy 246, following signs for Santa Barbara. This is another gorgeous region of horse ranches and neighboring vineyards. The towns are small, charming and country-western: **Santa Inez**, **Los Olivos**, **Ballard**—all with a main street, a few charming shops and restaurants, and the ever-present horse and feed store.

Just outside Santa Inez, Hwy 246 merges with Hwy 154, which takes you through the heart of this beautiful landscape and the lush green valley gives way to hills as the road climbs through the mountains up the San Marcos Pass. Rounding the crest of the pass, you see **Santa Barbara** stretched out below, hemmed between the mountains and the sea. The red-tile roofs and abundance of palm trees add an affluent look to this prosperous town. Santa Barbara is one of California's loveliest cities. The homes and public buildings show a decidedly Spanish influence and make such a pretty picture—splashes of whitewashed walls, red-tiled roofs, and palm trees snuggled against the Santa Ynez Mountains to the east and stretching to blue waters of the Pacific to the west.

A pleasant introduction to Santa Barbara is to follow the driving tour published by the Chamber of Commerce. You can probably pick up a brochure at your hotel or by calling the Chamber of Commerce at 805-965-3023 or *www.sbchamber.org*. The route is well marked and gives you an overall glimpse of the city as you drive by beaches, the wharf, the old downtown area, and affluent suburbs. The brochure also outlines what is called the "Red-Tile Walking Tour," which guides you through the town's beautiful streets. It takes discipline to stay on the path as you pass the multitude of shops filled with so many tempting things to buy. The highlight of the tour is the **Santa Barbara County Courthouse**, a magnificent adobe structure with a Moorish accent. You definitely must not leave town without visiting the splendid **Mission Santa Barbara**, which is located at the rise of the hill on the northern edge of town. This beautiful church with two bell towers faces a large park laced with rose gardens. As in many of the other missions, although the church's main purpose is for religious services, a museum is incorporated into the complex with examples of how life was lived when the Spaniards first settled in California.

When your allotted stay in Santa Barbara draws to a close, it is a little less than a 100-mile drive to the Greater Los Angeles area. The vast **Los Angeles** basin is crisscrossed by a network of freeways, which confuses all but the resident Southern Californian. Frustrating traffic jams during the morning and afternoon rush hours are a way of life. Therefore, plot the quickest freeway route to your destination and try to travel during the middle of the day in order to avoid traffic. Los Angeles does not offer a wide selection of inns, but there are many attractive, modern hotels where you can stay. The Greater Los Angeles area has an incredible wealth of places to visit and things to do. Sightseeing suggestions are described in the *Leisurely Loop of Southern California* itinerary.

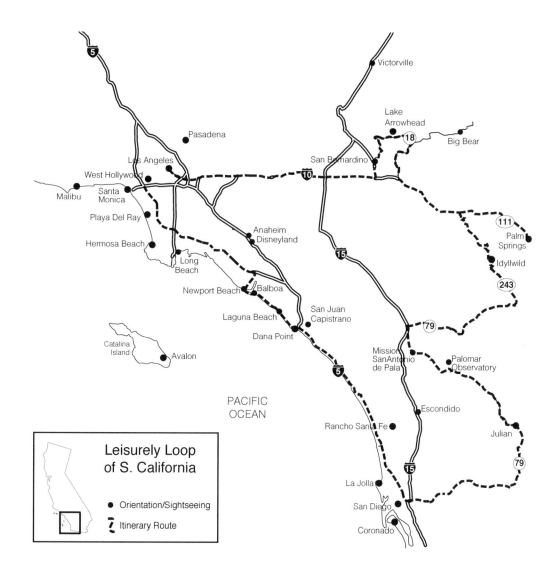

Victorville

Lake
Arrowhead

18

Big Bear

Pasadena

San Bernardino

10

Los Angeles

West Hollywood

Malibu

Santa
Monica

111

Palm
Springs

Playa Del Ray

Idyllwild

Anaheim
Disneyland

Hermosa Beach

15

243

Long
Beach

Newport Beach

Balboa

San Juan
Capistrano

Laguna Beach

79

Dana Point

Catalina
Island

Avalon

Mission
SanAntonio
de Pala

Palomar
Observatory

5

PACIFIC
OCEAN

Escondido

Julian

Rancho Santa Fe

Leisurely Loop
of S. California

79

15

● Orientation/Sightseeing

La Jolla

Itinerary Route

San Diego

Coronado

33

Leisurely Loop of Southern California

Disneyland

Los Angeles and San Diego are popular destinations, attracting travelers from around the world to a wealth of sightseeing treats. But in addition to visiting these justifiably famous cities, we hope to entice you to venture out into the countryside to explore lesser-known sightseeing gems: quaint Balboa Island with its handsome yachts, charming La Jolla with its idyllic beaches, picturesque Julian exuding its Gold Rush heritage, secluded Idyllwild nestled in the mountains, glamorous Palm Springs where movie stars still steal away, beautiful Arrowhead with its crystal-clear lake. Perhaps nowhere else can you discover within only a few short miles such a rich tapestry of places to visit—all so different, all so appealing. White-sand beaches, forests with towering pines, deserts rimmed with snow-peaked mountains, bountiful orchards, historical mining towns, and shimmering blue lakes all await your discovery.

Recommended Pacing: Greater Los Angeles is an enormous metropolis of cities and suburbs connected by an overwhelming maze of very busy freeways—during the commuter rush hours it can take hours to get from one side of the city to the other. Choose a hotel or motel close to the principal attraction you are visiting in Los Angeles and use it as a base for your other sightseeing. If you are just visiting Disneyland, stay in the area for two nights—the more attractions you want to include, the longer the recommended stay: if you include San Diego or La Jolla, add two nights; if you visit Palm Springs, add another and possibly include one additional night for Lake Arrowhead. **The itinerary route is also outlined on Map 1 at the front of the book.**

Weather Wise: The weather along the coast is warm year-round and there is very little winter rain. Julian has a more temperate climate—though sometimes in the summer it has the odd very hot day and in the winter the occasional snowfall. Palm Springs can be boiling hot, but with a dry heat, during the summer; and is ideal in the winter, with warm days and cool mountain-desert nights. Lake Arrowhead is a mountain resort with warm summer weather and snow in winter.

If you are going to be staying for an extended period of time in **Los Angeles**, supplement this guide with a book totally dedicated to what to see and do. Take a look at the wealth of things to do in LA on *www.lacvb.com*. We are not going to attempt to detail all of Los Angeles's sightseeing possibilities, but just briefly mention a few highlights.

Disney Concert Hall: Over 16 years in the making, this is a magnificent building with futuristic stainless steel curves reflecting the bright southern California sun. Designed by California architect Frank Gehry and every bit as exciting as his Guggenheim Museum in Bilbao, Portugal, the hall is home to the Los Angeles Philarmonic. Self-guided audio tours are available. Open daily, 135 North Grand Avenue, Los Angeles, 213-972-7211, *www.musiccenter.org*.

Disneyland: The wonderland created by Walt Disney needs no introduction. What child from two to ninety-two has not heard of this Magic Kingdom, home to such lovable characters as Mickey Mouse, Donald Duck, Pluto, and Snow White? The park is a fantasyland of fun, divided into various theme areas. You enter into Main Street, USA and from there it is on to Tomorrowland, Fantasyland, Frontierland, and Adventureland, each with its own rides, entertainment, and restaurants. California Adventure, Disney's newest theme park, is located right next door to the main park. Disneyland is open every day of the year and is located at 1313 Harbor Boulevard in Anaheim. (714-781-4565, *www.disney.go.com*)

The Farmers Market and **The Grove:** From its humbler beginnings as farm stands in the fields of the 1930s the **Farmers Market** has grown to a permanent complex of clapboard stalls linked to the adjacent shopping center, The Grove, by a double-decker trolley. The market still sells wares, fresh produce and baked goods but what attracts locals and tourists alike are the stands which offer every imaginable delicacy from gourmet Mexican and Cajun cuisine to fresh pressed peanut butter and orange juice and, of course, gourmet coffee. By contrast with the simple market **The Grove** is a glitsy Disney-style shopping street of various architectural styles from Las Vegas art deco to Italianate—you'll find a great many of your favorite stores here. Located at Fairfax Avenue and W. Third Street, Los Angeles, 323-933-9211, *www.farmersmarketla.com* and 323-900-8080, *www.thegrovela.com*.

The Getty Center: Climbing aboard the electric tram that takes you up to the Getty's mountaintop location, you soon realize that this is not your usual museum visit. Arriving at the central plaza of gleaming white travertine rock and walking up the broad staircase, you soon discover there is so much more than museum exhibits. There is the architecture to admire, exquisite gardens to stroll in, inviting tree-lined pathways to follow, places to dine, quiet corners for contemplation, reflecting pools to gaze in, and spectacular views across the city to the ocean. The exhibition galleries house collections of European paintings (Van Gogh's *Irises*, Monet's *Wheatstacks,* and David Hockney's *Pearblossom Hwy No 2* being amongst the more well known), drawings (Michelangelo's *The Holy Family with Infant St. John the Baptist*), sculpture (lots of Greek and Roman antiquities), illuminated manuscripts, decorative arts (there's a wonderful collection of Louis XIV furniture), photographs, and changing exhibits. Admission is free. You do not need a reservation for the museum BUT you do need a parking reservation (fee for parking). Often parking reservations have to be made several weeks in advance. There is no convenient street parking. Buses—MTA Metro bus #561 (213-626-4455, *www.mta.net*) and Santa Monica Big Blue Bus #14 (310-451-5444, *www.bigbluebus.com*)—stop at the Getty Center. Closed Mondays and holidays, the museum is open weekends 10 am to 9 pm and weekdays 10 am to 6 pm or 9 pm. (310-440-7300, *www.getty.edu*)

The Getty Villa is modeled after a first-century Roman country house, the Villa dei Papiri in Herculaneum, Italy. The villa was buried by the eruption of Mt. Vesuvius in A.D. 79, therefore the architects based their villa, and its landscaping, on elements from other ancient Roman houses. The Getty Villa houses the J. Paul Getty Museum's collection of approximately 44,000 Greek, Roman, and Etruscan antiquities. Over 1,200 works are on view in 23 galleries devoted to the permanent collection, with five additional galleries for changing exhibitions. You can tour with a "wand" or sign up on arrival for guided tours of the architecture and garden, an overview tour or an in depth look into one particular piece in the collection. Located at 17985 Pacific Coast Highway, Malibu CA 90272. Access to the Getty villa is only from the northbound, right hand lane, of the Pacific Coast Highway. You need a reservation for the museum, last minute reservations are often available online. There is a fee for parking. There is no convenient street parking. Open Thursday to Monday 10 am to 5 pm. Closed Tuesdays, Wednesdays and holidays. (310-440-7300, *www.getty.edu*)

Huntington Library, Art Gallery, and Botanical Gardens: The home and 207-acre estate of the late Henry Huntington are open to the public and should not be missed by any visitor to the Los Angeles area. Huntington's enormous home is now a museum featuring the work of French and English 18th-century artists. What makes the museum especially attractive is that the paintings are displayed in a homelike setting surrounded by appropriately dramatic furnishings. Nearby, in another beautiful building, is the

Huntington Library—a real gem containing, among other rare books, a 15th-century copy of the Gutenberg bible, Benjamin Franklin's handwritten autobiography, and marvelous Audubon bird prints. The gardens of the estate merit a tour in themselves and include various sections such as a rose garden, a Japanese garden, a camellia garden, a cactus garden, an English garden, and a bonsai garden. Located at 1151 Oxford Road in San Marino, the estate is open Tuesday through Friday noon to 4:30 pm, and Saturday and Sunday 10:30 am to 4:30 pm. For information on special events and shows call 626-405-2100, *www.huntington.org*.

Hollywood Boulevard—Mann Chinese Theatre, Kodak Theatre, El Capitan Theater: There has been a renaissance of the heart of tinsel town. The glitzy new Highland and Hollywood shopping center houses the **Kodak Theatre**, home to the Academy Awards. You can easily recognize the spot where they unfurl the famous red carpet, threading its way through the indoor shopping mall past the pillars posting the names of Academy Award movies of the year. Tours of the sparkling theatre building itself are available, *www.kodaktheatre.com*. You can catch a distant glimpse of the famous **Hollywood sign** from the outdoor upper deck of the shopping complex. Next door visit the fantasy of Chinese pagodas and temples that comprise **Mann's Chinese Theatre.** The courtyard is filled with famous cement hand- and footprints from legends such as John Wayne and Marilyn Monroe. For the price of a movie ticket (or tour) you can see the lavish interior. The Chinese Theatre may not be the best-preserved theater in Hollywood, that honor goes to the nearby Disney **El Capitan Theater** whose 1926 interior is now in fine fettle and comes complete with a state of the art projection and sound system, *www.elcapitantickets.com*. The sidewalk along Hollywood Boulevard is inlaid with stars dedicated to the celebrities (some obscure, some that are household names) who made Hollywood great. Located at the junction of Hollywood and Highland Boulevards. Discounted parking (with validation) is available beneath the Hollywood and Highland complex, enter on Orange.

Le Brea Tarpits: Learn what Los Angeles was like between 10,000 and 40,000 years ago when animals such as saber-toothed tigers and mammoths roamed the area, only to become trapped in the asphalt deposits that bubble to the surface in Hancock Park. Excavation of the pits started in 1908. Located amongst the rolling lawns each fenced excavation provides details of the prehistoric animals that were found there. Visit in summer and you can see the excavation of Pit 91 in action, watching paleontologists wrestle remains from the sticky tar. Most of the fossils are displayed in the adjacent Page Museum where you can watch recent finds being classified and examined. Of special interest is a tank that recreates how animals became stuck in the sticky La Brea asphalt, frantically trying to escape from an oily grave. Visitors can even touch a massive leg bone of an extinct giant ground sloth. 5801 Wilshire Boulevard, Los Angeles, 323-934-7243, *www.tarpits.org*.

NBC Television Studios: Los Angeles is the television capital of the world. To get an idea of what goes on behind the screen, visit the NBC Television Studios and take their one-hour tour that gives you a look at where the stars rehearse, how costumes are designed, how stage props are made, and what goes into the special effects. The tour also visits some of the show sets. The studios are located at 3000 West Alameda Avenue in Burbank. (818-840-3537)

The Norton Simon Museum of Art: The Norton Simon Museum of Art is without doubt one of the finest private art museums in the world, set in a beautiful Moorish-style building accented by a reflecting pool and manicured gardens. Norton Simon and his actress wife, Jennifer Jones, share their incredible collection of art including paintings by such masters as Rubens, Rembrandt, Raphael, Picasso, and Matisse. The museum, open Thursday through Sunday noon to 6 pm, is located at 411 West Colorado Boulevard in Pasadena. (626-449-6840, *www.nortonsimon.org*)

El Pueblo de Los Angeles: With all the clamor and glamour of modern-day Los Angeles, it is easy to forget that this city was originally a *pueblo* founded in 1781 to grow food for the Spanish soldiers guarding this distant territory for their king. You catch a glimpse of the town's history in El Pueblo de Los Angeles, a little bit of Mexico where Hispanic people sell colorful Mexican souvenirs and operate interesting restaurants on **Olivera Street**. The 44-acre complex of old buildings (some dating back to the 1780s) has been restored and is now a state park. Be sure to visit **Plaza Firehouse**-the oldest firehouse in Los Angeles, the **Chinese American Museum** with its historic Chinese herbalist display on the ground floor and rotating art exhibits on the upper floors, and **Mission Nuestra Señora Reina** founded in 1781. El Pueblo is located opposite **Union Station** (impressive art-deco building), on the Red Line Metro at 125 Paseo de la Plaza, Los Angeles. (213-628-1274, *www.cityofla.org/elp*)

Rodeo Drive: Rodeo drive is as much a tourist destination as it is a deluxe shopping street. It is great fun to browse the windows of Gucci, Armani, Harry Winston, Tiffany's, Hermes and the like. At the southern end of Rodeo Drive, where it joins Wilshire Boulevard, is Via Rodeo, a curvy cobblestoned street designed to resemble an Italian via—perfect for picture-taking. Located in Beverly Hills at Wilshire Boulevard and Rodeo Drive, Red Line buses run along Wilshire.

Warner Brothers Studios: Do a little celebrity snooping on a VIP tour of the backlot sets, sound stages, crafts shops and prop warehouses of one of Hollywood's famous movie studios. No two tours are alike—it depends on what is open and available but chances are you will get to visit the sound stage of a current Warner Brothers production and stroll down Midwest Street, made famous in the musical *A Music Man*, now home to the *Gilmore Girls*. (818-846-1403)

Universal Studios: Visiting Universal Studios, the biggest, busiest movie studio in the world, is like going to a vast amusement park and there is so much to see and do that you must spend a whole day here. Included in the admission price is a two-hour tram journey that takes you around the 420-acre lot, out of the real world and into make-believe: along the way you venture inside the Curse of the Mummy's Tomb, encounter the howling fury of King Kong, and tremble in a terrifying 8.3 earthquake. Water World, a live sea war spectacular, Back to the Future, a time-travel ride from the age of the dinosaurs to 2015, and Backdraft's raging firestorm thrill you with their excitement, while the Animal Planet Live show and the re-creation of the zany Lucille Ball sitcoms give you the chance to laugh away all that adrenaline in your blood. New in 2002 is the Spider Man Rocks rock 'n' roll stunt show. The studios are just off the Hollywood Freeway at the Universal Center Drive exit. (*www.universalstudios.com*)

It takes only a couple of hours to whip down the freeway between Los Angeles and San Diego but, instead, follow our sightseeing suggestions and dawdle along the way to enjoy some of southern California's coastal attractions en route.

Drive south from Los Angeles on Hwy 405, the San Diego Freeway, until you come to Hwy 73, the Corona del Mar Freeway, which branches to the south toward the coast. Take this, then in just minutes you come to Hwy 55, Newport Boulevard. Exit here and stay on the same road all the way to **Newport Beach**. Soon after crossing the bridge watch for the sign to your right for Newport Pier. (In case you get off track, the pier is at the foot of 20th Street.) Try to arrive mid-morning so that you can capture a glimpse of yesteryear when the **Dory Fleet** comes in to beach, just to the right of the pier. The Dory Fleet, made up of colorfully painted, open wooden fishing boats, has been putting out to sea for almost a hundred years. It is never certain exactly what time the fleet will come in (it depends upon the fishing conditions), but if you arrive mid-morning, the chances are you will see the fishermen preparing and selling their catch of the day from the back of their small boats. If seeing all the fresh fish puts you in the mood for lunch, walk across the street to the **Oyster Bar & Grill**—the food is excellent and the clam chowder truly outstanding.

From Newport Beach, continue south along the long, thin peninsula: the next community you come to is **Balboa**. In the center of town there is a clearly signposted public parking area next to Balboa Pier: leave your car here and explore the area. The beach is beautiful, stretching the entire length of the peninsula, all the way from the southern tip to beyond Newport Pier. Stroll along the beach and then walk across the peninsula (about a two-block span) to the Balboa Pavilion, a colorful Victorian gingerbread landmark smack in the center of the wharf. Next to the pavilion are several booths where tickets are sold for cruises into the harbor. One of the best of these excursions is on the *Pavilion Queen*, which makes a 45-minute loop of the bay. Buy your ticket and, if you have time to spare until the boat leaves, wander around the nostalgic, honky-tonk boardwalk with its cotton candy, Ferris wheel, saltwater taffy shops, and penny arcade. But be back in time to board your boat because the Balboa harbor cruise should not be missed. The trip is a boat fancier's dream: over 9,000 yachts are moored in the harbor. Also of interest are the opulent homes whose lawns stretch out to the docks where their million-dollar cruisers are moored.

A block from the Balboa Pavilion is the ferry landing—you cannot miss it. After your cruise, retrieve your car and follow signs to the Balboa Ferry. You might have to wait in line a bit because the little old-fashioned ferry takes only three cars at a time. When your turn comes, it is just minutes over to **Balboa Island**, a delightful, very wealthy community. Park your car on the main street and poke about in the pretty shops.

From Balboa Island there is a bridge across the harbor to the mainland. Almost as soon as you cross the bridge, turn right, heading south on Hwy 1 through the ritzy community of **Corona del Mar**. Although there is still a quaintness to the area, exclusive boutiques, expensive art galleries, palatial homes, and trendy shops hint at the fact that this is not the sleepy little town it might appear to be.

From Corona del Mar, Hwy 1 parallels the sea, which washes up against a long stretch of beach bound by high bluffs. The area seems relatively undeveloped except for its beach parks. About 11 miles south of Corona del Mar the road passes through **Laguna Beach**, famous for its many art galleries, pretty boutiques, and miles of lovely sand. In summer, from mid-July through August, Laguna Beach is usually packed with tourists coming to see the Pageant of the Masters, a tableau in which town residents dress up and re-create paintings. Two dozen living paintings are staged each evening and viewed by spectators in an outdoor amphitheater.

Continue south along the Coastal Hwy. Soon after passing Dana Point, take the turnoff to the east on Hwy 5 to **San Juan Capistrano**. Watch for signs directing you off the freeway two blocks to **Mission San Juan Capistrano**. This mission, founded by Father Junipero Serra in 1776, has been carefully restored to give you a glimpse of what life was like in the early days of California. Although located in the center of town, the mission creates its own environment since it is insulated by lovely gardens and a complex of Spanish adobe buildings. Another point of special interest at San Juan Capistrano is that the swallows have chosen it as "home," arriving every March 19th (Saint Joseph's Day) and leaving October 23rd. Visit the mission and then retrace your route to Hwy 5 and continue south about an hour to San Diego.

The San Diego Visitors Bureau (619-232-3101) will send you a packet of valuable information for touring its many attractions. The San Diego Trolley makes it easy and fun to get around San Diego and its environs—you can actually ride from Old Town to the Mexican border. **San Diego** offers a wealth of attractions and amusements—on the following pages we feature some of our favorites in the San Diego area. (Find out more at *www.sandiego.org*.)

Balboa Park: Balboa Park is without a doubt one of the highlights of downtown San Diego. Attractions within the park include the **San Diego Zoo**, one of the finest in the world (619-234-3153, *www.sandiegozoo.org*). For a good orientation of the zoo take either the 40-minute bus tour or the aerial tramway. Most of the more than 3,000 animals live within natural-style enclosures with very few cages. The Children's Zoo is especially fun, with a nursery for newborn animals and a petting zoo. But Balboa Park offers much more than its splendid zoo. There are fascinating museums and exhibits within the 1,400-acre park: the **Museum of Man**, the **Aerospace Museum**, the **San Diego Museum of**

Art, the **Timken Art Gallery**, the **Natural History Museum**, the **Reuben H. Fleet Space Theater and Science Center**, the **Hall of Champions**, the **Museum of Photographic Arts**, and the beautiful wooden **Botanical Building**:. Most of the museums are housed in picturesque Spanish-style buildings. (619-239-0512, *www.balboapark.org*)

Coronado: While in San Diego take the bridge or the ferry over to Coronado, an island-like bulb of land tipping a thin isthmus that stretches south almost to the Mexican border. Here you find not only a long stretch of beautiful beach, but also the Del Coronado Hotel, a Victorian fantasy of gingerbread turrets and gables. The Del Coronado, locally referred to as "The Del," is a sightseeing attraction in its own right and makes an excellent choice for a luncheon stop.

The Embarcadero: The Embarcadero is the downtown port area located along Harbor Drive. From here you can take a harbor cruise or visit one of the floating museums tied up to the quay, part of the San Diego Maritime Museum. These include the *Star of India*, built in 1863, a dramatic tall-masted ship that carried passengers and cargo around the world. (619-234-9153, *www.sdmaritime.com*)

La Jolla: Be sure to visit La Jolla, "The Jewel," a sophisticated town just north of San Diego. Classy shops and restaurants line the streets and on a warm sunny day there is nowhere more perfect for an informal lunch and water views than George's Ocean Terrace (858-454-4244). La Jolla is home to a branch of the University of California and within its Scripps Institution of Oceanography are an excellent aquarium and museum featuring marine life from California and Mexico. Another very interesting museum is the **Museum of Contemporary Art** with its spectacular ocean views, interesting exhibits, and delightful café (858-454 3541, *www.mcasd.org*). Just down Prospect Street from the museum visit the landmark **John Cole's Bookstore** set in a historic house overlooking the ocean. However, what really makes La Jolla so special is her setting—beautiful white-sand beaches sheltered in intimate little coves. You may prefer to stay here rather than in San Diego.

Legoland: A Mecca for children between the ages of two and eight, this is the first Legoland in the United States and is modeled on the famous one in Denmark. All the attractions are built of, or themed on, the colorful Lego bricks. From fun rides to opportunities to see the production of the famous bricks and the chance to buy every available Lego product, this is a theme park that Lego enthusiasts will not want to miss. Located in Carlsbad 30 miles north of San Diego, 760-918-5346, *www.legoland.com.*

Mexico: Mexico lies just south of San Diego. Do not judge the whole of Mexico by its border town of Tijuana, but if you would like to have a *taste* of Mexico, take one of the "shopping and sightseeing" tours that leave from downtown for the short drive to the border. You can drive across the border, but the bus tour removes the hassle from the trip.

Old Town: Old Town is where San Diego originated. The area has been designated as a city park and several square blocks are accessible to pedestrians only. Make the Historical Museum your first stop and orient yourself by viewing a scale model of San Diego in its early days. Old Town is most interesting to visit as many of the buildings are open as small museums, such as the Machado-Stewart Adobe, the Old School House, and the Seeley Stables (an 1860s stage depot with a good display of horse-drawn carriages). If you are in Old Town at mealtime, you can choose from many attractive restaurants. Just southeast of the intersection of Hwys 5 and 8, parking is well signposted.

Mission San Diego de Alcala: The oldest of the chain of missions that stretches up the coast is Mission San Diego de Alcala. The mission was originally closer to San Diego but was moved to its present site (10818 San Diego Mission Road) in 1774. To reach the mission, head east on Hwy 8—it is signposted to the north of the highway beyond the intersection of Hwy 15. (619-283-7319, *www.missionsandiego.com*)

Seaport Village: Adjacent to the Embarcadero is Seaport Village, a very popular tourist attraction and fun for adults and children alike. Situated right on the waterfront, it has little paths that meander through this 23 acre village of shops and restaurants built in a colorful variety of styles from Early Spanish to Victorian. Street artists display their talents to laughing audiences.

Sea World: San Diego's marine display is in Mission Bay Park. Set in a 150-acre park which includes a 1-acre children's playland, Sea World features one of California's famous personalities, Shamu, the performing killer whale who delights everyone with her wit and aquatic abilities. Penguin Encounter is a particularly fun exhibit where you watch comical penguins waddling about in their polar environment, while Shark Encounter presents one of the largest displays of sharks in the world and provides the terrifying thrill of being surrounded by these efficient killing machines as you walk through an acrylic tube. (800-380-3203, *www.seaworld.com*)

Wild Animal Park: This is a branch of the San Diego Zoo 30 miles north of the city near Escondido—truly a zoo on a grand scale. The animals roam freely in terrain designed to match their natural habitat. You feel as if you are on a safari in Africa as you watch for lions and other animals while you tour the park on the Wgasa Bush Line Monorail tour. There are also several open theaters where animal shows are presented. (619-234-6541, *www.wildanimalpark.org)*

Leaving San Diego, Hwy 8 takes you east and winds through shrub-filled canyons dotted with ever-expanding housing suburbs. About 30 minutes after you leave the city, watch for the sign for Hwy 79 where you turn north toward Julian. The road weaves through an Indian reservation and the scenery becomes prettier by the minute as you climb into the mountains and enter the **Cuyamaca Rancho State Park**. There are not many opportunities to sightsee en route, but if you want to break your journey, you can pause at the park headquarters and visit the Indian museum or the museum at the **Old Stonewall Mine**. Leaving the park, the road winds down into Julian.

Julian is a small town that can easily be explored in just a short time. What is especially nice is that, although it is a tourist attraction, the town is not "tacky touristy." Rather, you get the feeling you are in the last century as you wander through the streets and stop to browse at some of the antique shops, visit the small historical museum in the old brewery, and enjoy refreshment at the soda fountain in the 1880s drug store. If you want to delve deeper into mining, just a short drive (or long walk) away on the outskirts of town is the **Eagle Mine**, founded by pioneers from Georgia, many of them soldiers who came here after the Civil War. Tours are taken deep into the mine and a narration gives not only the history of the mine, but the history of Julian.

If you are in Julian in the fall, you can enjoy another of Julian's offerings—apples. Although you can sample Julian's wonderful apples throughout the year (every restaurant has its own special apple pie on the menu), the apple becomes king during the fall harvest. Beginning in October and continuing on into November, special crafts shows and events are held in the Julian Town Hall. If you visit one of the packing plants on the edge of town you can buy not only apples, but every conceivable item that has apples as a theme.

It is only a short drive north from Julian on Hwy 79 to **Santa Ysabel** where you turn right at the main intersection. At this junction you see **Dudley's Bakery**, a rather nondescript-looking building that houses a great bakery: loyal customers drive all the way from San Diego just to buy one of their 21 varieties of tasty bread. As you leave Santa Ysabel you come to **Mission Santa Ysabel**, a reconstructed mission that still serves the Indians. This is one of the less interesting missions, but you may want to see the murals painted by the local Indians.

About 7 miles after leaving the mission, Hwy 79 breaks off to the east and you continue north on Hwy 76. In five minutes you come to Lake Henshaw. Just beyond the lake turn northeast (right) on East Grade Road, which winds its way up the mountain to the **Palomar Observatory**. Just near the parking area is a museum where you learn about the observatory through photos and short films. It is a pleasant stroll up to the impressive white-domed observatory, which houses the Hale telescope—the largest in the United States. A flight of steps takes you to a glass-walled area where you see the giant telescope whose lens is 200 inches in diameter, 2 feet thick, and took 11 years to polish.

After viewing the observatory, loop back down the twisting road to the main highway and, when it intersects with Hwy 76, turn northwest (right), driving through hills covered with groves of avocado and orange trees. In about 12 miles you come to **Pala** and the **Mission San Antonio de Pala:**. Established in 1810, it is one of the few remaining active *asistencias* (missions built in outlying areas to serve the Indians). The mission is small, but the chapel is very beautiful in its rugged simplicity enhanced by thick adobe walls, rustic beamed ceiling, and Indian paintings. A bell tower stands alone to the right of the chapel, a picturesque sight. To the left are a simple museum and a souvenir shop.

From Pala it is about a ten-minute drive north on S16 to Temecula. Just before you enter town the road intersects with Hwy 79 and you head east for 18 miles to Aguanga where Hwy 371 takes you northeast for 21 miles to Hwy 74. As you head north on 74 the mountain air becomes sweeter and the scenery increasingly prettier as you enter the forest. In about 12 miles you see signs for **Idyllwild** to the northeast. Turn here on Hwy 243 and very soon you come to the small resort tucked into the mountains high above Palm Springs. Homely little restaurants, antique stores, and gift shops make up the town.

Leaving Idyllwild, continue north on Hwy 342 to Banning where you turn east (right) on Hwy 10. In about 12 miles you come to Hwy 111 where you turn right and follow signs to Palm Springs (about a ten-minute drive). **Palm Springs** was first discovered by the Indians who came to this oasis to bathe in the hot springs, which they considered to have healing qualities. The same tribe still owns much of Palm Springs and rents their valuable real estate to homeowners and commercial enterprises. The hot springs are still in use today. During the winter season the town is congested with traffic and the sidewalks are crammed with an assortment of people of every age, size, and shape dressed in colorful,

sporty clothes. Palm Springs used to be deserted in summer when the days are very hot. However, more and more tourists are coming in June, July, and August, attracted by the lower hotel rates. Although the temperature in the summer months is frequently well above 110 degrees, it is a dry heat and not unbearable in the mornings and balmy evenings. In fact, due to the altitude, evenings often require a sweater. So if your visit is in summer, plan your sightseeing for early and late in the day.

In addition to the pleasures of basking in the sun or playing on one of the many golf courses in the area, Palm Springs offers a variety of sightseeing. The most impressive excursion is to take the **Aerial Tramway** (located just north of town off Hwy 111) from the desert floor up 2½ miles into the San Jacinto Mountains. In summer you go from sizzling heat to cool mountain forests, while in winter you go from desert to snow. The weather atop the mountain is often more than 40 degrees cooler than in Palm Springs, so remember to take the appropriate clothing. At the top are observation decks with telescopes, a restaurant, and miles of hiking trails. (888-515-TRAM, *www.pstramway.com*)

If you enjoy deserts, be sure not to miss the **Living Desert Wildlife and Botanical Park** (open only in the mornings in summer) where 6 miles of trails wind through different types of desert that are found in the United States. Tour booklets are available at the entrance to assist you along the trails, 760-346-5694, *www.livingdesert.org*. If you are interested in the rich and famous, join a bus tour that drives by the outside of their magnificent homes. Many movie stars have second homes in Palm Springs.

Palm Springs is a convenient place to end this itinerary because it is a quick, easy drive on the freeway back to Los Angeles. But, if time permits, squeeze in one more contrasting destination, the exclusive Alpine resort of Lake Arrowhead.

Leave Palm Springs and head north on Hwy 111 for about 10 miles to Hwy 10 and turn west for Banning. Approximately 20 miles past Banning at Redlands, exit from the freeway on Hwy 30 and drive north for a few minutes until Hwy 38 travels into the hills. As the road begins to climb up from the valley the scenery becomes prettier with every curve—the dry desert brush is gradually left behind, replaced by evergreen trees. At the town of Running Springs turn west on Hwy 18. This is called the **Rim of the World Highway**, a road where sweeping vistas of the valley floor can be glimpsed through the clouds. Be aware that fog often hovers around this drive and then, instead of admiring beautiful views, you creep along in thick, gray mist.

Lake Arrowhead village is a cluster of restaurants and shops along the lakefront. The lake is bordered by magnificent estates. The magnet of Lake Arrowhead is not any specific sightseeing, but rather the outdoors experience: although lakefront and beach access is restricted and private, you can take leisurely walks through the forest, picnic in secluded parks, explore the lake by paddle boats, or rent bicycles for a bit of fresh-air adventure. You can also take the hour-long ride on the steamer that circles the lake.

When it is time to complete your itinerary, retrace your path back to the valley and follow Hwy 10 back into Los Angeles. Unless you encounter unexpected traffic, the trip should take about two hours.

North From San Francisco, Almost To The Oregon Border

● Orientation/Sightseeing

⌇ Itinerary Route

Redwood NP

Trinidad

Eureka

Ferndale   Scotia

Humboldt Redwoods SP (101)

Garberville

Leggett

(1)   (101)

Fort Bragg   Skunk RR   Willits

Mendocino

Ukiah

(20)

(128)

Cloverdale

(1)

Fort Ross   Healdsburg

Santa Rosa   Sacramento

PACIFIC OCEAN

Inverness

Point Reyes NS   San Rafael

(1)   (101)

Muir Beach

San Francisco

Mount Shasta   (3)

(299)   Weaverville

Redding

(5)

51

North from San Francisco, almost to the Oregon Border

Mendocino

If your heart leaps with joy at the sight of long stretches of deserted beaches, rugged cliffs embraced by wind-bent trees, sheep quietly grazing near crashing surf, and groves of redwoods towering above carpets of dainty ferns, then this itinerary will suit you to perfection. Nowhere else in California can you travel surrounded by so much natural splendor. Less than an hour after crossing the Golden Gate Bridge, civilization is left far behind you and your adventure into some of California's most beautiful scenery begins. The first part of this route includes many well-loved attractions: Muir Woods, the

Russian River, Sonoma County wineries, the Mendocino Coast, and the Avenue of the Giants. Then the route becomes less "touristy" as it reaches the Victorian jewel of Ferndale and the bustling town of Eureka, and concludes in the coastal hamlet of Trinidad.

Recommended Pacing: You can cover the distance between San Francisco and Mendocino in a day. It is approximately a four-hour drive if you are traveling inland on Hwy 101 and then cutting west over at Cloverdale on Hwy 128 back to the coast and Hwy 1 just south of Mendocino. It is approximately a six-hour journey if you follow Hwy 1 as it hugs the coast all the way north. However, if time allows, follow our routing and spend a night just north of San Francisco near Point Reyes National Seashore (more if you want to take advantage of the hiking and biking trails), and a night or two in the Healdsburg/Russian River area before arriving in Mendocino. Allow two nights for the Mendocino area and two nights for the Eureka area. **The itinerary route is also outlined on Map 3 at the front of the book.**

Weather Wise: The weather along California's northern coast is unpredictable: beautiful warm summer days suddenly become overcast when the fog rolls in (July and August). The prettiest months are usually June, September, and October. Rain falls during the winter and spring, while fall enjoys beautiful crisp, clear days.

San Francisco, a city of unsurpassed beauty, is a favorite destination of tourists and it is no wonder: the city is dazzling in the sunlight, yet equally enchanting when wrapped in fog. The setting is spectacular: a cluster of hills on the tip of a peninsula. San Francisco is very walkable and if you tire, a cable car, bus, or taxi is always close at hand. In the *San Francisco to Los Angeles via the Coast* itinerary we give you enough sightseeing suggestions to occupy you for a week.

Avoiding commuter hours and congestion, leave San Francisco on the **Golden Gate Bridge** following Hwy 101 north. After you cross this famous bridge, pull into the vista point for a panoramic view of this most lovely city. For another spectacular detour, take the very first exit after the viewing area, Alexander Avenue, turn left back under the freeway, and continue as if you are heading back onto the Golden Gate Bridge but, instead, take a quick right to the **Marin Headlands**. Some of the city's most spectacular skylines are photographed from the vantage point of these windswept and rugged headlands looking back at the city through the span of the Golden Gate. The road continues through the park and eventually winds back to Hwy 101. Information and maps are available at the visitors center located in the old Fort Barry Chapel. (415-331-1540). Not to be missed is the **Marine Mammal Center**, where injured seals and other marine animals are nursed back to health by a multitude of volunteers. (415-289-7325, *www.tmmc.org*)

After returning to Hwy 101, continue on to the Mill Valley exit. Circle under the freeway and follow signs for Hwy 1 north. As the two-lane road leaves the town behind and winds up through the trees, watch closely for a sharp right turn to **Muir Woods**. The road takes you high above open fields and down a steep ravine to the Muir Woods entrance and car park where a park volunteer gives out a map and information. Near the park entrance a cross section of a trunk of one of the stately giant coastal redwoods gives you an appreciation of the age of these great trees. Notations relate the tree's growth rings to significant historical occurrences during the tree's lifetime: 1066—the Battle of Hastings, 1215—the Magna Carta, 1492—the discovery of America, 1776—the Declaration of Independence. But this tree is only a baby—some date back over 2,000 years. Your brochure guides you on the walk beneath the redwoods or you can take a guided tour with one of the rangers. Allow about an hour for the park, longer if you take a long walk or just sit on one of the benches to soak in the beauty.

Leaving the park, continue west to the coastal road, Hwy 1. Turn left and then, almost immediately, right. There is a small sign marked **Muir Beach**, but it is easy to miss. Just before you come to the beach you arrive at the **Pelican Inn**, a charming re-creation of an English pub that fortunately also offers lodging (415-383-6000). The adjacent Muir Beach is a small half-moon beach bound at each end by large rock formations.

Return to Hwy 1 and head north along a challenging, winding section of this beautiful coastal road. The road descends to the small town of **Stinson Beach** where by entering the state park you can gain access to a fabulous stretch of wide white sand, bordered on one side by the sea and on the other by grassy dunes. This is a perfect spot to stretch and enjoy a walk along the beach.

Leaving Stinson Beach, the road curves inland bordering **Bolinas Lagoon**, a paradise for birds, and then leaves the water and continues north for about 10 miles to the town of Olema. At Olema you leave Hwy 1 and take the road marked to Inverness, just a short drive away.

If the weather is fine, allow time to explore **Point Reyes National Seashore**, a spectacular wilderness area stretching along the sea (*www.nps.gov/pore*). If you happen to be in the area on a weekend, in addition to taking advantage of the free ranger programs, call ahead (415-663-1200) to inquire about special field trips (such as tidepool studies, bird watching, and sights and sounds of nature) that are offered for a fee. The ranger station, located in a handsome redwood building at the entrance to the park, has maps, leaflets, books, a museum, and a movie theater where a presentation gives interesting information on the park.

Point Reyes Lighthouse

Be sure to stop here before your explorations to obtain a map and study what you want to see and do. A short stroll away from the ranger station is the "earthquake trail" where markers indicate changes brought about by the 1906 earthquake. Also within walking distance is the **Morgan Ranch** where Morgan horses are raised and trained for the park system. If the weather is clear, a drive out to **Point Reyes Lighthouse** is a highlight that should not be missed. As you drive for 45 minutes across windswept fields and through dairy farms to the lighthouse you realize how large the park really is. When you arrive, it is a ten-minute walk from the parking area to the viewing area. From there, steps lead down to the lighthouse. Be prepared: it is like walking down a 30-story building and once down, you have to come back up! In late fall and spring it is a perfect place from which to watch for migrating gray whales.

After a visit to the lighthouse, look on your map for **Drakes Bay**, one of the many beaches along this rugged strip of coast, and named for the explorer seeking lands for Queen Elizabeth I of England. He is purported to have sailed into the bay on the *Golden Hinde* and christened it Nova Albion, meaning New England. If you are hungry, there is a café at Drakes Bay where you can have a bite to eat. Another interesting stop is at the **Johnson Oyster Company** on Sir Francis Drake Boulevard—a sign directs you to it on the left on the drive toward Point Reyes Lighthouse. Stop to see the demonstration of how oysters are cultivated in the bay for 18 months before being harvested.

If you choose to continue on to the northernmost point of the peninsula, travel Pierce Point Road, which ends at the Tule Elk Range. Before 1860, thousands of tule elk roamed here but were hunted to extinction; then in 1978 two bulls and eight cows were successfully reintroduced and now the herd numbers over 300. Trails lead through this wilderness and research area to the Tomales Point Bluff or a shorter distance down to McClures Beach and Elephant Rock.

Retrace your route through the park to **Point Reyes Station** where the **Station House Café**, a delightful restaurant with delicious, imaginative food, beckons you into its dining room or tranquil, brick-paved, cottage-garden patio. Continue north on Hwy 1 as the road winds through fields of pastureland and dairies and then loops back and follows for a while the northern rim of **Tomales Bay**, providing lovely vistas across the water to the wooded hills and the town of Inverness. About a 20-minute drive brings you to the village of Marshall. Soon after, the road heads inland through rolling ranch land bound by picket fences, passing the towns of **Tomales** (the **Tomales Bakery**, located in the old barbershop and open Thursday to Sunday, is worth visiting) and Valley Ford before turning west to Bodega Bay and the small town of **Jenner**. From here it is about a 15-minute drive to **Fort Ross**. "Ross" means "Russian" and this is the site where the Russians, in the early part of the 19th century, built a fort to protect their fishing and fur interests in California. After browsing through the museum, follow the footpath through the woods and enter the courtyard bounded by the weathered wooden buildings where the settlers lived and worked. Be sure not to miss the pretty Russian Orthodox chapel in the southeast corner of the compound. When you have finished roaming through the encampment, take the dramatic walk along the bluffs above the ocean. (707-847-3286)

Leaving the fort, retrace your path to Jenner and follow Hwy 116 inland along the banks of the **Russian River**. This is a tranquil stretch of road, passing through dense forests that open up conveniently to offer views of the very green water of the Russian River. (In winter after heavy rains the river can become a rushing torrent—no longer green and tranquil.) On weekends this road is very congested, but midweek and off-season this is a very pretty drive. The largest resort along the river is **Guerneville** and just a few miles beyond the town you come to the **Korbel Winery** (13250 River Road, Guerneville), a picturesque, large building banked with flowers. Three Korbel brothers came to this area from Bohemia to harvest the redwoods and ended up harvesting grapes. Korbel is famous for sparkling wines and the tour and video presentations are especially interesting. Tours of the historic champagne cellars last a little under an hour and are offered daily every hour on the hour between 10 am and 3 pm—to be safe, call to double-check the schedule. There is also a delicatessen and a pretty rose garden nestled on the slope to the left of the winery. The winery is open daily between 9 am and 4:30 pm and offers complimentary tasting. (707-824-7000, *www.korbel.com*)

Sampling champagne at Korbel will whet your appetite for more local wines. Leaving the winery, continue for a short distance along River Road, watching for a left-hand turn for Westside Road (if you go over the bridge, you have gone too far). Westside Road winds its way to Healdsburg, past vineyards, meadows with cows grazing, pretty apple orchards, and several wineries, including **Hop Kiln Winery** (6050 Westside Road, Healdsburg), which is open for tasting until 5 pm. The architecture at Hop Kiln (which, unsurprisingly, was originally built for drying beer hops) is very interesting, with whimsical chimneys jutting into the sky (707-433-6491, *www.hopkilnwinery.com)*. The nearby **Rochioli Winery**, (6192 Westside Road, Healdsburg) offers tasting and tours by appointment (707-433-2305). Nearby **Healdsburg** has an attractive main square lined with quaint shops and restaurants. Make at stop at **Oakville Grocery** on the square for lunch, picnic supplies and gourmet treats.

Leaving Healdsburg, follow Hwy 101 north for the half-hour drive to Cloverdale where you take Hwy 128 heading northwest toward the coast. At first the road twists slowly up and over a rather steep pass. After the summit, the way becomes more gentle as you head down into the beautiful **Anderson Valley**, well-known for its delicious wines. Wherever the hills spread away from the road, the gentle meadows are filled with vineyards. If time permits, stop at the **Navarro Winery**, housed in an attractive contemporary building where complimentary wine tasting is offered (707-895-3686, *www.navarrowine.com*). As the road leaves the sunny open fields of grapes, the sun almost disappears as you enter a majestic redwood forest, so dense that only slanting rays of light filter through the trees. Upon leaving the forest, Hwy 128 soon merges with the coastal Hwy 1 (about a 60-mile drive from where you left Hwy 101). Here you join Hwy 1 going north along the coast through **Albion** and **Little River**, and then on to Mendocino.

Mendocino is an absolute jewel: a New-England-style town built upon headlands that jut out to the ocean. It is not surprising that the town looks as if it were transported from the East Coast because its heritage goes back to adventurous fishermen who settled here from New England, and, upon arrival, built houses like those they had left behind. (In fact, the "New England" setting, seen in the popular television series *Murder She Wrote,* was filmed here.) Tucked into the many colorful wood-frame buildings you find a wealth of art galleries, gift shops, inns, and restaurants. (Mendocino Coast Chamber of Commerce, 707-961-6300, *www.mendocinocoast.com.*)

Do not let your explorations stop at the quaint town, but venture out onto the barren, windswept headlands—a visit to Mendocino would not be complete without a walk along the bluffs. In late fall or spring there is an added bonus: spouts of water off the shoreline are an indication that gray whales are present.

Mendocino makes a most convenient base for exploring the coast. However, if breathtaking views are more important to you than quaint shops and restaurants, then stay overnight instead 16 miles south of Mendocino in **Elk**, a tiny old lumber town hugging the bluffs along one of the most spectacularly beautiful stretches of the sensational Mendocino coastline. Elk has several places to stay that are described in detail in the inn section of this guide—each has its own personality, each has a magnificent ocean view. Note: If you choose to overnight in Elk instead of the town of Mendocino, when Hwy 128 merges with Hwy 1, go south to Elk instead of north to Mendocino.

Staying in this area, you could most successfully be entertained by doing absolutely nothing other than soaking in the natural, rugged beauty of the coast. However, there are some sightseeing possibilities:

Whale watching is a must if you are here between Christmas and April when the gray whales migrate along the coast. We thoroughly enjoyed the two-hour whale-watching trip that we took from **Noyo Harbor** with **Telstar Charters**, owned and operated by Randy and Charan Thornton (Charan handles the reservations and Randy pilots the boat). Randy also takes people deep-sea fishing for crab, salmon, cod, and albacore year-round. (707-964-8770, *www.gooceanfishing.com*)

Fort Bragg. This is a sprawling town that, when compared to the quaintness of Mendocino, has little to offer architecturally except for an extremely colorful fishing harbor. At 18220 N. Hwy One you find the 47 acres of the **Mendocino Coast Botanical Gardens**. The mild, rainy winters and cool summers provide ideal growing conditions for the flowers, trees and shrubs, including 4,000 spring-blooming rhododendrons, fuchsias, Japanese maples, roses and more. The gardens are open daily between 9 am and 5 pm. (707-964-4352, *www.gardenbythesea.org*)

Much of Fort Bragg's history can be viewed at the **Guest House Museum,** located on the corner of Main (Highway 1) and Laurel streets. Built for the Fort Bragg Redwood company in the 19th century, the building later became the Union Lumber Company guest house and now houses artifacts, photos and exhibits from the town's early days.

Just behind the museum you find the **Skunk Railroad**, which runs between Fort Bragg and Willits (*www.skunktrain.com*). During the summer months you can take either the all-day trip, which makes the complete round trip to Willits, or a half-day trip leaving in the morning or the afternoon. The train follows the old logging route through the redwood forests. The outing is especially fun for children. (800-866-1690.)

Leaving the Mendocino area, continue to follow the coast north and enjoy a treasury of memorable views: sometimes the bluffs drop into the sea, other times sand dunes almost hide the ocean, and at one point the beach sweeps right up to the road. At Rockport, Hwy 1 turns inland and twists and turns its way through forests and over the coastal range on 20 miles of narrow winding road. Arriving at **Leggett** (just before the junction with Hwy 101), look for a sign to your right indicating a small, privately-owned redwood park where you can drive through a hole in a redwood tree.

From Leggett continue north along Hwy 101, signposted for Eureka. However, rather than rushing all the way up Hwy 101, follow the old highway, called the **Avenue of the**

Giants, that weaves through the **Humboldt Redwoods State Park**. This is a 33-mile-long drive, but we suggest you select the most beautiful section by skipping the first part and joining the Avenue of the Giants at Myers Flat. As you exit at Myers Flat the two-lane road passes a few stores before entering a spectacular glen of redwoods. A lovely section of the forest is at **Williams Grove**. Stop at the nearby park headquarters and obtain a map that directs you off the Avenue of the Giants to **Rockefeller Forest** the oldest glen of redwoods left in the world—some date back over 2,000 years. The trees are labeled and a well-marked footpath guides you through the forest to the Big Tree, an astounding giant measuring 17 feet in diameter and soaring into the sky, and to the Flat Iron Tree (another biggie with a somewhat flattened-out trunk) located nearby in an especially serene grove.

About ten minutes after rejoining Hwy 101, exit to **Scotia**. Established in 1869, the picturesque town's little redwood homes are dominated by the lumber mill. You will find the small shopping center worth visiting just for the sake of seeing the redwood building constructed from pillars made of whole tree trunks. Drive to the **Scotia Museum**—an all-redwood building styled after a Grecian temple with redwood-tree pillars (bark and all) instead of marble. The museum displays photos, artifacts, and machinery used in the logging camps. Open weekdays Memorial Day to Labor Day. (707-764-2222.)

Returning to Hwy 101, about a 10-mile drive brings you to the Ferndale exit. Founded in 1852, **Ferndale** is the westernmost town (more of a village than a town) in the continental United States. Downtown, with its gaily painted Victorian buildings, has changed very little since the 1890s. **Main Street** is a gem, lined with delightful little galleries and stores—a favorite being the irresistible candy shop where you view, through the window, hand-dipping of delectable chocolates. Many visitors enjoy the **Repertory Theater** on Main Street where some excellent plays are produced (707-786-5483). Epitomizing the colorful character of the town is the **Gingerbread Mansion.** Stop at Ferndale's **Museum** to learn more about her past as you tour Victorian rooms and see displays of old dairy and smithying equipment. (Shaw and 3rd Street, open Tuesday through Saturday 11 am to 4 pm and Sunday 1 to 4 pm, 707-786-4466.)

Centerville Beach is 5 miles west of Ferndale on Centerville Road (turn right on Ocean Avenue at the end of Ferndale). Here you have 9 miles of beaches backed by dairy farms to the north and steep cliffs to the south. Watch for harbor seals in the breakers and tundra swans, which congregate in the Eel River bottoms north of Centerville Road from mid-November to February.

Leaving Ferndale, retrace your way to Hwy 101 and continue north for the 10-mile drive to **Eureka**. The area surrounding the 101 is full of fast-food chains, gas stations, and commercial establishments, but a portion of this large town, the **Old Town**, is well worth a visit (G and D between 1st and 3rd). On the northwestern edge of this restored project lies the ornate **Carson Mansion** (2nd and M), the most photographed, ornate, Victorian mansion in northern California.

About 20 miles beyond Eureka, exit the 101 for the coastal hamlet of **Trinidad**. Although its houses are now mostly of modern architecture, Trinidad Bay has an interesting history. It was discovered by the Portuguese in 1595, claimed by the Spaniards in 1775, flourished in the 1850s gold rush as a supply port for the miners, and was later kept on the map by logging. Now Trinidad is a sleepy little cluster of homes nestled on the bluffs overlooking a sheltered cove where an untouristy wharf stretches out into the bay. Next to the wharf is the **Seascape Restaurant** where you can dine on fish straight from the little fishing boats. Stroll the mile-long path along the headlands enjoying the views and in winter the crashing rollers.

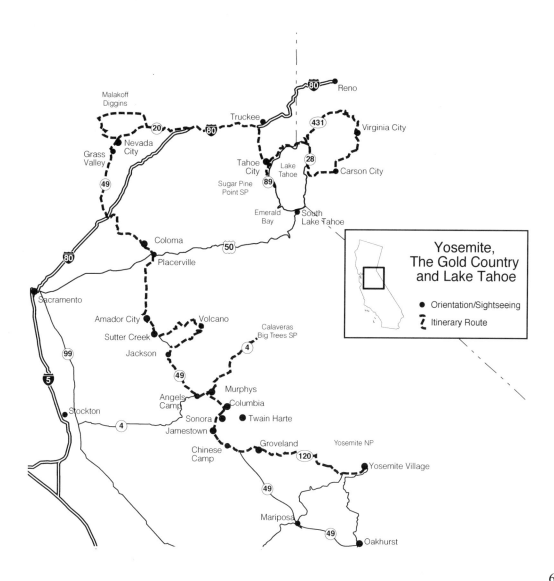

Malakoff
Diggins

⟨20⟩

Truckee

⟨80⟩ Reno

⟨431⟩

Virginia City

Nevada
City

Grass
Valley

⟨80⟩

Tahoe
City

Lake
Tahoe

⟨28⟩

Carson City

⟨49⟩

Sugar Pine
Point SP

⟨89⟩

Emerald
Bay

South
Lake Tahoe

⟨80⟩

Coloma

⟨50⟩

Placerville

Sacramento

Amador City

Volcano

Calaveras
Big Trees SP

Sutter Creek

⟨99⟩

Jackson

⟨4⟩

⟨5⟩

⟨49⟩

Stockton

Angels
Camp

Murphys

Columbia

⟨4⟩

Sonora

Twain Harte

Jamestown

Chinese
Camp

Groveland

Yosemite NP

⟨120⟩

Yosemite Village

⟨49⟩

Mariposa

⟨49⟩

Oakhurst

Yosemite,
The Gold Country
and Lake Tahoe

● Orientation/Sightseeing

Itinerary Route

Yosemite, the Gold Country & Lake Tahoe

Half Dome, Yosemite

This itinerary features two of California's most spectacular natural attractions, majestic Yosemite National Park and beautiful Lake Tahoe, and links them together by one of California's best-kept secrets—the spirited, nostalgic, Gold Rush towns, which string along the Sierra foothills. These colorful towns date back to 1848 when the cry went up that gold had been found at Sutter Creek, precipitating the rush to California by men eager to make their fortunes. Overnight, boom towns sprang up around every mining camp, with a cluster of similar-style saloons, restaurants, hotels, dance halls, and homes. Gold Rush fever quickly cooled and many of the towns were left, quietly forgotten, until tourists rediscovered their charm. Today these benignly neglected towns have been spruced up and bustle with activity: antique shops, art galleries, nifty boutiques, attractive restaurants, and appealing inns are tucked into old Victorian houses lining sleepy streets. The highway that runs through the mother lode country is numbered 49 after the gold-seeking miners who were known as the Forty-Niners.

Recommended Pacing: We recommend a minimum of two nights in Yosemite and suggest that you try to stay at accommodation in the park (see following page). Either before or after visiting Yosemite, you have a perfect opportunity to explore California's Gold Rush Country. Rather than backtracking, plan to progress through the region, spending at least one night in the south and one night in the north. From the northern region of the Gold Country it is a logical continuation on to Lake Tahoe. Many people enjoy Lake Tahoe as a resort and will spend at least a week here, basking on its sandy beaches in the summer and skiing down the snow-covered peaks that ring its waters in the winter. If you are visiting Lake Tahoe as a tourist, we recommend a two-night visit. **The itinerary route is also outlined on Map 5 at the front of the book.**

Weather Wise: Heavy snow is the norm at Tahoe and Yosemite during the winter, while most of the Gold Rush towns are beneath the snow line and experience heavy winter rains. During summer months the days are hot in Yosemite and Tahoe, and several degrees warmer in the Gold Country.

As you read through this itinerary, please be aware that each of the areas featured could well be a destination in itself. Yosemite and Lake Tahoe are especially popular resorts and an entire vacation could easily be dedicated to either one. If that is your desire, just extract from the itinerary the portion that suits your interests. However, the Gold Country is not as well known and makes a super link between Yosemite and Tahoe—or, for that matter, a great destination in its own right.

Since Yosemite makes a most convenient first-night stop from either San Francisco or Los Angeles, driving directions are given from both so that you can tailor the trip to your own needs. Much of the first day of this itinerary is spent driving to Yosemite National Park, about a four- to five-hour drive from San Francisco or a six- to seven-hour drive from the Greater Los Angeles area. A brief description of what to see and do during your stay in San Francisco is included in *San Francisco to Los Angeles via the Coast*, while the list of attractions of the much larger, more sprawling Los Angeles are included in *Leisurely Loop of Southern California.*

Leave San Francisco east over the Bay Bridge, in the direction of Oakland. Once across the bridge, stay in the middle lane and follow signs for Hwy 580, heading east, signposted Stockton. Stay on Hwy 580 for about 48 miles until you come to Livermore where Hwy 580 meets Hwy 205, which you take, continuing east, following signs for Manteca. Near Manteca, take Hwy 120 east, directly to the northern gate of Yosemite National Park. Total driving distance is about 200 miles.

Leave Los Angeles heading north on Hwy 5 until you come to the junction of Hwy 99, which you take north (signposted Bakersfield). Continue on Hwy 99 to the north edge of Fresno where you take Hwy 41 north, directly to the southern gate of Yosemite National Park. Total driving distance is about 300 miles.

The main attractions of the over 1,000 square miles of **Yosemite National Park** lie within the narrow 7-mile-long **Yosemite Valley**, which is where you should try to stay if at all possible. A two- or three-night stay in the park is recommended. From hotels through tented cabins, all accommodations in Yosemite are controlled by the **Yosemite Concessions Services (YCS)**—for information call 209-372-0200. It is necessary year-round to make reservations well in advance by phoning 559-252-4848 or *www.yosemitepark.com*. Visit their homepage on the National Park Service website at *www.nps.gov*.

From the stately and very expensive **Ahwahnee Hotel**, through lodges, cabins, tented camps, and regular campsites, Yosemite has accommodations to suit every pocketbook. If your taste in hotels runs to grand, stay at The Ahwahnee. **Yosemite Lodge** provides more moderately priced accommodations in both cabins and motel/hotel-type rooms. Still less expensive are the tented camps that provide canvas tents on wooden board floors (you do not need sleeping bags since beds and linens are provided). The budget choice is regular camping. But please remember—space is very limited in every category and reservations are essential.

While the attractions of staying in the valley cannot be denied, a more relaxed, serene, country atmosphere pervades the **Wawona Hotel**, located within the park, but about a 30-mile drive south of the valley on Hwy 41. With its shaded verandahs overlooking broad rolling lawns, the hotel presents a welcoming picture. Bedrooms with private bathrooms are at a premium—most rooms use communal men's and women's bathrooms (sometimes situated quite a distance from your bedroom).

Yosemite Valley, an awe-inspiring monument to the forces of nature, is bounded by magnificent scraped granite formations—**Half Dome**, **El Capitan**, **Cathedral Rock**, **Clouds Rest**—beckoning rock climbers from around the world. And over the rocks, cascading to the valley far below, are numerous high waterfalls with descriptive names such as Bridalveil, Ribbon, Staircase, and Silver Strand. Below the giant walls of rock the crystal-clear River Merced wends its way through woodlands and meadows of flowers. Undeniably, this is one of the most beautiful valleys anywhere in the world.

Your first stop should be the information center to obtain pamphlets, books, and schedules. The park service offers a remarkable number of guided walks, slide shows, and educational programs—look over the possibilities and select the ones that most appeal to you.

Once you are in the valley, park your car and restrict yourself to travel aboard the free shuttle buses as you can do most of your sightseeing by combining pleasant walks with shuttle-bus rides. Alternative modes of transportation are on horseback on guided trips and by bike (bicycles can be rented in the park). Because the valley is flat, it has miles of paths for biking—a very unstrenuous, efficient way of getting around.

Be warned that during the summer months Yosemite Valley is jammed with cars and people—spring and fall are much more civilized times to visit.

Within the park, but beyond the valley floor, are many areas of great natural beauty. Situated just inside the park's southern perimeter is the **Mariposa Grove** of giant sequoias. It was here that John Muir, the great naturalist who fathered the idea of the national park system, persuaded President Theodore Roosevelt to add the 250-acre grove of trees to the Yosemite park system. A tram winds through the grove of sequoias as the driver tells the stories of these giant trees—some of the largest in the world.

To the south of the valley Hwy 41 climbs for about 10 miles (stop at the viewing point just before the tunnel) to the Glacier Point turnoff. It is a 15-mile drive to the spectacular **Glacier Point**—a vista point over 3,000 feet above the valley floor. From Glacier Point everything in the valley below takes on Lilliputian proportions: the ribbon-like River Merced, the forest, meadows, and waterfalls all dwarfed by huge granite cliffs. Beyond the valley a giant panorama of undulating granite presents itself. The ideal time to visit for taking photographs is early in the morning or evening. Rangers at Glacier Point offer evening interpretive programs.

Leave Yosemite by the northern gate on Hwy 120 to **Groveland**, a handsome old town shaded by pines. The nearby town of Big Oak Flat is little more than a couple of houses and the crumbling IOOF (International Order of Odd Fellows) building strung along the road. As Hwy 120 drops steeply down 5 miles of twisting road to Hwy 49, the shady pine forests of the mountains give way to rolling, oak-studded foothills, the typical scenery of the Gold Country.

Heading north on Hwy 49, detour through **Chinese Camp**, home to over 5,000 Chinese miners in the 1850s and now almost a ghost town sleeping under a profusion of delicate Chinese Trees of Heaven.

The main street of **Jamestown** is off Hwy 49 and therefore free of thoroughfare traffic. With its wooden boardwalks, balconies, and storefronts, Jamestown has managed to retain much of the feel of the Gold Rush days. Inviting shops, particularly the emporium, merit a browse, the western-style saloons are full of local color, and the **1859 National Hotel** as well as the **Jamestown Hotel** have been restored to a beauty such as the Gold Rush days never witnessed. Just above Main Street on Fifth Avenue is the **Railtown 1897 State Historic Park** where visitors can see old freight and passenger cars, steam trains, and the roundhouse. Rides on an old steam train are offered on summer weekends. (209 984-3953)

Leaving town, continue up the main street and cross Hwy 49 onto Jamestown Road, a peaceful little byway that avoids the congestion of Sonora, and takes you through the countryside to Columbia. Follow signs for Columbia or, wherever a junction is unmarked, continue straight. A 15-minute drive brings you to Parrot Ferry Road on the outskirts of the town.

In the 1850s **Columbia** was one of the largest towns in California, with many saloons, gaming halls, and stores. Today the main street is closed to car traffic and has been restored as a state park to reflect the dusty, raucous days when Columbia was the "gem of the southern mines." The renovated buildings of Main Street are like exhibits that make learning fun. Be sure to visit the Wells Fargo office, fire station, candy store, mining museum, and concession shops where costumed citizens sell goods appropriate to the period. You can enjoy a cold sarsaparilla at the saloon, munch candy rocks at the Candy Kitchen, and pan for gold at the mining shack. It is great fun to climb aboard a stagecoach for a ride through the town or take a tour to the Hidden Treasure Mine.

City Hotel, Columbia

Both the Fallon and City Hotel have been restored to mirror the look of two of Columbia's hotels in Gold Rush days. The City Hotel on Main Street has a less ornate Victorian decor, reflecting the Columbia of the 1860s.

Parrot Ferry Road leads north from Columbia, crosses the dam and continues through hilly countryside in the direction of Murphys. If you would like to try your hand at rappelling into the largest cavern in California, you have the opportunity at **Moaning Cavern**. (You can, of course, take the saner descent down a spiral staircase into a room capable of holding the Statue of Liberty.) The rappel is exciting, and with outfitting, instruction, and a boost of confidence, you descend through a small opening into the well-lit cavern—a most exhilarating experience.

From the caves a short drive brings you to Hwy 4 where you turn east (right) and travel a very short distance to **Chatom Vineyards** where you can sample their wines and picnic under their shady arbor. (*www.chatomvineyards.com*, 800-435-8852)

Leaving Chatom a 20 mile drive brings you to **Calaveras Big Trees State Park**, a 6,000-acre preserve of forest including two magnificent stands of sequoia trees. A 45-minute self-guided tour takes you through the North Grove and the nearby visitors center provides information and history on these mammoth trees. If you have time and interest, you can visit the more distant South Grove of giant sequoias. (*www.bigtrees.org*)

Leaving the park, retrace your route down Hwy 4 and detour into **Murphys**, the most stylish of Gold Rush towns where boutiques and restaurants shelter under locust and elm trees and the **Old Timers' Museum** reflect its Gold Rush heritage. Well signposted from the center of town is another cavern complex, **Mercer Caverns**, with rooms of stalactites, stalagmites, and other interesting limestone formations. You might also want to detour to a beautiful winery, **Ironstone Vineyards,** set on the hill outside Murphys. (Turn off Main Street up the road to the side of Murphy's Hotel and follow signs.) A visit here is much more than wine tasting for there's a mining museum (you can go gold panning), deli, jewelry store and theater with a grand organ used in the days of silent movies. Complimentary tours are offered daily at 11:30 am, 1:30 pm, and 3:30 pm (no 11:30 am tour during winter months). The winery is open daily between 10 am and 5 pm (closed at Christmas and Thanksgiving). Ironstone Vineyards is located at 1894 Six Mile Road, Murphys. (209-728-1251, *www.ironstonevineyards.com*)

At the junction of Hwys 4 and 49 sits **Angels Camp**, a pleasant town with high sidewalks and wooden-fronted buildings. Today Angels Camp's fame results not from mining, but from the frog-jumping contests held every May. There is even a monument to a frog taking the place of honor on the main street and brass plaques set in the sidewalk honoring the frogs who have won the jumping contest over the years.

Leave Angels Camp traveling north on Hwy 49 through **San Andreas** where nearly all evidence of Gold Rush days has been obliterated by modern shopping centers and commercial businesses. On the outskirts of the town Hwy 49 makes a sharp turn to the east (right), which is signposted Jackson. A 7-mile drive brings you to **Mukulumne Hill**, which in its heyday was one of the more raucous mining towns, though now it's a sleepy place. Turn off Hwy 49 and loop through town past the Hotel Leger and turn left in front of the crumbling IOOF (International Order of Odd Fellows) building, then through the residential area and back onto the main road.

Jackson still supports roughly the same population as it had during the Gold Rush—consequently, modern shopping centers and sprawling suburbs are the order of the day. To visit the old town turn right at the first stop sign in town which curves through the old downtown along Main Street. Set above the old town in a Victorian home is the **Amador County Museum**, 225 Church Street. The various rooms have rather eclectic exhibits from the Gold Rush era: for example, the kitchen is full of 19th-century cookware while a small upstairs bedroom displays Indian baskets. Set in an adjacent building is a scale working model of the North Star Stamp Mill, which crushes tiny stones.

Retrace your route to where you turned off Hwy 49 and turn left on Hwy 88 signposted for Lake Tahoe and Pine Grove. Just outside Pine Grove turn left (signposted for your next two destinations, Indian Grinding Rock State Park and Volcano) and follow a pretty back road to **Chaw'se Indian Grinding Rock State Park**. A giant slab of limestone has over 1,000 grinding mortars worn into it by Indian women grinding acorn meal. A typical Miwok village has been built nearby with a ceremonial roundhouse and various tree-bark dwellings. The adjacent cultural center, built in the style of an Indian roundhouse, has interesting displays from several local Indian tribes.

Just a short drive takes you past the turnoff for Sutter Creek and into **Volcano**, one of the smallest (population 100) Gold Country towns, which boasted the first lending library and theater group in the state. Now it is a tiny one-street town whose most impressive building is the three-storied, balconied **Saint George Hotel**. Several weathered building fronts give an impression of what the town looked like in more prosperous days. Three miles beyond the town lies **Daffodil Hill** where over 25,000 daffodils provide a colorful spring display.

Follow the narrow wooded ravine alongside Sutter Creek as it twists down to the town of the same name. **Sutter Creek** rivals Nevada City and Murphys as the loveliest of the Gold Rush towns. Its main street is strung out along busy Hwy 49 but somehow the bustling traffic does not detract from its beauty. False wooden storefronts support big balconies, which hang over the high sidewalks of the town. Today many of the quaint wooden buildings are home to antique, craft, and gift shops.

Amador City and **Drytown**, the first two towns you encounter after leaving Sutter Creek as you head towards Placerville on Hwy 49, have an old-world charm and are worth exploring. However, following thereafter is a string of commercial towns that are of little interest to the tourist although the intervening countryside is still most attractive. Follow Hwy 49 as it weaves through the commercial sprawl of **Placerville.** As Hwy 49 winds down into town take a right at the bottom on the hill to explore the town's restored Main Street. If it is lunchtime head for A Main Street Café. Cross Hwy 50 and then follow the 49 as it climbs out of town.

It is an 8-mile drive along Hwy 49, through apple orchards and woodlands, to Coloma where the Gold Rush began. Set on the banks of the American River, the scant remains of the boom town of **Coloma** are preserved as **Marshall Gold Discovery State Historic Park**. It all began in 1848 when James Marshall discovered gold at **Sutter's Sawmill**. The remaining historic buildings are scattered over a large area, each separated by expanses of green lawn and picnic places along the banks of the river. The residential part of town is a sleepy little cluster of attractive houses set back from the river—it is hard to believe that there was once a population of over 10,000 here. The museum shows a short film on gold discovery and provides information for a self-guided tour. A duplicate of Sutter's original sawmill, looking like a big shed, sits on the bank of the river. For a change of transportation, a number of companies offer one-day rafting trips down the most famous section of the South Fork of the American River. We thoroughly enjoyed the trip that we took with **Beyond Limits Adventures**. It's a class 3 (intermediate) section of river that combines pretty scenery and whitewater as your raft plunges into Satan's Cesspool, Hospital Bar, and Ambulance Driver. (Minimum age seven, season April to October, 800-234-7238, *www.rivertrip.com.*)

Nevada City

Auburn lies 20 miles farther north along Hwy 49, which weaves through its town center, crosses Hwy 80, and continues as a fast, wide road for approximately 24 miles into Grass

Valley. An alternative, far more attractive, and just a few miles longer route, is to take Hwy 80 north to the Colfax-Grass Valley exit and follow Hwy 174 through pretty woodlands and orchards into Grass Valley. (The following sightseeing suggestion, Empire Mine State Park, is signposted on your left as you near town.)

Grass Valley has a booming economy and sprawls far beyond its historic boundary. Its old downtown buildings housing everyday stores attest to its prosperity. Save town explorations for adjacent Nevada City and concentrate on Grass Valley's **Empire Mine State Park** at the southern end of town. This hard-rock mine is the oldest and richest in California. From startup in 1850 to closure in 1956, an estimated 5,800,000 ounces of gold were extracted. Wander through the yard to see the historic buildings (excellent displays) and take a peek down the mainshaft. Tours are given through the opulent **Empire Cottage** where you see how William Bourne, the wealthy mine owner, lived when on vacation or visiting his mine interests. (530-273-8522)

The adjacent town of **Nevada City** is as handsome as Grass Valley is functional. The old mining stores and saloons have been cleverly converted into eateries ranging from family-style cafés to gourmet restaurants, antique stores, boutiques, bookstores, and the like. Old-fashioned gas lamps light the streets at night, providing a perfect backdrop for a horse-drawn-carriage ride. Many settlers came here from the east bringing with them the deciduous trees of their home states, so Nevada City is one of the few places in California that has the glorious fall foliage. A great many events occur in Nevada City including the popular Victorian Christmas (Thanksgiving to Christmas—roast chestnuts and carolers), Summer Nights, and the Teddy Bear Convention (April). The town also hosts parades such as the Joe Cain Parade (Mardi Gras), markets, festivals, and tours that give you plenty of excuses to visit this delightful spot at all times of the year.

As a conclusion to your Gold Country explorations, take a 45-mile round trip to **Malakoff Diggins** where high-powered jets of water were blasted at a mountainside to extract gold. The method was very successful, but it clogged waterways for miles and left a lunar-like landscape where there had once been a forested mountainside. This is a very pleasant summer-evening trip, but rather than run the risk of returning down narrow country roads in the dark, make the loop as you leave Nevada City for Lake Tahoe. The route is quite well signposted, but it gives you reassurance to have in hand the map from Nevada City Chamber of Commerce. (530-265-2692, *www.nevadacitychamber.com*)

Go north on Hwy 49, following it through wooded countryside for 11 miles to the marker directing you right to Malakoff Diggins (signposted Tyler Foote Crossing Road). The narrow paved road leads you through the forest and, just as you are beginning to wonder quite where you are going, a signpost directs you right down a dirt road into **North Bloomfield**, a town of white-painted houses and buildings set behind picket fences under forest shade. (Several buildings have been restored as museums and the ranger station is a useful informational stop.) The road through town leads to the diggins proper, a vast landscape of awesome scars. If the weather is inclement, turn back at this point and return to Nevada City by way of the paved highway. Otherwise, continue along the well-maintained dirt road (forking left and downhill at junctions), which leads you down through some lovely scenery to a narrow wood-and-metal bridge spanning a rocky canyon of the South Yuba River where you pick up the paved road that brings you back to Hwy 49 on the outskirts of Nevada City.

Leave Nevada City on Hwy 20 east, a freeway which soon becomes a two-lane highway passing through forests and along a high ridge giving vistas of the Sierras. As Hwy 20 ends, take Hwy 80 towards Truckee, a fast freeway that climbs into the Sierra mountains through ever-more-dramatic rugged scenery.

The freeway climbs over **Donner Pass** and by **Donner Lake**, both named in honor of the group of settlers led by George Donner who in 1846 became snowbound while trying to cross the Sierra Nevada in late fall. Harsh conditions and lack of food took many lives and resulted in the survivors resorting to cannibalism.

Take Hwy 89, the Tahoe City exit, and follow it alongside the rushing **Truckee River** to its source, **Lake Tahoe**. Tucked in a high valley, Lake Tahoe is a vast, blue, icy-cold lake ringed by pine forests and backed by high mountains. The lake has about 70 miles of shoreline, a maximum depth of 1,645 feet, and a summer temperature of about 65 degrees. When people from the San Francisco Bay Area say they are "going to the mountains," Tahoe is usually where they're heading. While certain enclaves have their share of hot dog stands, McDonald's restaurants, and glitzy gambling casinos, there are many unspoilt areas where you can enjoy the exquisite beauty of the lake and its surrounding stunning scenery. For bikers and joggers, a marvelous, seemingly endless trail traces a path along the lakefront and down the Truckee River.

Tahoe City combines rustic, folksy shops, restaurants, and everyday stores with two quite interesting tourist attractions: Fanny Bridge and the Gatekeeper's Cabin. **Fanny Bridge** is very close: just turn right at the supermarket, and there it is. You will see immediately the derivation of "Fanny" when you see the tourists leaning over the railing to watch the trout gobble up the food tossed to them. On the same side of the bridge where the fish feed, outlet gates are opened and shut to control the level of the lake—the entire flow of water exiting from Lake Tahoe is regulated here as the water runs into the Truckee River. The other attraction of Tahoe City, the **Gatekeeper's Cabin**, sits on the bank of the Truckee. The rustic old cabin, once home to the man who controlled the river level, is now an attractive small museum operated by the local historical society.

Hugging the shoreline, Hwy 89 opens up to ever-more-lovely vistas as the road travels south. Nine miles south of Tahoe City brings you to **Sugar Pine State Park** with its many miles of hiking trails, and camping and picnic sites. In summer you can tour the nicely furnished Ehrman Mansion, once the vast lakeside summer home of a wealthy San Francisco family.

You will know by the sheer beauty of your surroundings when you are at **Emerald Bay**. The road sits hundreds of feet above a sparkling, blue-green bay and miles of Lake Tahoe stretch beyond its entrance. Center stage is a small wooded island crowned by a stone teahouse. A 1½-mile trail winds down to the lake—it seems a lot farther walking up—and in summer you can tour **Vikingsholm**, the 38-room lakeside mansion built in 1929 and patterned after a 9th-century Norse fortress. It is the finest example of Scandinavian architecture in America and is filled with Norwegian furniture. (*www.vikingsholm.com*)

Emerald Bay

Just beyond Emerald Bay a trail leads from the parking lot up a ¼-mile steep trail to a bridge above the cascading cataract of **Eagle Falls**, which offers fantastic views of Lake Tahoe. A mile farther up the trail is **Eagle Lake**, in an isolated, picture-perfect setting.

A memorable outing from Tahoe is a day trip to Nevada's silver towns, Virginia City and Carson City. Leaving Tahoe City, follow the northernmost shore of the lake across the Nevada state line and take Hwy 431 from Incline Village over Mount Rose to the stoplight at Hwy 395. Cross the highway and go straight ahead up the winding Geiger Grade, Hwy 341, to **Virginia City**. Built over a honeycomb of silver mines, in its heyday Virginia City had a population of over 30,000. Its wooden sidewalks, colorful saloons (you must visit the Bucket of Blood Saloon), and false-front buildings with their broad balconies make it a town straight out of a John Wayne movie. The stores sell everything from homemade candy to western boots and several have been reconstructed as museums. You can walk up to the old cemetery, take a steam-train ride, or tour a mine.

Leaving town, travel on through Gold Hill and Silver Hill to Hwy 50 where you turn south for the 7-mile drive to **Carson City**, the state capital. The town itself has little of interest except for the **Nevada State Museum**, just across the street from the Nugget Casino on the main road (open 8:30 am to 4:30 pm daily). The highlight of the museum is the re-created silver mine in the basement. You walk along rail car lines in semi-darkness, past exhibits of miners at work and mine machinery—a lot safer than going down a working mine. (775-687-4810)

To return to Tahoe, go south on Hwy 395, the main street of town, to Hwy 50 west. Turn right and when you come to Lake Tahoe turn right, following the lake to Tahoe City.

Leaving Lake Tahoe, it is a fast four- to five-hour freeway drive, via Hwy 80, to the San Francisco Bay Area. If you are going to Los Angeles, take Hwy 80 to Sacramento and Hwy 5 south to Los Angeles—a fast eight- to nine-hour drive.

Yosemite, the Gold Country & Lake Tahoe

Wandering Through
The Wine Country

- Orientation/Sightseeing
- Itinerary Route

Napa Valley
1. Hess Collection
2. Jarvis Winery
3. Trefethen Vineyards
4. Domaine Chandon
5. Goosecross Cellars
6. Plumpjack
7. Opus One
8. Robert Mondavi
9. Beaulieu Vineyards
10. Nichelini Winery
11. Rutherford Hill
12. V. Sattui Winery
13. Beringer Vineyards
14. Frank Family
15. Schramsberg
16. Sterling Vineyards
17. Clos Pegase
18. Château Montelena
19. Vincent Arroyo

Sonoma Valley
20. Landmark Vineyards
21. Château St. Jean
22. Kunde Winery
23. Benziger Winery
24. Buena Vista
25. Gloria Ferrer Winery
26. Viansa Winery

81

Wandering through the Wine Country

The Napa Valley

The Napa and Sonoma Valleys, just north of San Francisco, have earned a well-merited reputation for the excellence of their wines and many of the wineries are open to the public for tours and tasting. But there is so much more to lure you here than sampling wines—informative tours, exquisite artwork, historic buildings, movie memorabilia, and beautiful scenery abound. A visit to the wine country makes a pleasant excursion any time of year. In summer the days are long and warm, perfect for bike rides, picnics, music festivals, concerts, and art shows. As summer days give way to the cooler afternoons and crisp evenings of fall, the lush foliage on the thousands of acres of grapevines turns to red, gold, and yellow—a colorful reminder that it is time for harvest. You can sense the energy of the crush as vintners work against the clock and weather to pick grapes at their prime. In winter, cool days are often washed by rain, but this is also an excellent time to visit since this is "off season" and the winery tours will be almost private as you travel from one vineyard to the next. Spring is glorious: mustard blossoms paint the valleys yellow, contrasting dramatically with the dark bark of the vines laced with the delicate green of new leaves.

Recommended Pacing: You cannot follow this complete itinerary in a day trip from San Francisco but you certainly can visit both the Napa and Sonoma wine regions in a day—it takes about an hour to drive from San Francisco to the southern boundary of either valley and a day trip would allow you to visit a winery or two and get the flavor of the region. However, since the valleys are so beautiful and to allow adequate time for leisurely tastings, we suggest that you select a base (because of their close proximity you can select either valley) and stay for a minimum of two nights. Please do not try to follow this itinerary just as we have described it—it encompasses more wineries than you can possibly do justice to in a week. Instead, use it as a framework to plan your own trip: select those wineries that appeal to you (you can check out the wines they produce on their websites) and plot your route on a detailed map. **The itinerary route is also outlined on Map 4 at the front of the book.**

Weather Wise: The Napa and Sonoma Valleys have very similar climates. Summer days can be scorching hot and roads are often clogged with visitors. Autumn gives way to mild, sunny days, cooler afternoons, and crisp evenings. From autumn to spring you can expect some rain although many days will be sunny. In winter, temperatures are mild yet several degrees cooler than in the nearby San Francisco Bay Area.

Note: Gone are the days when you could turn up at a winery and expect a tour. Most now require advance reservations, particularly in the summer. We have tried to be as accurate as possible when giving information about tour costs and tastings, but things change, so be certain to contact each winery in advance of your arrival.

This itinerary wends up the Napa Valley and back down the Sonoma Valley. In the Napa Valley there are two parallel roads that stretch along its length—Hwy 29 and the Silverado Trail. Hwy 29 is the busier and wider of the two. The Silverado Trail, more scenic, less commercial, hugs the eastern hills, offering a welcome escape from traffic. Our suggested route crisscrosses back and forth between Hwy 29 and the Silverado Trail, and then travels west to follow a path south through the Sonoma Valley.

From San Francisco, travel east on Hwy 80 across the San Francisco-Oakland Bay Bridge. After crossing the bridge, stay in the left-hand lane and follow Hwy 80 in the direction of Sacramento for 30 miles. Four miles after crossing the Carquinez Bridge, take Hwy 37 (the Marine World Parkway exit) for 2½ miles to Hwy 29 (Sonoma Blvd). Turn right towards Napa and stay on Hwy 29 into the town.

Napa sprawls for several miles. Ignore its unappealing outskirts and head for downtown, which has really improved in recent years, adding some delightful restaurants and an attractive shopping precinct.

Take First Street through downtown to Hwy 29 (in the direction of Calistoga), turn left at the traffic lights on Redwood Road for the 6-mile drive to the **Hess Collection** winery (4411 Redwood Road, Napa, CA 94558). Leaving the town behind, travel ever higher up Mount Veeder though pretty wooded scenery with glimpses of distant vineyards. Watch for the sharp left-hand turn in the road after 4 miles. You emerge from the trees at the winery surrounded by rolling vineyards. Visiting here gives you the opportunity to enjoy a lovely garden with lily pond, wisteria-covered walkway, and wildflower garden, laid out in front of an early-20th-century winery.

When Mr. Hess purchased the winery in 1986 he set apart a portion of the historic ivy-covered stone structure to showcase a selection of his distinguished collection of paintings and sculptures. The production of wine and Mr. Hess's collection have been cleverly woven together and the visitors' tour encompasses wine production—fermentation vats, wooden barrels where the wine ages, and the bottling process—as well

Wandering through the Wine Country

as the art housed in two large galleries. Tasting costs are $10 for four wines. Open 10 am to 5:30 pm. 707-255-1144 or 877-707-4377, *www.hesscollection.com*.

Return to Hwy 29 and cross it onto Trancas, which after 1½ miles becomes Hwy 121 (signposted for Lake Berryessa). Follow this road for 4 miles as it climbs into the wooded hills. Watch for a gate on the left marking the **Jarvis Winery** entrance (2970 Monticello Road, Napa, CA 94559). The gates automatically open after you give your name and tour information (book well in advance—tour groups are limited). The tour is fun and the structure of the Jarvis Winery is different from that of any other you will see on this itinerary. It also produces excellent wines (Cabernet Franc, Cabernet Sauvignon, Chardonnay, and Merlot). All you see as you approach are two massive doors built into the hillside—it looks like an entrance into a bunker. But inside, another world opens up as you find yourself in a giant cave. You follow a path that forms a loop around the cavern, passing by an underground stream and a waterfall, and visit the Crystal Chamber, a grand reception hall. At the conclusion of the tour you sample fine wines at a small table surrounded by gilded chairs with red velvet upholstery. Five tours a day are offered. Based on demand, extra tours are sometimes added. 707-255-5280 or 800-255-5280, *www.jarviswines.com*.

Leaving the Jarvis Winery, retrace your tracks back down the hill to the Silverado Trail. Turn right (north) on the Silverado Trail and follow it to Oak Knoll Avenue, a left-hand turn down a road bounded by walnut trees and vineyards. Watch for a small signpost and large gates marking the right-hand turn for **Trefethen Vineyards** (1160 Oak Knoll Avenue, Napa, CA 94558). Trefethen Vineyards is housed in a wooden building dating back to 1886 and surrounded by towering oaks. This handsome complex is family owned and operated, proving that size is not a prerequisite for excellence. Open 10 am to 4:30 pm, tours are by appointment. 707-255-7700, *www.trefethen.com*.

Continue west on Oak Knoll Avenue for the very short distance to Hwy 29, which you cross, turning right on Solano Avenue, a quiet country road that parallels busy Hwy 29.

Solano Avenue ends on the outskirts of Yountville and ahead of you lies **Domaine Chandon** (1 California Drive, Yountville, CA 94559) where sparkling wine is made following the principles and rigid process dictated by the French *methode champenoise.* A wooden footbridge spans the creek-fed ponds and huge oak trees lead to the winery tucked back into the hillside. Complimentary tours are offered on the hour between 10 am and 6 pm. First you see the fermentation process in polished stainless-steel tanks and then continue on to observe the additional steps involved in making sparkling wine. In the cellar, bottles of sparkling wine are aged and riddled (turned). In the bottling room you see the process of freezing then disgorging the sediment, corking, cleaning, and labeling the bottles. A visit here shows French and Californian vintners sharing expertise and working side by side. After the tour enjoy a tasting of three to five wines for $16 to $22. Select your favorite and purchase a glass to enjoy on the adjacent terrace. There's an elegant restaurant that steps down the hillside and in sunny weather lunch is served on the patio. Open 10 am to 6 pm. 707-944-2280, *www.chandon.com.*

Leaving Domaine Chandon, turn left, go under Hwy 29, and turn left on Washington Street into the small town of **Yountville**. As the road divides (Washington left, Yount right) take the left-hand turn if you are in a shopping mood and turn immediately left into the car park of **Vintage 1870**, a complex of little shops and galleries housed in a charming old brick winery.

Return to Yount Street and follow it past the town's quaint houses, turning left onto Yountville Cross Road. After a mile turn left on State Lane for the half-mile drive to **Goosecross Cellars** (1119 State Lane, Yountville, CA 94559). This micro winery is a small family-run and -owned operation. Geoff Gorsuch and college roommate David Topper purchased it from Geoff's parents, who live in the cute house in front of the winery. Walk through the aging vats into the tasting room to sample red varietals and a Chardonnay. A very popular class in wine basics is offered every Saturday morning (advanced reservations needed). Open 10 am to 4:30 pm. 707-944-1986, *www.goosecross.com.*

Retrace your steps to Yountville Cross Road and turn left for the short drive up the Silverado Trail to Oakville Cross Road where you turn left. The first winery on your right is your destination, **Plumpjack** (620 Oakville Cross Road, Oakville, CA 94562). The fanciful theater-set style of the complex is a clue that this is a winery that flaunts tradition—they were front runners of eliminating corks in favor of screwtops even in their reserve Cabernets. Plumpjack derives its name from Shakespeare's portly character Jack Falstaff. Open for tasting 10 am to 4 pm, $10 per person. 707-945-1220, *www.plumpjack.com.*

Leave Plumpjack to your right and Oakville Cross Road takes you into the little town of **Oakville** where, as you turn right on Hwy 29, you see **Oakville Grocery** (on your right). If you plan to picnic, stop here for supplies and gourmet treats to accompany your winery purchases.

Just to the north of Oakville, on the right of Hwy 29, you soon come to **Opus One** (7900 Saint Helena Hwy, Hwy 29, Oakville, CA 94562) on your right. The winery is an exquisite showplace for the California Robert Mondavi family and the French Rothschild family. The gleaming white, circular structure looks a bit like a luxurious, futuristic coliseum. It certainly makes an impressive statement, and as you enter, is immediately obvious that no expense was spared in its construction. Tour and tasting $35, by appointment only. Tasting of their current vintage is $30. Tasting room is open from 10 am to 4 pm. 707-944-9442, *www.opusonewinery.com.*

Almost opposite Opus One you find the **Robert Mondavi** winery (7801 Saint Helena Hwy, Hwy 29, Oakville, CA 94562). This modern winery, with a statue of Saint Francis at its entrance, was styled after the Franciscan missions, with an open-arched entry framing an idyllic view of vineyards. Different tours are offered, varying in length and cost. The hour-and-a-half vineyard and winery tour is extremely informative and provides a good general introduction to the essentials of winemaking, $25. The spacious lawn at the back is the site of popular summer concerts. Reservations are recommended. Open 10 am to 5 pm. 707-968-2000 or 888-766-6328, *www.robertmondaviwinery.com.*

Continue north into Rutherford and just as you enter the town turn right to **Beaulieu Vineyards,** commonly known as BV (1960 Saint Helena Hwy, Hwy 29, Rutherford, CA 94573). Tours covering the history and production of their wines are offered. There's a fee for tasting. Open 10 am to 5 pm. 707-967-5200, *www.bvwines.com.*

Leaving BV, turn south (left) and then immediately left again onto Rutherford Cross Road for the scenic drive across the valley (following Hwy 128 towards Lake Berryessa). At the Silverado Trail, go right and immediately right again on Hwy 128 for the scenic 15-mile drive to **Nichelini** (2950 Sage Canyon Rd, Hwy 128, Saint Helena, CA 94574). This winery was founded by the Nichelini family in 1884 and is still in the same family today, making it the oldest family-operated winery in the Napa Valley. The building itself is of historical interest: showing off founder Anton Nichelini's stonemasonry, the hand-hewn stone wine cellar takes you back to the Ticino region of Switzerland. The old Roman-type press, constructed by Anton himself and in use until 1956, is the centerpiece of the visitor area. It is believed to be the only one of its kind still standing at a California winery. Open Saturdays and Sundays, 10 am to 5 pm, for wine tasting, picnicking, and bocci ball. 707-963-0717, *www.nicheliniwinery.com.*

Returning to the Silverado Trail, head north (right) for a short distance, taking the first right-hand turn on Rutherford Hill Road, which winds up past Auberge du Soleil, to the **Rutherford Hill** winery (200 Rutherford Hill Road, Rutherford, CA 94573), housed in a weathered redwood barn draped with roses and wisteria and surrounded by olive groves and shady woodlands. This is THE place to head for if you want to enjoy a picnic (bring your own food) for surrounding the winery are three shady picnic areas with fabulous views and lots of tables. Rutherford Hill winery is considered the leading producer of Merlot in the Napa Valley. The tour, $20, offered at 11:30 am, 1:30 pm, and 3:30 pm, includes a visit to the vast wine caves. Guides are knowledgeable about the winery and visitors are encouraged to ask questions. Open 10 am to 5 pm. 707-963-1871, *www.rutherfordhill.com.*

From Rutherford Hill travel north on the Silverado Trail, cross over to Hwy 29 on Zinfandel Lane, and then jog north on Hwy 29 (approaching the town of Saint Helena) to visit the **V. Sattui** winery found on your right (111 White Lane Street, Saint Helena, CA 94574). Sattui winemaking history dates back to 1885 when Vittorio Sattui founded the winery in the North Beach district of San Francisco. Great-grandson Daryl Sattui revived the family tradition in 1973 by moving the winery to Saint Helena. Currently 15 vintage-dated wines are produced, all of which are sold exclusively at the winery or by mail order. With a lovely garden setting, this is an attractive winery with an excellent gift shop where you can also purchase picnic supplies, selecting from over 200 different kinds of cheeses, homemade salads, pâtés, breads, and desserts. There is also a wonderful picnic spot, with tables set on the lawn beneath shady trees. You are welcome to look into the cellars or, when wine is being bottled, watch the bottling line in action—there are no formal tours. Tastings offered. Open 9 am to 6 pm in summer, 9 am to 5 pm in winter. 707-963-7774, *www.vsattui.com.*

Opposite V. Sattui you find **Dean and Deluca**, an upmarket store for purchasing kitchenware, wine, cheese, and all manner of picnic supplies.

In **Saint Helena** Hwy 29 becomes the town's Main Street, lined with elegant stores, boutiques, and restaurants. Detour east two blocks off Main Street via Adams Street to the **Silverado Museum**, housed in a wing of the town's library. Dedicated to Robert Louis Stevenson, the little museum chronicles his life and contains books, paintings, and Stephenson memorabilia. Open 10 am to 4 pm, closed Mondays.

As Hwy 29 leaves the northern residential area of Saint Helena, turn left into **Beringer Vineyards** (2000 Main Street, Hwy 29, Saint Helena, CA 94574). Set on a knoll, surrounded by landscaped grounds, the magnificent Rhine House was built as a replica of the German home that Frederick and his brother Jacob left behind when they emigrated. A 45-minute guided tour is offered every half hour, Monday through Friday between 10 am and 5 pm (from November to March the last tour is at 4 pm), Saturday and Sunday starting at 9:30 am (availability is on a first-come, first-served basis). Tours emphasize the historical aspect of the winery and include a visit through the tunnels and caverns where the wine is aged in barrels. Tours costs vary. The tasting fee is $10 to $25. 707-963-4812, *www.beringer.com*.

Four miles north, turn right off Hwy 29 onto Larkmead Lane to visit the **Frank Family Vineyards** (1091 Larkmead Lane, Calistoga, CA 94515). A vineyard has been on this spot since 1884. The main building was refurbished with local sandstone in 1906 and the resulting sturdy edifice is considered an archetype of the local wine country. Owners Richard Frank and Koemer Rombauer purchased the property from the Hans Kornell company, which is famous for its sparkling wines, and five types are still crafted in the champagne style, though nowadays the focus of the winery has shifted to the production of a superb range of still red and white wines. Tasting is free of charge. Open 10 am to 5 pm. 800-574-9463 or 707-942-0859, *www.frankfamilyvineyards.com*.

Returning to Hwy 29, take the first left, signposted Peterson Lane, and turn immediately up a driveway for the 1-mile drive up through woodlands to **Schramsberg Vineyards** (1400 Schramsberg Road, Calistoga, CA 94515). Built in 1862, Schrambsberg is the first hillside winery built in the Napa Valley and was featured by Robert Louis Stevenson in his chronicles of the wine country. Over 2 miles of tunnels are devoted to the production of sparkling wine and tours are by appointment only. In conjunction with the tour, wine tasting is offered at a charge of $35 for samples from four cuvees. Open 10 am to 4 pm. 707-942-4558, *www.schramsberg.com*.

Back on the 29, you soon see your next destination, **Sterling Vineyards** (1111 Dunaweal Lane, Calistoga, CA 94515), a complex of low, white buildings crowning the hill to your right. Turn right on Dunaweal Lane to reach them. From the winery you can savor panoramic views looking down through tall pines to a checkerboard of vineyards. Access to Sterling is possible only by an aerial tramway (the first tram is at 10:30 am, the last at 4:30 pm). A fee of $20 is charged for the tram and a tasting. A self-guided tour leads you through the maze of rooms that comprise the winery and concludes with the tasting. A very pleasant feature here is the melodic sound of bells originally from a London church, that ring out every half hour. *www.sterlingvineyards.com* 800-726-6136.

Across the street, **Clos Pegase** (1060 Dunaweal Lane, Calistoga, CA 94515) is a joy for those who love stunning architecture, sculpture, and fine wine. When owner Jan Isaac Shrem, a Paris-based businessman and art collector, turned 50, he decided to move to Napa Valley and take up viticulture. Shrem enlisted the help of Michael Graves, who designed the structure with influences that range from ancient Rome to art deco. The result is an exquisite building that the *Washington Post* called "America's first monument to wine as art." Sculptures are placed on the edge of the vineyards, on the lawns, and in the winery. Tours are complimentary (11 am and 2 pm) and reservations are not required, but be aware that the afternoon weekend tour tends to be crowded. Several tasting options are offered. Open 10:30 am to 5 pm. 707-942-4981, *www.clospegase.com.*

Our favorite Napa Valley town, **Calistoga**, bounded by rugged foothills and vineyards, is just a few miles north at the intersection of Hwy 29 and Hwy 128. Its main street, Lincoln Avenue, is lined on both sides by attractive shops and numerous restaurants. This charming town has been famous ever since Spanish explorers arrived in 1823 and observed Indians taking mud baths in steamy marshes. Sam Brannan, who purchased a square mile of land at the foot of Mount Saint Helena, gave the town its name: he wanted the place to be the "Saratoga of California" and so called it Calistoga. He bought the land in the early 1860s and by 1866 was ready to open his resort of a few cottages and palm trees. The oldest surviving railroad depot in California, now shops, received its first trainload of passengers when they came to Calistoga for the much-publicized opening of Sam Brannan's resort. For more than a hundred years, Calistoga has attracted visitors from all over the world, primarily for its hot springs and spas. People came in search of its glorious, healing waters long before the region became a popular destination for its wineries.

There are many excellent spa facilities and two kinds to choose from: with "heavy" mud and without. Among other places, traditional mud tubs are available at **Dr. Wilkinson's**

Hot Springs, 707-942-4102, *www.drwilkinson.com,* and **Indian Springs**, 707-942-4913, *www.indianspringscalistoga.com.* Excellent spas include **Lavender Hill** (small and cute, great for couples and friends), 707-942-4495, *www.lavenderhillspa.com,* and **Mount View Spa** (in the Mount View Hotel), 707-942-5789, *www.mountviewspa.com.*

Whenever we go to Calistoga, we always make a point of visiting **Old Faithful Geyser**, one of only three such regularly erupting geysers in the world. It erupts at intervals varying between 15 and 50 minutes, throwing a spume of about 4,000 gallons of water over 60 feet into the air. This is certainly an interesting phenomenon, although the staging is a bit honky-tonk. Old Faithful can be viewed from 9 am to 5 pm (9 am to 6 pm during daylight savings time). To reach the geyser, travel north from Calistoga on Hwy 128 to Tubbs Lane, turn right onto Tubbs Lane, and in half a mile you see the entrance to the geyser on your left. Cost $10, 707-942-6463, *www.oldfaithfulgeyser.com.*

Just beyond the geyser is the very interesting **Château Montelena** winery (1429 Tubbs Lane, Calistoga, CA 94515), founded in 1882 by Alfred Tubbs who brought over a French architect to build an "authentic" French château (you'll see that the architect took a little artistic license with this instruction). Enjoy a tasting ($25), see the exterior of the château and wander round the lake, resplendent with swans and a bridge leading to a tea house on an island. 707-942-5105, *www.montelena.com.*

A very personal wine-tasting experience is offered by the nearby **Vincent Arroyo** winery (2361 Greenwood Avenue, Calistoga, CA 94515). Proceed to the end of Tubbs Lane, turn right and first right on Greenwood Avenue, and the winery is on your right. This small, friendly, winery offers you the chance to taste wine from the barrel and secure purchases from future bottlings. "JJ", the resident black lab, offers an amusing addition to your visit, for once she observes a barrel tasting in progress, she drops a ball (or two) at your feet and climbs high on the barrel stacks waiting for you to throw the ball for her to retrieve. You can also sample and purchase estate-produced olive oil. By appointment only, hours vary. 707-942-6995, *www. vincentarroyo.com.*

Leaving Calistoga, take the Petrified Forest Road (which becomes Calistoga Road) west to the outskirts of Santa Rosa, forsaking the Napa Valley for the neighboring Sonoma Valley. The road climbs and winds a scenic 12 miles through forest and past meadows where cattle graze next to orchards. You may wish to stop at the rather commercial **California Petrified Forest**, a grove of redwoods that was petrified by ash from the volcanic eruption of Mount Saint Helena over 6,000,000 years ago.

On the residential outskirts of Santa Rosa, turn left on Hwy 12 in the direction of Sonoma. This road travels down the center of Sonoma Valley, often referred to as the "Valley of the Moon" after Jack London's famous novel of the same name.

Your first destination in this lovely valley, **Landmark Vineyards**, lies 6½ miles to the south (101 Adobe Canyon Road, Hwy 12, Kenwood, CA 95452). Tucked up against the hillside, the winery enjoys spectacular views of towering Sugarloaf Ridge from its beautifully landscaped courtyard, lakeside picnic grounds (bring your own picnic), and vineyards, which you tour in a wagon pulled by massive Belgian dray horses (Saturdays only, May to October, noon to 3 pm). As an accompaniment to wine tasting, you enjoy beautiful gardens and the opportunity to play bocci ball. Tasting $5 to $10. Open 10 am to 4:30 pm. 707-833-0053 or 800-452-6365, *www.landmarkwine.com*.

The neighboring **Château St. Jean** (8555 Sonoma Hwy, Hwy 12, Kenwood, CA 95452) lies snug against the hillside. An extremely pretty road winds up through vineyards to the strikingly beautiful winery and main house surrounded by lush lawns. With the exception of its mock tower, Château St. Jean is Mediterranean-French in its architecture. Be careful to pronounce its name as the English "Jean" since the winery is named after the founder's wife, Jean Sheffield. A booklet outlines a self-guided tour of the courtyard garden, which leads to the visitors' center, a combination tasting room and gift shop. Tastings are $10. Luxury wine tastings are available in the château. Open 10 am to 5 pm. 707-833-4134, *www.chateaustjean.com*.

Your next winery is the nearby **Kunde Winery** (10155 Sonoma Hwy, Kenwood, CA 95452) whose founder, Louis Kunde, settled in the Sonoma Valley in 1904. The present-day winery, which re-creates an 1883 barn that previously stood on the same site, houses a reception area with wine tasting and a small gift shop. Tasting, $10 estate wines, $20 reserve wines, is available between 10:30 am and 4:30 pm. Complimentary tours of the barrel-aging caves, which feature half a mile of interconnecting tunnels, are available approximately every hour on Fridays, Saturdays, and Sundays. 707-833-5501, *www.kunde.com.*

Travel south on Hwy 12 for several miles before taking a turnoff to the right to **Glen Ellen**. In the center of this small, quaint, wooded town turn right for Jack London State Park. Before you reach the park, stop to visit the Benziger Winery found on the right.

Trolley at Benziger Winery

The **Benziger Winery** (1883 London Ranch Road, Glen Ellen, CA 95442), set on a wooded knoll, is a fun, family-run winery. If it's close to lunchtime, take advantage of picnic tables set under redwood trees (bring your own food). Before you walk up to the tasting room, follow the informative self-guided vine tour next to the parking lot. Benziger offers tours ($15) every half hour. You climb aboard a trolley pulled by a bright-orange tractor for a tour of the vineyards, which lasts approximately 45 minutes. After the tour taste some of their wines. 888-490-2739, *www.benziger.com*.

Continue on up the hill to **Jack London State Park** where Jack London is buried. This lovely wooded park was established as a tribute to the famous author who had such an impact on the Sonoma Valley. This strikingly handsome man lived a life of rugged adventure and wrote passionately about life's struggles and how to survive them with integrity. In the 16 years prior to his death at age 40 he wrote 50 novels, which were immensely popular and are today considered classics. Two of his more renowned novels are *Call of the Wild* and *Sea Wolf*. This park offers a fitting tribute to Jack London, a courageous, dynamic man, full of life and concern for others. Open all year 9:30 am to 5 pm (7 pm in summer). *www.parks.sonoma.net/jlpark.html*.

In the park you can visit the ruins of Wolf House (London's dream house, which mysteriously burned to the ground the night of its completion), Beauty Cottage (the cottage where London wrote much of his later work is staffed from noon to 4 pm on weekends), and the House of Happy Walls (the home that Charmian London built after her husband's death, open 10 am to 5 pm). This last building is now an interesting museum depicting London's life through numerous photographs, writings, and furnishings that belonged to the author. From the museum, paths lead to the other homes and the gravesite. After visiting the park, return on Arnold Drive into Glen Ellen, turn right, and travel south (past the Sonoma State Home) to Madrone where you turn left, crossing over to Hwy 12, which takes you into Sonoma.

Sonoma is a gem of a town. By simply exploring the boundaries of its main square you will glimpse some of California's most important periods in history. (A small admission fee is charged to tour Sonoma's historic buildings.) On the square's northern edge sits the **Sonoma Barracks**, a two-story adobe building that was the Mexican provincial headquarters for the Northern Frontier under the command of General Vallejo. The adjacent wood-frame **Toscano Hotel** has been restored and on weekends guides lead interesting tours through the rooms. The nearby **Mission San Francisco Solano de Sonoma**, the last Franciscan mission built in California, was restored in the early 1900s. If you visit during the week, you may see elementary-school children, dressed as missionaries with their simple cloaks and rope ties, experiencing history "hands on" as they work with crafts and tools from the days of the missionaries. One hall of the mission houses an unusually beautiful collection of watercolor paintings depicting several of California's missions. The long, low adobe building across the way, the Blue Wig Inn, originally built to house soldiers assigned to the mission, enjoyed a more colorful existence as a saloon and gambling room during the Gold Rush days. *www.parks.sonoma.net/sonoma.html.*

Mission San Francisco Solano de Sonoma

Wandering through the Wine Country

In addition to the historic sites on Sonoma's plaza, there are numerous shops and boutiques to investigate, including some wonderful specialty food stores where you can purchase picnic supplies. The **Sonoma Cheese Factory** on Spain Street is interesting to visit.

Leaving the square, go east on Napa Street for 2 miles to Old Winery Road where you turn left to visit the region's oldest winery, **Buena Vista** (18000 Old Winery Road, Sonoma, CA 95476), built in 1857. Nestled in a wooded glen, the old ivy-covered buildings are very picturesque with arched caverns and stone walls. Picnic tables are set under the trees (bring your own food and be prepared for quite a crowd in the summer). There's a self-guided tour, tastings $10. Open 10 am to 5 pm. 800-926-1266 or 707-938-1266, *www.buenavistacarneros.com*.

General Vallejo, the military commander and director of colonization of the Northern Frontier (until the Bear Flag Revolution established California as a free and independent republic), lived nearby with his wife and their 12 children. **General Vallejo's Home,** "Lachryma Montis" (translated to mean mountain tear, an adaptation of the Indian name given to a free-flowing spring that surrounds the property), is well signposted on the outskirts of town on Spain Street. In its day this lovely Victorian-style house was considered one of the most elegant and lavishly decorated homes in the area, and is still attractively furnished. *www.parks.sonoma.net/sonoma.html*.

Leave Sonoma south on Broadway (Hwy 12), continuing on to Hwy 121 towards San Francisco.

A short drive brings you to the **Gloria Ferrer Winery** (23555 Hwy 121, Sonoma, CA 95476). The Ferrer family, who brought expertise in making Spanish sparkling and table wines, hails from Catalonia, Spain and, consequently, the winery resembles a small Catalonian village. A wide road sweeps up to the winery through the vineyards. Three tours a day are offered, $10. They start from the spacious tasting room whose windows look out over the vineyards and valley. Most of the narrative is given in a room decorated with winemaking instruments from the Ferrers' winery in Spain. The riddling of the bottles to capture the sediment is explained, and then you go to the observation room to see the process of freezing then disgorging the sediment, corking, cleaning, and labeling the bottles of sparkling wine. The tour then descends into a maze of interconnected wine-storage tunnels. It is awesome to stand next to towering heights of stacked bottles. The tour concludes back in the tasting room. Wine tasting is $5 to $10 per glass. 707-933-1917, *www.gloriaferrer.com.*

One more winery awaits you before you return to San Francisco. Just a short drive from the Gloria Ferrer Winery you come to the **Viansa Winery** and Italian marketplace (25200 Hwy 121, Sonoma, CA 95476). Founded in 1990 by Vicki and Sam Sebastiani, Sam being a third-generation Sonoma Valley winemaker, this lovely winery produces Italian varietals, all of which are sold exclusively at the winery or by mail order. The hilltop location is especially inviting with its shaded picnic tables (for food bought on site) overlooking acres of vineyards and wetland. In the marketplace you can purchase gifts, wine, and delicious food items prepared daily in the Viansa kitchen, or sample one of the many pantry foods set out for tasting. A tour of the cellar is offered at 3 pm and includes a tasting, cost $10. Open 10 am to 5 pm. 707-935-4700, *www.viansa.com.*

From the Viansa Winery it is less than an hour's drive back to San Francisco by continuing along Hwy 121 to Hwy 37 and onto Hwy 101, which takes you over the Golden Gate Bridge into the city.

Places to Stay

The location of the Albion River Inn is impressive—right on the bluff overlooking the bay where the Albion River meets the Pacific Ocean. Know that you deserve the best, splurge, and request one of the six especially lovely rooms with spa tubs. All guestrooms offer sweeping views of the inlet where the fishing boats bob about in the ever-changing tides. Most have private decks. All rooms are spacious, romantic, beautifully decorated, and very private and all have fireplaces and binoculars for whale watching. Other extras include robes, complimentary wine, newspapers, and coffee makers. There's a New England feel to the place: softly hued clusters of cottages perched on the cliffs fronted by grassy meadows. Gardens filled with brightly colored flowers line the walkways and the quiet is broken only by the sound of the sea and the deep-throated call of the foghorn. The lovely Albion River Inn Restaurant with its award-winning wine list, and single malt collection, is adjacent to the inn and shares the remarkable views. A hearty breakfast is served including juices, homemade breads, and other specialties of the house. *Directions:* From "Cloverdale" drive west on Hwy 128 to Hwy 1, and north 3 miles to Albion. The inn is on the northwest side of the Albion bridge.

ALBION RIVER INN
Owners: Flurry Healy & Peter Wells
3790 N. Hwy 1
P.O. Box 100
Albion, CA 95410, USA
Tel: (707) 937-1919, Fax: (707) 937-2604
Toll Free: (800) 479-7944
22 Rooms, Double: $195–$325
Minimum Stay Required: 2 nights on weekends
Open: all year, Credit cards: all major

Rarely do we promote resorts in our book, but the stunning location of the Seascape Resort prompted us to make an exception. This sprawling complex of seven buildings rests on the bluffs overlooking the Monterey Bay.The beach is a short walk down a private paved path (or take the golf-cart shuttle if you prefer) and there are three pools with outdoor Jacuzzis. Guests can choose from studios, one-bedroom suites, or two-bedroom villas. Suites are decorated and furnished in a beach motif and offer private balconies with ocean (or property) view, fireplace, kitchenette, and TV. Families are easily accommodated in the larger villas. Sanderlings Restaurant in the main building with its spectacular ocean views is named after the scurrying shorebirds. Lots of extras are available (often for rent): firepits at sunset, boogey boards and wetsuits, bikes, beach umbrellas and chairs. Walk for miles along the beach, visit the Monterey Bay Aquarium, Santa Cruz Beach Boardwalk, and golf on one of the nearby courses. Directions: About 9 miles south of Santa Cruz, take the San Andreas Road exit off Hwy 1 and go west to the first stop sign where you turn right and follow Seascape Boulevard to the Ocean and the resort. *Directions:* About 9 miles south of Santa Cruz, take the Larkin Valley Road exit off Hwy 1 and go west on San Andreas Road. Turn right on Seascape Boulevard.

SEASCAPE RESORT–MONTEREY BAY
Manager: Jim Maggio
One Seascape Resort Drive
Aptos, CA 95003, USA
Tel: (831) 688-7109, Fax: (831) 685-0615
Toll Free: (800) 929-7727
285 Rooms, Double: $320–$652*
*Breakfast not included: $15
*Service: Resort fee $18–$25 daily
Open: all year, Credit cards: all major

Staying at the Inn on Mt. Ada is like stepping into a fairy tale—suddenly you are "king of the mountain." This is not too far from reality, since the inn is the beautiful Wrigley family mansion (chewing gum, you know), their vacation "cottage" built high on the hill overlooking Avalon harbor. If you arrive by ferry at Catalina Island, you cannot miss the house: the mansion appears like a wedding cake to your left above the harbor. The inn is expensive, but money seems almost immaterial, because, once through the door, you have bought a dream. You are truly like a pampered guest in a millionaire's home, with not a hint of commercialism (until you pay the bill) to put a damper on the illusion. The lounges and dining room are exquisite: decorated with traditional furniture and fabrics appropriate to the era when the house was built. Upstairs are six individually decorated bedrooms, the grandest having a fireplace, sitting area, and a terrace with breathtaking views of the harbor. Rates include all the extras such as complimentary use of your own golf cart, a full scrumptious breakfast, and lunch. Coffee, tea, soft drinks, beer, wine, champagne, ice cream and freshly baked cookies are always available in the dining room and butlers pantry. *Directions:* By boat from Long Beach, San Pedro, and Newport Beach. By helicopter from Long Beach and San Pedro.

INN ON MT. ADA
Owners: Susan Griffin & Marlene McAdam
398 Wrigley Road
P.O. Box 2560
Avalon, CA 90704, USA
Tel: (310) 510-2030, Fax: (310) 510-2237
Toll Free: (800) 608-7669
6 Rooms, Double: $375–$780*
Minimum Stay Required: 2 nights on weekends
*Includes breakfast, lunch & appetizers
Closed: Jan, Credit cards: AX, MC, VS

The lovely Ballard Inn is located in the Santa Ynez Valley, a lush region of rolling hills planted with vineyards or sectioned off with white picket fences. Set just off the road, the Ballard Inn was built as an inn but carries the appearance of a gracious sprawling residence. White picket fences enclose its narrow front garden and a wide porch winds round it. The dining room, serving bountiful breakfasts and gourmet dinners (open to the public Wed through Sun evenings), is located just off the entry to the right. To the left, another cozy room is perfect for afternoon hors d'oeuvres and weekend wine-tasting. Venture on into the sitting room where large, deep sofas steal you away for lazy conversations in front of an open fireplace. Guestrooms are located upstairs or in a neighboring wing just off the graveled driveway. Rooms are comfortable and attractively decorated, each with a small bathroom. Bikes are available and maps provides for pedaling quiet country roads. If you like horses, ask about the neighboring miniature horse farm. We visited in spring when every mother was matched with a tiny foal—adorable. *Directions:* From Hwy 101, take the Solvang exit, following Route 246E through Solvang to Alamo Pintado. Turn left, drive 3 miles to Baseline Avenue, then turn right. The inn is on the right side.

BALLARD INN
Owners: Budi & Chris Kazali
2436 Baseline Avenue
Ballard, CA 93463, USA
Tel: (805) 688-7770, Fax: (805) 688-9560
Toll Free: (800) 638-2466
15 Rooms, Double: $245–$315*
*Service: 10%
Minimum Stay Required: 2 nights on weekends
Closed: Christmas, Credit cards: all major
Select Registry

Deetjen's Big Sur Inn, a collection of rustic houses amongst the redwoods was built in the early 1930s by Helmuth Deetjen, who crafted the cabins in the style of his native Norway. If you are looking for the amenities of a modern hotel, Deetjen's will definitely not be your cup of tea. However, those who appreciate old-fashioned charm and the splendor of nature will love this very special property—it exemplifies the lifestyle of those who first came to the magnificent Big Sur area to enjoy a gentle life, uncluttered by possessions. Guestrooms have individual names and characters. Hand-hewn doors (without locks) open to a medley of varying room configurations, all warmed by fireplaces, wood-burning stoves, or electric heaters. The rooms, decorated with antique accents and rustic fabrics, are charming in their utter simplicity. Walls are paper-thin—whispering becomes second nature so that everyone can enjoy the surrounding peace and quiet. The dining room, divided between four low beamed rooms, serves excellent food—produce is organic and, as far as possible, from local growers. Feast on blueberry pancakes or eggs benedict for breakfast (often the chance to meet interesting locals) and duck breast or fresh local fish for dinner. There's lots of opportunity for hiking and staff can give you directions on how to get to secluded beaches. *Directions:* Located on the east side of Hwy 1, 30 miles south of Carmel and about 3 miles south of Big Sur.

DEETJEN'S BIG SUR INN
Manager: Torrey Waag
48865 Hwy 1
Big Sur, CA 93920, USA
Tel: (831) 667-2377
20 Rooms, Double: $95–$200*
*Breakfast not included: $8–$14
Minimum Stay Required: 2 nights on weekends
Open: all year, Credit cards: MC, VS

Ventana is surrounded by 240 acres of meadows and forests on Big Sur, a rugged stretch of coast where the hills plunge down to meet the crashing waves below, but there is nothing rugged about Ventana Inn and Spa—a sophisticated resort where guests are pampered and provided with every luxury. After check-in a golf cart takes you and your luggage to your room, found in one of 12 natural-wood buildings. The decor varies (depending upon which section you are in) but each guestroom has the same ambiance with natural-wood paneling, luxurious fabrics, and leather chairs. All rooms have a large terrace with a latticed wood screen and a fireplace (be sure to request real logs if this is important to you)—some have private soaking tubs or hot tubs on the deck and the suites have jetted soaking tubs in the bathrooms. All have a pretty view to the hills and forest or to the sea on the horizon. Wine and cheese are served in the afternoon and a continental breakfast of pastries and fruit is set out each morning but can also be delivered to your room. There are two large swimming pools with adjacent Japanese bath (some areas are designated as clothing-optional), and a luxurious spa with facials and massages. Massages are also available in the privacy of your room. Walk the forest path (or arrange for a van) to take you to dinner at Cielo's restaurant. *Directions:* Thirty miles south of Carmel on the east side of Hwy 1, just south of the Big Sur State Park.

※ ▰ ✄ CREDIT ¶ @ Υ P ⑪ ⊘ ✿ ≈ ⌲ ஃ ⊥ 秄 ⵗ

VENTANA INN & SPA
Manager: Tina Harlow
Hwy 1
Big Sur, CA 93920, USA
Tel: (831) 667-2331, Fax: (831) 667-2419
Toll Free: (800) 628-6500
60 Rooms, Double: $600–$1350
Open: all year, Credit cards: all major

The Chateau de Vie is a delightful hideaway—a small pseudo French country château surrounded by vineyards just to the north of Calistoga. Wine, cheese and hors d'oeuvres are enjoyed on the back deck for most of the year, and in winter fireside in the sitting room. If you are feeling energetic hop into the pool or take a walk through the surrounding vineyards. Relax, under the stars, in the secluded Jacuzzi tub at the edge of the vineyard. After waking up to the coffee or tea that arrives outside your door in the morning, mosey down to the handsome dining room with its forest-green walls and large window seat or to the back deck for a gourmet repast of fresh-baked scones and fruit followed by a cooked breakfast that will equip you for a full day of sightseeing. All of the guestrooms overlook the pretty garden and are appealingly decorated in bold colors and textures. We loved the spaciousness and privacy of our top-floor room. *Directions:* From Calistoga take Hwy 128 north. At Tubbs Lane, go ¼ mile farther, turn right along a small lane and the Chateau de Vie is the first house on your right.

CHATEAU DE VIE
Owners: Felipe Barragan & Peter Weatherman
3250 Hwy 128
Calistoga, CA 94515, USA
Tel: (707) 942-6446, Fax: (707) 942-6456
Toll Free: (877) 558-2513
4 Rooms, Double: $229–$429
Open: all year, Credit cards: all major

Christopher's Inn is located in an easy-to-find, walk-to-everything spot in the quaint town of Calistoga with its boutiques and delightful restaurants. Owner Christopher Layton has employed his considerable architectural talents in developing this charming and secluded haven right next to Hwy 29. Guestrooms come in a wide range of types and sizes and are priced accordingly, so be sure to specify exactly what you want. The oh-so-cozy queen- and king-bedded rooms have private entrances and are nicely decorated—room 10 is a particularly nice example. At the other end of the spectrum are the splendid French suites, sumptuously attired in the manner of a luxurious château, with decadent bathrooms where you can soak in two-person Jacuzzi tubs before flickering firelight. The quietest, more basic, accommodation is found in a pair of two-bedroom cottages, each with a trundle bed in the sitting room—these face a peaceful suburban street and are perfect for family reunions or small groups of friends. In the morning a basket is delivered to your room with a bounty of delicious breakfast treats. The Laytons are personable, helpful innkeepers. *Directions:* Coming north on Hwy 29, the inn is 500 yards before the blinking intersection light.

CHRISTOPHER'S INN
Owners: Christopher & Adele Layton
1010 Foothill Boulevard
Calistoga, CA 94515, USA
Tel: (707) 942-5755, Fax: (707) 942-6895
Toll Free: (866) 876-5755
21 Rooms, Double: $185–$465
2 Cottages: $330 daily
Open: all year, Credit cards: all major

In the 1970s Monica Bootcheck, Tom Stimpert, and Bob Beck shared a three-apartment houseboat in Sausalito. Their friendship endured and 20 years later, along with their spouses, they pooled their talents of architecture, contracting, interior design, and marketing and built the Cottage Grove Inn. The inn is a complex of 16 individual cottages tucked into a beautiful grove of century-old Siberian Elm trees. The property reflects the nostalgic charm of yesteryear. From the outside each of the sweet, doll-house-like cottages has a similar appearance, with a clapboard exterior painted a warm dove gray, accented by deep-coral-colored shutters and crisp white trim. A romantic porch stretches across the front of each cottage with two white wicker rockers just begging you to relax with a good book. Inside, each cottage has its own personality, achieved through decorative accessories, beautiful wall colors, fine fabrics, lovely linens, and high-quality furnishings. Another bonus: each has a wood-burning fireplace and an enormous bathroom featuring a wonderful, deep Jacuzzi tub big enough for two (and cozy bathrobes). A romantic place to hide away with someone you love. *Directions:* From Hwy 29, turn east on Lincoln. Just before the road curves left as it leaves town, you will see the inn on your left.

COTTAGE GROVE INN
Manager: Donna Johnson
1711 Lincoln Avenue
Calistoga, CA 94515, USA
Tel: (707) 942-8400, Fax: (707) 942-2653
Toll Free: (800) 799-2284
16 Cottages: $250–$445 daily
Open: all year, Credit cards: all major

Calistoga   Meadowlark Country Inn   Map: 4

Privately tucked away on a 20 acres just one mile from Calistoga's shopping and dining, you find Meadowlark, an elegant Napa Valley retreat. Cross the white covered bridge and enter the restful haven created by Kurt Stevens and Richard Flynn. Seven, air-conditioned, rooms are your home from home. All are tastefully furnished, with some with four-poster pencil beds and French doors leading to their own deck or terrace. All are equipped with TV, VCR and en suite marble tile bathrooms featuring whirlpool tubs for two. The two suites have sitting rooms equipped with sleeper sofas for an extra guest. Meadow Cottage provides a perfect weekend (or longer!) hideaway retreat for two with its large bedroom/sitting area, kitchen and private deck. The larger cottage, adjacent to the pool area comes complete with marble bathroom, its own kitchen and dining area, fireplace and French doors to views across the meadow. A gourmet breakfast is served in the main house. The (clothing optional) mineral pool, hot tub and sauna have spacious flagstone terraces to soak up the California sunshine in secluded privacy. Licensed therapists provide in-house massage. Well-behaved dogs are welcome. Meadowlark is hetero and gay friendly. *Directions:* From Hwy 101, take the River Road/Guerneville exit and turn right onto Mark West Springs Road. Follow it to the end and turn left towards Calistoga onto Petrified Forest Road, the inn is on your right.

MEADOWLARK COUNTRY INN
Owners: Kurt Stevens & Richard Flynn
601 Petrified Forest Road
Calistoga, CA 94515, USA
Tel: (707) 942-5651, Fax: (707) 942-5023
Toll Free: (800) 942-5651
8 Rooms, Double: $165–$285
2 Cottages: $315–$425 daily
Open: all year, Credit cards: all major

Places to Stay   109

As an alternative to the bed and breakfasts near Cambria's shops and galleries, the Blue Whale Inn offers guests more privacy plus the opportunity to stroll for miles along Moonstone Beach. Inside the inn, picture windows showcase expansive ocean views in the dining and common rooms. It is here that guests are served a delicious gourmet breakfast, cookies in the afternoon, with local wines and cheese and appetizers in the evening. Behind the main building are the guestrooms, buffered from the parking area by a border of flowers and opening at an angle to capture a distant ocean view. Know you deserve the best and request the Tuscany Suite with its two sided fireplace dividing the sitting room from the bedroom which, like the magnificent bathroom, enjoys ocean views. The large bedrooms all have country decor, light-pine furnishings, chintz and floral fabrics, and canopy beds. Each is well equipped with a fireplace, television, telephone, refrigerator, and a top-of-the-line bathroom with Jacuzzi tub. Motels line the beach frontage but, without a doubt, the Blue Whale Inn is the best of the bunch. The owners and staff are friendly and helpful, extending a warm welcome to both their new and many returning guests. *Directions:* Turn west off Hwy 1 north at the exit sign for Moonstone Beach. Follow Moonstone Beach Drive past the hotels that line this coastal frontage to the Blue Whale Inn.

BLUE WHALE INN
Owners: Marguerite & Thomas Nunn
6736 Moonstone Beach Drive
Cambria, CA 93428, USA
Tel: (805) 927-4647, Toll Free: (800) 753-9000
7 Rooms, Double: $315–$470
Open: all year, Credit cards: all major

This pretty little Victorian is suspended in a delicious time warp at the heart of historic Cambria with its galleries, shops, and restaurants. A gate in the picket fence opens to a brick walkway leading through the garden to the small porch and entry. Inside, the decor is refreshing, clean, light, and minimalist, with soft white walls and the warm patina of natural pine floors, and there's a remarkable collection of photos and uncluttered memorabilia of all the house's occupants. The five tasteful guestrooms have snug en suite shower rooms, queen size beds, fireplaces and hand made furniture. Request my favorite, the Garden Room. Sit out on your balcony and enjoy your own private access to the winding little paths of the garden. At the front of the inn, the Parlor Room, once used as a school classroom, is now a pretty bedroom with a bay window and bird's-eye-maple furnishings. Rent the entire house for family re-unions, weddings or get togethers. Breakfast is set in the parlor and trays provided if you want to eat in your room. Enjoy a complimentary tasting of wines from small private vineyards at Fermentation, just across the road. Dine next door (we do) or walk to other good Cambria restaurants. Check in at the Shop Next Door, an excellent excuse to purchase some of Bruce's well-chosen country-style furniture. Cambria with all its shops and restaurants is on your doorstep. *Directions:* From Hwy 1 turn east on Burton Drive to Cambria Village.

SQUIBB HOUSE
Owner: Bruce Black
4063 Burton Drive
Cambria, CA 93428, USA
Tel: (805) 927-9600, Fax: (805) 927-9606
Toll Free: (866) 927-9600
5 Rooms, Double: $125–$185
Open: all year, Credit cards: all major

The Inn at Depot Hill, just two blocks up the hill from the beach and picturesque village of Capitola-by-the-Sea, dates back to 1901 when it was built as a Southern Pacific railroad station. The property does not sit on a large lot, so the grounds are minimal. Inside, the inn's imaginative decor reflects the theme of first-class train travel at the turn of the century: the bedrooms are handsomely decorated and named after different parts of the world—as if a guest were taking a railway journey and stopping at different destinations. My favorite is the unexpectedly Oriental Kyoto room, tucked away in a secluded corner complete with Buddha, reflecting pool, Asian antiques, and a huge soaking tub. The rooms feature many caring touches such as cutwork-lace sheets and pillowcases, and sumptuous feather beds. There is a wealth of other amenities including televisions VCR/DVD players, luxurious marble bathrooms, some Jacuzzi tubs on private outdoor patios, and even mini-televisions in all of the bathrooms. An elegant full breakfast is served either in the dining room, the romantic walled garden, or your room. Complimentary early-evening wine and hors d'oeuvres and late-evening desserts and port are served from the dining-room buffet. *Directions:* South on Hwy 1 from Santa Cruz. Take the Park Avenue exit, turn right and go 1 mile. Turn left onto Monterey, then immediately left into the inn's driveway.

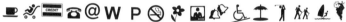

INN AT DEPOT HILL
Manager: Claire Whitelaw
250 Monterey Avenue
Capitola, CA 95010, USA
Tel: (831) 462-3597, Fax: (831) 462-3697
Toll Free: (800) 572-2632
12 Rooms, Double: $209–$349
Open: all year, Credit cards: all major

Dogs (and cats) are welcome to join their owners at Cypress Inn, just blocks from the village's famous beach, shops, galleries, and restaurants. On a recent visit, three dogs enjoyed each others' company by the fire in the beautifully vaulted living room while their owners' read the morning papers. Built in 1929 in the Spanish mission-style, the hotel has, in recent years, received a complete facelift including all 44 rooms. "Terry's" (named after principal owner, leading lady Doris Day's son, Terry Melcher) is a great place to enjoy breakfast, scrumptious afternoon teas, light dinners and lunches. Smartly decorated in beiges and creams, the majority of the bedrooms are not large. Suites 221 and 222 are the most spacious with separate bedrooms and living rooms, verandas, and bathrooms with circular jetted tubs. My favorite room is 215, large and airy, featuring a four-poster king bed, fireplace and private deck with distant ocean views. Guestrooms located off the central courtyards are particularly attractive, several with fireplaces and air conditioning. Carmel is an especially dog- friendly town where Rover can run free on the beach. Many stores welcome pooches with treats and water bowls, and several restaurants offer doggie menus. *Directions:* From Hwy 1, take the Ocean Avenue exit then turn left on Lincoln. Cypress Inn is on your left on the corner of Lincoln and 7th Street. Park in front to unload. The hotel has a car park on the next block.

CYPRESS INN
Owners: Doris Day & Dennis Levett
Manager: Nancy Slade
Lincoln & 7th, P.O. Box Y
Carmel, CA 93921, USA
Tel: (831) 624-3871, Fax: (831) 624-8216
Toll Free: (800) 443-7443
44 Rooms, Double: $150–$575
Open: all year, Credit cards: all major

Built in 1912 the Lamp Lighter is one of the oldest inns in California. It has an ideal location just steps from the beach and the town. Painted white with blue trim and set in a pretty garden the Lamp Lighter is one of Carmel's most photographed inns. Hansel & Gretel is the largest with a bedroom downstairs and a loft that opens up to the living room below with its wood-burning fireplace. Bluebird has a ground floor bedroom and twin beds tucked in a loft. Early Bird is our particular favorite, one spacious room bathed with light through a large window. Next door, Katydid is the smallest. Treetop is an especially private room nestled at the back of the garden with a private deck accessed through the closet. Next to the tiny reception area is the most luxurious accomodation, the Concours Suite. Set under a lofty white painted ceiling and beams, it has a lovely large living room warmed by a wood burning fireplace, a spacious bedroom nook partitioned off by drapes and a luxurious bath. A breakfast of muffins, juice and yogurt is delivered to your room. Dogs are welcome. There's also a coffee maker, fresh fruit, candy and a decanter of sherry. *Directions:* Take Highway 1 to Ocean, turn west. The Lamp Lighter is located on the south side, at Camino Real. Park your car in the municipal car park opposite.

THE LAMP LIGHTER
Owner: Dennis LeVett
Manager: Bobby Richards
Southeast corner of Ocean Ave & Camino Real
P.O. Box AF
Carmel, CA 93921, USA
Tel: (831) 624-7372, Fax: (831) 620-1424
22 Rooms, Double: $185–$450
Open: all year, Credit cards: all major

The lovely L'Auberge Carmel was built in 1929 and has maintained its charming Old-World architecture with its white façade, pitched gabled roof and green shutters. The hotel's location is ideal, only a half block from Carmel's famous Ocean Avenue with its many shops, restaurants and art galleries. And it is just a few short blocks to the beach. L'Auberge is the dream of David and Kathleen Fink who also run the popular Bouchée and Cantinetta Luca restaurants. This luxurious little gem of a hotel is a member of the prestigious Relais and Châteaux hotel group and has received too many awards to list. The European-inspired décor is elegant and the service top notch. Many of the guestrooms open to the hotel's charming central brick patio where breakfast is served on warm days. The spacious bedrooms are all tastefully decorated and include the finest amenities, such as brocade feather beds, flat-panel TVs, radiant heated floors in the bathrooms and French windows. The restaurant is famous in Carmel and you can make a trip out of simply enjoying his multi-course tasting menus. Each course is a labor of love, using local produce and items from the hotel's garden. The dining room has only 12 tables and is open to the public for dinner and to hotel guests for breakfast and lunch. *Directions:* Follow Ocean Avenue through the village, turn left at Monte Verde, the inn is a half block on your left.

L' AUBERGE CARMEL
Owners: Kathleen & David Fink
Manager: Lisa Dias
Monte Verde (Between Ocean & 7th)
P.O. Box J
Carmel, CA 93921, USA
Tel: (831) 624-8578
20 Rooms, Double: $300–$650
Open: all year, Credit cards: all major
Relais & Châteaux

The Mission Ranch, which in days long past was a working farm, was bought and renovated with great sensitivity for its heritage by Clint Eastwood. The inn is located on 22 acres, quite a long walk from the center of Carmel, yet a world away in tranquility (sheep graze in the big meadow between the hotel and the beach). The ranch offers a wide range of accommodations in terms of setting, views, and price. The least expensive guestrooms are found in the old barn (simple rooms facing the parking lot), while the premier rooms (an assortment of king and queen-bedded) are found in small meadow-front cottages. The latter have fireplaces and private porches with old-fashioned rocking chairs that invite you to watch the sunset over the sea. There's also a very private bunkhouse cottage (handicap accessible), an adorable honeymoon cottage, and six bedrooms in the charming old farmhouse with its ornate Victorian-style living room (perfect for family reunions. A Continental buffet breakfast is served in the restaurant—you can eat outdoors in warm weather. For exercise, there are six tennis courts and a workout room, plus, of course, a lovely beach within a 15-minute walk. Guests often walk along the beach into town. Carmel mission is just up the road. *Directions:* From Hwy 1, turn west onto Rio Road, then left at the Mission and wind round the Mission to the ranch.

MISSION RANCH
Manager: Theresa Jung
26270 Dolores
Carmel, CA 93923, USA
Tel: (831) 624-6436, Fax: (831) 626-4163
Toll Free: (800) 538-8221
31 Rooms, Double: $120–$300
Open: all year, Credit cards: all major

Tucked off Carmel's principal shopping street a few blocks up from the beach, the Monte Verde and Casa de Carmel face each other across Monte Verde Avenue in the heart of Carmel. Casa De Carmel, a two-story, cream-stucco building, set under a tile roof, is positioned perpendicular to the street and guestrooms all enjoy an outside entrance through Dutch doors, either off the parking lot that fronts it, or the second floor balcony. At Casa de Carmel the price differential simply reflects the bed size. Second floor rooms offer more privacy. Front corner rooms (1 on the first floor, 5 above it) are a bit larger, have king beds and enjoy side windows. Monte Verde is more French/western in style with stucco painted walls in the main house and small wooden cottages bordering the back patio. Room 6 is a spacious suite with 2 queen beds, a sitting room and beautiful bathroom. All the bedrooms are priced according to their size—there are a variety of twins, queens and kings. All the bedrooms have a snug sitting area where you enjoy a breakfast of muffins, yogurt and juice—left for your convenience in the in-room refrigerator. There's also a coffee maker, fresh fruit, candy and a decanter of sherry. After a day of sightseeing or shopping enjoy wine and cheese on the terrace at Monte Verde. *Directions:* From Hwy 1 in Carmel, turn west on Ocean and travel down to Monte Verde and turn south.

MONTE VERDE & CASA DE CARMEL
Manager: John McCord
On Monte Verde between Ocean and 7th
P.O. Box 394
Carmel, CA 93921, USA
Tel: (831) 624-6046, Fax: (831) 624-6904
Toll Free: (800) 328-7707
16 Rooms, Double: $150–$400
Open: all year, Credit cards: all major

The Normandy Inn exudes the charm and storybook quality that make this town so famous. As you walk down the main street toward the ocean, you cannot help stopping and smiling at this whimsical inn, which stretches for almost two blocks in the heart of town. Over the years it has grown to include not only the two-story building where the reception parlor, breakfast room, and many of the bedrooms are located, but also several cozy cottages and three houses—each house has three bedrooms, two bathrooms, and a kitchen. If you want to splurge, ask for one of the adorable cottages. Happily, although the buildings vary architecturally, there is a pleasing continuity of style that harmoniously blends them. The gardens too are really pretty. Carmel is famous for its flowers—shops and hotels all vie to outdo their neighbors with the finest floral displays, but the Normandy Inn wins the prize. Like the exterior, the guestrooms have a similarity of feel, with wrought iron headboards and dark mahogany furniture. This is an extremely well-run, friendly small hotel (with a swimming pool!) where guests are warmly greeted, a continental breakfast is included, sherry is offered in the afternoon, and there is plenty of off street parking. *Directions:* Leave Hwy 1 at Ocean Avenue. The Normandy Inn is on your left, just past Monte Verde.

NORMANDY INN
Owner: Max Hoseit
Ocean Avenue & Monte Verde
P.O. Box 1706
Carmel, CA 93921, USA
Tel: (831) 624-3825, Fax: (831) 624-4614
Toll Free: (800) 343-3825
48 Rooms, Double: $79–$600
Open: all year, Credit cards: all major

Three blocks from the ocean, Sea View Inn is within easy walking distance of the much-photographed Carmel beach. You can catch glimpses of the water through the trees from the inn's third floor. This large Victorian house has always been an inn. Deep-red-colored board-and-batten wainscoting accented by a plate rail displaying antiques and interesting bric-a-brac sets the welcoming mood for the living room and adjacent parlor where continental breakfast, afternoon tea and coffee, and evening wine and sherry are served. Both rooms are warmed by cozy fireplaces. Games, books, and magazines add a comfortable, lived-in feel. The largest bedrooms are found on the second floor. Room 6 has an elegant decor with an Oriental rug, Ralph Lauren prints, and white window shutters. Room 7 has a dramatic Oriental-style four-poster bed draped with blue-and-white chinese-motif fabric. The four tiny bedrooms tucked under the steeply slanting attic ceilings on the third floor provide the very snuggest of accommodation. Each is lavishly decorated in a Provence floral print gathered into canopies and covering huge bed pillows. With it's location in Carmel's premier residential area it is delightful walk to the restaurants and shops in town. *Directions:* Take the Ocean Avenue exit from Hwy 1 to Camino Real and turn left—Sea View Inn is just after 11th Street on the left.

SEA VIEW INN
Owners: Diane & Marshall Hydorn
Manager: Margo Thomas
Camino Real between 11th & 12th Streets
P.O. Box 4138
Carmel, CA 93921, USA
Tel: (831) 624-8778, Fax: (831) 625-5901
8 Rooms, Double: $120–$205
Open: all year, Credit cards: all major

Carmel's quaint gingerbread architecture, profusion of colorful flowers, and tall, shady trees are all happily combined at the Vagabond's House. Set around a flagstone courtyard shaded by a giant oak tree and surrounded by ferns, azaleas, camellias, and rhododendrons, the inn is made up of a group of attached storybook English cottages, brick and half-timbered, topped by a thick shake roof, making this one of Carmel's most appealing-looking inns. Most of the guestrooms open directly onto the courtyard with its fountain and abundance of flowers including colorful fuchsias cascading from hanging boxes set in the oak tree. All of the bedrooms have inviting coordinating fabrics. Every bedroom has at least two antique clocks, all have sherry, several have a small kitchen and many have their own cozy sitting nook and fireplace. In the morning you phone reception to let them know when you would like a breakfast tray brought to your room. Dennis LeVett, the owner, has a collection of British toy soldiers which he displays in the lounge. It is a quiet location and a short walk to the shops and restaurants of Carmel. Pets are welcome. *Directions:* Take the Ocean Avenue West exit from Hwy 1, turn right on Dolores Street, and go three blocks to 4th Street. The Vagabond's House Inn is on the corner of 4th Street and Dolores.

VAGABOND'S HOUSE INN
Manager: Barbar Uboe
Dolores & 4th Street
P.O. Box 2747
Carmel, CA 93921, USA
Tel: (831) 624-7738, Fax: (831) 626-1243
Toll Free: (800) 262-1262
13 Rooms, Double: $165–$275
Open: all year, Credit cards: all major

Set high above the shore just south of Carmel, at the northern gateway to Big Sur, sits the little coastal community of Carmel Highlands. Coastal views are the name of the game at the Tickle Pink Inn and the reservations folks are particularly helpful and happy to discuss each and every vista. Whether spotting whales while sipping wine on the terrace (there is an excellent cheese and wine hour), soaking in views from your Jacuzzi tub, or gazing at coastal vistas from in front of your crackling log fire, there is a spectacular view for you. The utilitarian-like structure belies an absolutely charming interior with quality decor in restful, muted colors. Relax by the fire, borrow a movie, soak up the view from your private deck. Newspapers are delivered to your door—request breakfast to accompany them or make your own selections from the extensive breakfast buffet which we always enjoy on the heated patio. For complete seclusion opt for the Senators Cottage, the onetime two bedroom cottage of Senator and Mrs. Tickle. As the inn's motto says, "Rest a bit for 'tis a rare place to rest at." Just up the road are the 1,250 acres of our favorite state reserve, Point Lobos, known as the greatest meeting of land and water in the world—be sure to visit. *Directions:* Take Hwy 1 south from Carmel for 4 miles. Highland Inn and the Tickle Pink Inn share the same driveway, Highland Drive, on the east side of the highway.

TICKLE PINK INN
Manager: Krysty Parker
155 Highland Drive
Carmel Highlands, CA 93923, USA
Tel: (831) 624-1244, Fax: (831) 626-9516
Toll Free: (800) 635-4774
34 Rooms, Double: $279–$549
1 Cottage: $529–$599 daily
Open: all year, Credit cards: all major

Our favorite place to stay in the Carmel Valley is the spectacular Bernardus Lodge. This gorgeous boutique hotel has only 57 rooms, and the quality and service are unsurpassed. The charming terracotta and mustard colored buildings are scattered around the property which is set among the hotel's vineyards and breathtaking flower gardens. The lobby is cozy and invitingly decorated with wonderful antiques, rich deep sofas and large fireplaces that always seem to be lit. There is no formal check-in desk at this fine property; guests are simply greeted at the door with a glass of Bernardus' fine wine and personally escorted to their room. The spacious guest rooms are simple and elegant with every amenity imaginable. The rooms feature crisp white linens, feather beds, 2-person tubs and French doors leading to a private patio or terrace. The hotel has two restaurants offering exceptional food: One of them, Marinus, is rated one of the top three restaurants in California. There is much to do in the area, including, a visit to the Bernardus tasting room just two miles down the road or the charming towns of Carmel and Pebble Beach, just 20 minutes away by car. However you might opt not to leave this beautiful property with its restaurants, spa, heated pool, tennis court and croquet lawns. *Directions:* From Hwy 1 turn east on Carmel Valley Rd. Travel 10 miles and the property is on your left just after the turnoff for Los Laurlas Grade.

❄ 💳 ☎ @ W P ⑪ 🚫 ❀ ≈ 🚶 🖼 ⚓ 🕴 👫

BERNARDUS LODGE
Manager: Michael Oprish
415 Carmel Valley Road
Carmel Valley, CA 93924, USA
Tel: (831) 658-3400, Fax: (831) 658-3584
Toll Free: (888) 648-9463
57 Rooms, Double: $415–$1970*
*Breakfast not included: $20–$30
*Service: Resort fee $20 per day
Open: all year, Credit cards: all major

The Coloma Country Inn, a handsome early-American farmhouse, was built in 1852, four years after gold was discovered at Sutter's Mill, just down the street. Today Coloma is a sleepy little village where the scant remains of the heady Gold Rush days are separated by wide green lawns sloping up from the American River, giving it the air of being a well-kept park. The Coloma Country Inn sits in the middle of the park, its wraparound porch inviting guests to relax and sip a glass of wine while soaking in the beauty of the surrounding tranquil countryside. Your room might feature a balcony or brick patio with a rose garden. Lavender is an especially spacious upstairs bedroom. An 1898 carriage house offers a suite with its own flowering courtyard, sitting room, and kitchenette—perfect for families. Behind the inn is a cheerful pond with a colorful collection of wild ducks begging to be fed from the dock. The surrounding Gold Country holds many great attractions and in addition to exploring the historic sites, or hiking or biking on the many mountain and river trails, outdoor activity abounds. The South Fork of the American River offers Class III rapids for exciting but safe whitewater rafting. *Directions:* Take Hwy 50 from Sacramento to Placerville and exit on Hwy 49, going north for 8 miles to Coloma.

COLOMA COUNTRY INN
Owners: Marjorie & Craig Sandborn
345 High Street
P.O. Box 502
Coloma, CA 95613, USA
Tel: (530) 622-6919, Fax: (530) 626-4959
6 Rooms, Double: $125–$245
Open: all year, Credit cards: none

The Blue Lantern Inn, perched on a bluff offering unparalleled views of the fascinating harbor of Dana Point and the blue Pacific, is an outstanding inn on southern California's Riviera. The inn is designed in a Cape Cod style—a most appealing building whose many gables, towers, and jutting rooflines create a whimsical look. The façade is painted a soft gray made even prettier by its crisp white trim. Each of the 29 guestrooms is individually decorated—some with light-pine, some with wicker, others with dark-mahogany furniture. The traditional-style furnishings complement the beach-side setting. Each room has a gas log fireplace and spacious bathroom with jetted spa tub. Many of the rooms capture magnificent views of the sea. A full signature breakfast is served buffet style each morning in the sunroom, a cheerful room where sunlight streams through the wall of windows or outside on the view terrace. Wine and hors d'oeuvres are served every afternoon, often in the book-lined library. Other amenities include an elevator, conference rooms, on site spa treatments and a well-equipped exercise room. A Four Sisters Inn. *Directions:* From the Pacific Coast Hwy 1, turn west on Street of the Blue Lantern and go one block.

BLUE LANTERN INN
Manager: Lin McMahon
34343 Street of the Blue Lantern
Dana Point, CA 92629, USA
Tel: (949) 661-1304, Fax: (949) 496-1483
Toll Free: (800) 950-1236
29 Rooms, Double: $180–$600
Open: all year, Credit cards: all major

Deep within Lassen National Park lies Drakesbad Guest Ranch, set in an idyllic high mountain valley. A broad sweep of grassy meadow cut by a tumbling river gives way to towering pines rising to rocky peaks. There's no electricity at Drakesbad—the warm glow of a kerosene lamp lights your cozy paneled bedroom. Furnishings are simple: polished pine-log chairs and beds topped by quilts, simple country curtains, and a pine dresser and bedside table. Our favorite rooms are in the little cabins that nestle at the very edge of the meadow with their smart modern bathrooms and French doors opening to a tiny deck where you can sit and watch the deer grazing at twilight. Other cabins nestle in the pines. Rooms upstairs in the main lodge have half-baths. Evenings are for books, games, and conviviality by the fireplace in the lodge, conversation around the campfire, or stargazing from the soothing warmth of the swimming pool, which is fed by the natural warmth of a hot spring. Start the day with yoga. Enjoy a theraputic massage, guided fly fishing, walks, horseback riding, and swimming. A bell is rung to announce meals, which are served in the rustic pine dining room whose tables are topped with flowery mats and napkins. It's a family place full of people who came as children returning year after year with children and grandchildren. Some even remember when guests slept in tents on the meadow. *Directions:* Take Hwy 36 to Chester. Turn left at the fire station and go 17 miles.

DRAKESBAD GUEST RANCH
Managers: Billie & Ed Fiebiger
End of Warner Valley Road
Drakesbad, CA 96020, USA
Tel: 866-999-0914, Fax: (530) 529-4511
19 Rooms, Double: $310–$358*
*Includes dinner, bed & breakfast
Open: Jun to Columbus Day, Credit cards: all major

The Elk Cove Inn, built on a bluff overlooking the Pacific Ocean, is an early example of Arts & Crafts architecture with gables, a gazebo, and a million-dollar view of cove and towering rock weathered by the crashing sea. In the main house, the dining room is set with tables in front of two walls of windows looking out to the spectacular coastline. The extensive breakfast buffet is presented on an antique pine buffet with lots of choices of fruit and a variety of cooked dishes. Enjoy complimentary "mix your own" cocktails and wine in the dining room and cozy fireplace sitting room overlooking the magnificent Pacific. All guests are greeted with a gift basket containing fruit, wine, snacks and the inn's famous giant homemade chocolate chip cookies. Pamper yourself at the European day spa which specializes in healing massage, soothing body treatments and hydrotherapy. Our favorite rooms are the four suites, particularly the upstairs ones with their high ceilings. Each has a large living room with a spectacular view, a spacious bedroom, a private deck, and a large bath equipped with Jacuzzi. There are six guest rooms in the main house and four cottages that enjoy ocean views through large picture windows. A private staircase leads down to the coastal path and from here a few steps lead you to the beach. *Directions:* Elk is 15 miles south of Mendocino, 6½ miles south of the junction of Hwy 128 on Hwy 1. The inn is on the south edge of Elk as the road winds down the hill.

ELK COVE INN & SPA
Owner: David Lieberman
6300 South Hwy 1
P.O. Box 367
Elk, CA 95432, USA
Tel: (707) 877-3321, Fax: (707) 877-1808
Toll Free: (800) 275-2967
15 Rooms, Double: $100–$395
Minimum Stay Required: 2 nights
Open: all year, Credit cards: all major

The Griffin House, a pretty little clapboard house painted Skyblue with white trim and with a white picket fence, dates back to the late 1800s when it served as the local doctor's office and pharmacy. Later, five cottages were added behind the office to house some of the lumbermen coming to the growing town of Elk. The garden cottages are pleasant and very good value for money, but truly outstanding are the dollhouse-like cottages on the edge of the bluff. In fact, these three separate cottages offer the most sensational views anywhere on the California coast. Two of them, named after early settlers of Elk, have a wood-burning stove, a sitting area, a wall of windows overlooking the coast, and a private redwood deck with chairs and table. The third oceanfront cottage, Matson, is the prize with its gas-flame stove, wooden floors, contemporary furnishings and private deck. These tiny cottages are cleanly simple in their decor, providing old-fashioned, basic comfort but with a vista so spectacular it fairly takes your breath away. The restaurant, its tables topped with white linen cloths, offers well priced meal choices. (hours vary). *Directions:* Off the west side of Hwy 1, at the center of Elk.

GRIFFIN HOUSE
Manager: Melaine Au
5910 South Hwy 1
P.O. Box 190
Elk, CA 95432, USA
Tel: (707) 877-3422, Fax: (707) 877-1853
8 Rooms, Double: $138–$247
7 Cottages: $138–$295 daily
Open: all year, Credit cards: all major

The Harbor House has a fantastic location on one of the most spectacular bluffs along the Mendocino coast. There is even a little path, with benches along the way, winding down the cliff to a secluded private beach. The home was built in 1916 as the home of the president of Goodyear Redwood Lumber Company, so it is no wonder that everything inside and outside is built of redwood. The inn is appealing, with the ambiance of a beautiful, elegant country lodge. You enter into a redwood-paneled living room dominated by a large fireplace, also made of redwood. An Oriental carpet, comfortable sofas, beamed ceiling, soft lighting, and a grand piano add to the inviting warmth. Doors lead from the lounge to the verandah-like dining room, stretching the length of the building, with picture windows looking out to the sea. A delicious set-price four-course dinner is served each evening at 7 pm and such is the reputation of the food that guests from other inns often dine here. A broad wooden staircase leads upstairs to spacious, sophisticated, beautifully furnished bedrooms that make you feel as if you are a guest in a private home. Our favorite accommodation is found in the four appealing little cottages set in the trees beside the main house—we particularly like Oceanstone and Seaview. *Directions:* From Hwy 101 take Hwy 128 west. At Hwy 1 turn left and drive south for 5 miles.

🍱 🏊 💳 🐕 @ W P ¶ 🚫 ⌂ ⚓ 🏋 🚶 ⛷ 🚴 ⛸ 🍇

HARBOR HOUSE INN
Owners: Eva Lu & Edmund Jin
5600 South Hwy 1
P.O. Box 369
Elk, CA 95432, USA
Tel: (707) 877-3203, Fax: (707) 877-3452
Toll Free: (800) 720-7474
10 Rooms, Double: $315–$490*
*Includes dinner, bed & breakfast
Open: all year, Credit cards: all major
Select Registry

Carter House Inns are made up of four buildings: the majestic Carter House, the adorable Bell Cottage and the Carter Cottage next door, and the adjacent Hotel Carter. The inns are the dream of Mark Carter who, after restoring several Victorian homes, chose to build his own (the Carter House), using the original plans for a Victorian house designed by the architect who built the Carson Mansion, a Victorian showplace in Eureka. All of their bedrooms are generously appointed with antique furniture, original artwork, and cozy flannel robes. While the Carter House offers the most delightful antique-filled rooms, if you are in the mood for something more sensuous, opt for a suite. The suites at the Hotel Carter offer large whirlpool tubs (in the bedroom) with marina views, fireplaces, king beds, large showers with two heads, entertainment centers, and well-stocked refrigerators (not complimentary). The inns restaurant 301 is a foodie destination. You can order a- la-carte or enjoy chef's prix fixe menu, a five-course feast complete with wine pairings. The 301 wine list features several thousand selections including wines from the Carter's own winery in Calistoga. *Directions:* Take Hwy 101 north to Eureka, where it turns into 5th Street. From 5th Street, turn left on L Street and go two blocks.

CARTER HOUSE INNS
Owners: Christi & Mark Carter
301 L Street
Eureka, CA 95501, USA
Tel: (707) 444-8062, Fax: (707) 444-8067
Toll Free: (800) 404-1390
32 Rooms, Double: $155–$610
Open: all year, Credit cards: all major
Select Registry

Ferndale is a jewel—a wonderfully preserved Victorian town 5 miles from the northern California coast. Happily, the town's most beautiful Victorian, a fantasy of ornate turrets and gables, is an inn: the Gingerbread Mansion. Walking through the parlors and breakfast room is like taking a step back into Victorian times. While the bedrooms continue the Victorian theme, I feel certain that the prude Victorians would be quite aghast at several of the more sensuous rooms. If money is no object, request the Empire Suite, an open-plan bedroom and bathroom combination where you can soak in a claw-foot tub in front of one of the two fireplaces, relish the complexity of operating a shower with eight heads, and sleep in a king-size bed where towering Ionic columns (pillars) soar to the rafters. Alternatively, request your room according to whether you want a tub in the room (Lilac), his-and-her tubs in the room (Gingerbread), fireplaces (five rooms), or a sleeping loft for a child (Hideaway). I particularly enjoyed the Garden Room with its fireplace, old-style bathroom, and French windows opening onto a private balcony overlooking the clipped hedges and colorful flowerbeds of the garden. *Directions:* From Hwy 101 north, take the Fernbridge/Ferndale exit, following signs to Ferndale. When you reach Main Street, turn left at Six Rivers and go one block.

GINGERBREAD MANSION
Owners: Juli & Robert McInroy and Susan & Vince Arriaga
400 Berding Street
P.O. Box 1380
Ferndale, CA 95536, USA
Tel: (707) 786-4000, Fax: (707) 786-4381
11 Rooms, Double: $155–$250
Open: all year, Credit cards: all major

The Farmhouse Inn provides accommodation and an excellent restaurant in the heart of the Russian River wine valley. Set back off the busy River Road the main house, circa 1872, resplendent in yellow and cream trim with chocolate shutters, is home to the restaurant, which serves breakfast daily and is open for fine dining Thursday through Monday. A hand-painted frieze of family members around the large dining area attests to the fact that this is a fifth-generation Forestville family. Two deluxe rooms in the main house have fireplaces and magnificent tubs with waterfalls. Eight nicely appointed guestrooms are found in a row of attached cottages across the gravel driveway. Dating back to 1899, these former workers' cottages have been transformed into havens of sumptuous modernity with feather beds, luxurious European linens, and immaculate white-tiled bathrooms (double jetted tubs), with clever touches such as garden windows that bring the wildflowers outside up close and personal. Most rooms have saunas and fireplaces, and the two suites each have a sizeable sitting area. Relax by the pool and pamper yourself with a relaxing massage in the full service spa. This is a great base for exploring the Russian River vineyards. *Directions:* From Hwy 101 take the River Road exit north of Santa Rosa and head west for a little over 7 miles. The Farmhouse Inn is on your left at the junction with Wohler Road.

FARMHOUSE INN
Owners: Catherine & Joe Bartolomei
7871 River Road
Forestville, CA 95436, USA
Tel: (707) 887-3300, Fax: (707) 887-3311
Toll Free: (800) 464-6642
18 Rooms, Double: $250–$650
Minimum Stay Required: 2 nights on weekends
Open: all year, Credit cards: all major

You would think you were in England instead of northern California when you first see the large Tudor-style Benbow Inn. The English theme continues as you step inside the lounge with its large antique fireplace flanked by comfortable sofas, antique chests, paintings, needlepoint, cherry-wood wainscoting, two grandfather clocks, potted green plants, and a splendid Oriental carpet. At tea time complimentary English tea and scones are served. The dining room, too, is very English: a beautiful, sunny room with beamed ceiling and dark-oak Windsor chairs. Both the reception hall and the dining room open out to a pretty courtyard overlooking the river. The traditionally decorated bedrooms vary in size—all the way up from small bedrooms located both in the main hotel and in an annex, which also opens onto the courtyard. The one disadvantage of the Benbow Inn is its proximity to the freeway, but loyal guests do not seem to mind. A wonderful feature here is the very special Christmas celebration with wondrous decorations, music, and dining (the whole month of December). The Benbow Inn is also justifiably proud to share the news of their award of excellence by the Wine Spectator. *Directions:* Drive north on Hwy 101. Just south of Garberville, take the Benbow exit—the hotel is on the west side of the freeway.

❄ ⚡ 💳 ☎ @ W P 🍴 🚭 🐾 ≋ ⚓ 🚶 🎿 ⛷

BENBOW INN
Owners: Teresa & John Porter
445 Lake Benbow Drive
Garberville, CA 95442, USA
Tel: (707) 923-2124, Fax: (707) 923-2897
Toll Free: (800) 355-3301
54 Rooms, Double: $99–$595*
3 Cottages: $160–$210 daily*
*Breakfast not included
Open: all year, Credit cards: all major

It is hard not to notice Beltane Ranch, a pale-yellow board-and-batten house encircled on both stories by broad verandahs, set on the hillside off the Valley of the Moon Road. Check in at the cozy country kitchen when you arrive: if no one is around, you will find a welcome note on the chalkboard hung by the back door. The house has no internal staircase, so each room has a private entrance off the verandah—which was probably very handy when this was the weekend retreat of a San Francisco madam. Incidentally, this also explains the southern architecture of the house as "madam" hailed from Louisiana. The bedrooms, decorated in family antiques, have a very comfortable ambiance. Bathrooms are basic. Chairs and hammocks are placed on the verandah outside each room and offer a wonderful spot to settle and enjoy peaceful countryside views beyond the well-tended garden. A small yellow cottage behind the main house with more contemporary decor enjoys a snug sitting room opening to a private patio and has breakfast delivered into its "silent butler." Beltane produces two varieties of wine grapes as well as its own olive oil. For the energetic, there are local walking trails and a tennis court. Beltane Ranch continues to remain a personal favorite. *Directions:* Beltane Ranch is on your right 1½ miles after passing the turnoff to Glen Ellen.

BELTANE RANCH
Owner: Alexa Wood
Manager: Anne Soulier
11775 Hwy 12 (Sonoma Hwy)
P.O. Box 395
Glen Ellen, CA 95442, USA
Tel: (707) 996-6501
8 Rooms, Double: $150–$220
Open: all year, Credit cards: none

On the main road that weaves through the quaint town of Glen Ellen, the Gaige House Inn is an elegant Victorian with a luxurious, contemporary interior. More Architectural Digest than Country Home, its crisp lines and Indonesian/Japanese details are the brainchild of your hosts, Ken Burnet and Greg Nemrow. They take great pride in their home and pay special attention to every little detail, from the bountiful gourmet breakfasts to the hand-ironed quality linens. I felt love at first sight for the Gaige Suite, an oh-so-spacious room with huge four-poster bed, massive deck, and decadent bathroom the size of my first apartment. Then we were swayed by the complete seclusion of the Creekside Suite with its private deck overlooking the creek and lavish bathroom. Although bowled over by the luxury of these premier rooms, we were also very impressed with the distinct personalities of all the other bedrooms. Eight new spa-suites are incredibly luxurious. The inn prides itself on its gourmet breakfasts. Languish by the pool or treat yourself to a spa treatment or massage on the secluded creekside deck or in the privacy of your room. *Directions:* Driving north on Hwy 12 from Sonoma, turn left on Arnold Drive, which is signposted to Glen Ellen. The inn is on the right, just before you arrive in town.

GAIGE HOUSE INN
Manager: Catherine Nelson
13540 Arnold Drive
Glen Ellen, CA 95442, USA
Tel: (707) 935-0237, Fax: (707) 935-6411
Toll Free: (800) 935-0237
23 Rooms, Double: $175–$650*
*Breakfast not included
Open: all year, Credit cards: all major

Groveland is a quaint Gold Rush town just half an hour from the west entrance to Yosemite, with Hwy 120 forming its one main street. It is a great place to overnight and take a day trip into the park. The Groveland Hotel offers the most comfortable accommodation in town. Fronting Main Street, the hotel is actually two buildings dating from 1849 and 1914 joined by a wraparound verandah. One building originated in the Gold Rush days, and the other got its start as a boarding house to accommodate the executives from San Francisco overseeing the building of the massive Hetch Hetchy water project. The Cellar Door dining room features elegant fare complimented by a comprehensive wine list personally selected by owner Peggy Mosely and stocked in her cellar of over 5,000 bottles. No two rooms are alike and all are decorated with a blend of antiques and attractive fabrics and their own jovial teddy bear. We especially liked Lyle's Room, a queen bedded room with a large bay window. There are two rooms, one with a queen, the other with twin beds, which each have only one small window and therefore no views, but they are a great value for their price. *Directions:* Groveland is two hours from Sacramento along the historic stretch of Hwy 120.

GROVELAND HOTEL
Owner: Peggy Mosley
18767 Main Street
P.O. Box 481
Groveland, CA 95321, USA
Tel: (209) 962-4000, Fax: (209) 962-6674
Toll Free: (800) 273-3314
20 Rooms, Double: $155–$295
Open: all year, Credit cards: all major
Select Registry

With a backdrop of towering redwood and pine trees, the weathered, wood-sided cottages of the North Coast Country Inn step up the hillside just off the east side of Hwy 1. Although it does not have ocean views, the inn's wooded setting is lovely and the accommodation is some of the best in the area. Sandy and Phil Walker use the original old farmhouse as their private residence and patterned the neighboring cottages after its rustic and appealing design. Each spacious guestroom cottage is attractive in its individual, country decor, enjoys its own private entrance off a porch or surrounding deck; and is equipped with a dining area (four guestrooms have kitchenettes), a wood-burning fireplace, and an en suite bathroom. I especially liked Aquitaine with its handsome four-poster bed, beamed ceiling, and large windows, though for the best view and complete privacy I would select either Southwind or Evergreen. Set aside time for the secluded hot tub set into a two-level redwood deck, magical at night under the beauty of the stars. A maze of pathways weaves upwards from the front lawn with its fruit trees into the redwoods to emerge at a sheltered meadow with a gazebo. *Directions:* Located at Hwy 1 and Fish Rock Road, 4 miles north of Gualala and ¼ mile north of Anchor Bay.

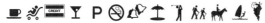

NORTH COAST COUNTRY INN
Owners: Sandy & Phil Walker
34591 South Hwy 1
Gualala, CA 95445, USA
Tel: (707) 884-4537, Fax: (707) 884-1833
Toll Free: (800) 959-4537
6 Rooms, Double: $195–$225
Open: all year, Credit cards: MC, VS

Beach House Hotel, 3½ miles from the town of Half Moon Bay, offers stunning views of the ocean and the boats of Princeton Harbor. Welcoming guests since 1997, Beach House Hotel has 54 lofts, each with a patio or balcony, with beach facing rooms (our favorites) boasting spectacular vistas of the entire 7-mile stretch of crescent-shaped coastline aptly named Half Moon Bay. Be aware that none ocean facing rooms are noisier, a busy highway runs just behind the hotel though double-paned windows have been installed to block its impact. Each loft is a tastefully decorated two-tiered suite with a king-size bed and sleeper-sofa. Designed with the guest's comfort in mind, every loft enjoys a wood-burning fireplace, wet bar, refrigerator, CD/stereo system, robes, and bathroom with double sinks and deep tub. If you are traveling with children, ask about their family accommodation—two neighboring lofts that share a common main door. For extra space and comfort, the 625-square-foot Half Moon Suite has two decks, vaulted ceilings, and a sitting area in the bedroom. Guests enjoy a complimentary continental breakfast buffet of croissants, muffins, scones, and fruit either on the outdoor patio or in their rooms. Beach House combines breathtaking views of the ocean with the comforts of a quality hotel. There's a small swimming pool and a large hot tub. *Directions:* From San Francisco take Hwy 1 south (about 25 miles). Beach House is on the right just after Pillar Point Harbor.

BEACH HOUSE HOTEL
Manager: Dana Dahl
4100 North Cabrillo Hwy
P.O. Box 129
Half Moon Bay, CA 94019-0129, USA
Tel: (650) 712-0220, Fax: (650) 712-0693
Toll Free: (800) 315-9366
54 Rooms, Double: $195–$435
Open: all year, Credit cards: all major

For those who love to be lulled to sleep by the rhythmic sound of crashing waves, the Cypress Inn, positioned directly across the road from the 5-mile-long sandy stretch of Miramar Beach, will be just your cup of tea. The Cypress Inn is a contemporary building with a weathered-wood façade with turquoise trim. Giving credence to the inn's name, a windswept cypress tree towers by the entrance. Inside, a native-folk-art theme prevails. As you enter, there is a snug sitting area to your left with wicker chairs and sofa grouped around a fireplace. Bedrooms in the main building tend to be on the cozy size and are delightfully decorated in inviting, bright colors. The large top-floor suite offers million-dollar ocean views and a rooftop patio. Each of the rooms has a television, gas-log fireplace, built-in bed with reading lamps, wicker chairs, writing desk, and glass doors opening onto private balconies overlooking the ocean. Our favorite rooms are the upstairs king-bedded rooms (Point Reyes and Mavericks) with magnificent ocean views in the adjacent Lighthouse building. We especially enjoyed Mavericks—named for the world-famous huge waves—with a surfboard hung over the bed and photos of Jeff Clark riding the waves. *Directions:* Cypress Inn is on Miramar Beach 25 miles south of San Francisco.

CYPRESS INN ON MIRAMAR BEACH
Manager: Gayle Colella
407 Mirada Road
Half Moon Bay, CA 94019, USA
Tel: (650) 726-6002, Fax: (650) 712-0380
Toll Free: (800) 832-3224
18 Rooms, Double: $199–$379
Open: all year, Credit cards: all major

Half Moon Bay is a delightful little beachside town just 45 minutes south of San Francisco, packed with interesting shops, galleries, and restaurants. One of the most attractive of several lovely Victorians along Main Street is the 1890s Old Thyme Inn, bordered by a white picket fence and named for the herb found in the inn's fragrant cottage garden. The seven bedrooms also take their names from the garden: Mint is decorated in shades of restful green, its queen four-poster decked with crisp white linens before a fireplace. For the most spacious of quarters, opt for the Garden Room, which has a queen four-poster bed, a Jacuzzi tub for two tucked into a corner of the room, and its own private garden entrance. Rick and Kathy really focus on a full breakfast served at the large round table in the parlor/dining area. The parlor displays a great many of Kathy's paintings and is the center of activity at the inn though on sunny evenings guest often enjoy wine and hors d'oeuvres on the patio. The beach is six blocks away and it's an easy stroll to places to eat that range from the adjacent Cetrella restaurant with its good food and jazz music to an excellent pizza parlor. San Francisco and the many nearby beaches are huge attractions. *Directions:* Half Moon Bay is on the coast 30 miles south of San Francisco. Old Thyme Inn is on Main Street—on the left as you go south.

OLD THYME INN
Owners: Kathy & Rick Ellis
779 Main Street
Half Moon Bay, CA 94019, USA
Tel: (650) 726-1616, Fax: (650) 726-6394
Toll Free: (800) 720-4277
7 Rooms, Double: $155–$325
Minimum Stay Required: 2 nights on weekends
Closed: Chrismas, Credit cards: all major

The Belle de Jour Inn, a complex of farm cottages built in 1873, has a rural, hillside setting just to the north of historic Healdsburg. The impeccably maintained complex has five cottages with guestrooms plus a single-story farmhouse, the home of Brenda and Tom, who run their small inn with great warmth and a professional eye to detail. The Caretaker's Suite has French doors opening onto a trellised deck and a pine four-poster, king-size canopy bed topped with Battenberg lace. The Terrace Room is charming, with a fireplace and a whirlpool tub for two, overlooking the terrace and valley. The Morning Hill Room is cozy with a fireplace and a shuttered window seat. The Atelier, with sitting room, is large and lovely. The Carriage House accommodates a magnificent deluxe, second-floor country suite with vaulted ceilings, plank-wood floors, antique pine furniture, fireplace, and a whirlpool tub for two in a large alcove—very romantic. All rooms have gas fireplaces, refrigerators, CD players, A/C, robes, and hairdryers—several have DVD players and direct satellite TV. A full country breakfast is served in the breakfast room. *Directions:* From Hwy 101 exit at Dry Creek Road then go east to Healdsburg Avenue. Turn left at the lights and go north for 1 mile. The entrance is directly across from the Simi Winery.

BELLE DE JOUR INN
Owners: Brenda & Tom Hearn
16276 Healdsburg Avenue
Healdsburg, CA 95448, USA
Tel: (707) 431-9777, Fax: (707) 431-7412
5 Cottages: $225–$355 daily
Open: all year, Credit cards: all major

Haydon Street Inn is set in a quiet neighborhood four blocks from Healdsburg's main plaza. The inn is most attractive: a soft-blue Victorian with a crisp, white trim, fronted by a white picket fence heavily laden with pink roses. The main house has a lovely living room, sitting room, and dining area for guests' use. The six bedrooms, one downstairs and five upstairs, are decorated with homey, Victorian-style furnishings and each one has their own private bath. The Turret Room, a smaller room, has a fireplace and lovely claw-foot soaking tub. The Rose Room on the first floor has a king and single bed, plus a Jacuzzi tub, fireplace, and comfortably accommodates three people. At the rear of the garden is a Victorian-style cottage with two king guest rooms upstairs. Each cottage room has a private entrance and beautiful pine floors. As an added touch of luxury, the bathrooms have double whirlpool bathtubs. Guests are welcome to relax on the patio and enjoy a glass of the wine with hors d'oeuvres that are served every day at 6 pm. John and Keren also prepare a full three course breakfast each morning. *Directions:* From Hwy 101 take the Central Healdsburg exit. Turn right on Matheson to Fitch, right on Fitch to Haydon, and left on Haydon.

HAYDON STREET INN
Owners: Keren Colsten & John Harasty
321 Haydon Street
Healdsburg, CA 94558, USA
Tel: (707) 433-5228, Fax: (707) 433-6637
Toll Free: (800) 528-3703
9 Rooms, Double: $175–$395
Minimum Stay Required: 2 nights on weekends
Open: all year, Credit cards: all major

Built in 1901, Healdsburg Inn on the Plaza recently underwent a complete renovation and in the process was transformed into the most delightful of retreats on Healdsburg's historic town plaza. The twelve spacious guest rooms feature high ceilings, original moldings, fireplaces, bay windows or balconies, excellent bathrooms (many with Jacuzzi tubs), as well as amenities such as air conditioning, phones and televisions. The streamlined décor in shades of cream and soft sage green takes advantage of the wealth of natural light indoors. The Carriage House, behind the inn, has a kitchen, hot tub and deck. Guests congregate in the sitting room overlooking the plaza. A bountiful breakfast is set on the buffet, coffee and tea are always available, fresh baked cookies never stay long in the cookie jar and hearty hors d'oeuvres and wine are served in an evening. Bikes are available for guests to use. From summer concerts in the outdoor bandstand to antique fairs and holiday tree lightings, all of the towns best events take place on the inn's doorstep. Guests are also surrounded by Healdsburg's stylish shops, galleries, tasting rooms and superb restaurants. A Four Sisters Inn. *Directions:* Leave Hwy 101 north at the Central Healdsburg exit. Drive down Healdsburg Avenue north and make a right on Matheson Street.

HEALDSBURG INN ON THE PLAZA
Manager: Jennifer Byrom
112 Matheson Street
Healdsburg, CA 95448, USA
Tel: (707) 433-6991, Fax: (707) 433-9513
Toll Free: (800) 431-8663
12 Rooms, Double: $250–$375
Open: all year, Credit cards: all major

The Honor Mansion, a soft-beige Victorian with white trim and a maroon door, sits behind a white picket fence on a residential street. Its formal Victorian façade gives not hint that this a destination in itself for behind the inn stretch acres of grounds that incorporate: a lap pool, tennis court, bocce ball courts, half-court basketball, competition croquet lawn, putting green, walking-jogging trail, a small vineyard and herb, flower and vegetable gardens. Accommodation comes in three distinct categories: bed and breakfast style rooms in the house, cottages and suites in the grounds. All are decorated and furnished to the highest of standards. The cottages and suites have the luxury of total seclusion, seven have spa tubs on private covered decks. Wherever you decide to stay, you will enjoy the very best, from lush robes to fine linens that make you want to just melt into bed. Enjoy wine and hors d'oeuvres in the evening and browse Steve and Cathi's personally rated list of nearby restaurants for dinner. *Directions:* From Hwy 101 exit at Dry Creek Road and turn right. At the first stoplight, Grove Street, turn right. The Honor Mansion is 1/2 mile down on your right.

HONOR MANSION
Owners: Cathi & Steve Fowler
14891 Grove Street
Healdsburg, CA 95448, USA
Tel: (707) 433-4277, Fax: (707) 431-7173
Toll Free: (800) 554-4667
13 Rooms, Double: $250–$600
Open: all year, Credit cards: all major
Select Registry

Madrona Manor, just a few minutes from the heart of Healdsburg, is secluded in 8 acres of glorious grounds. This fantasy vistorian mansion (on the National Register of Historic Places) was built in 1881 by John Alexander Paxton, a tycoon of great wealth. The mansion houses the reception area, several lounges, and a spacious dining room opening onto a large covered terrace. Antiques abound, emphasizing the Victorian mood of the home. A flight of stairs leads up to our four favorite second-story rooms, which are decorated with handsome Victorian furniture original to the house. Other guestrooms are found in the Carriage House, the Meadow Wood Complex, and the Garden Cottage (with its own private garden and sheltered deck). The Schoolhouse Suites are located in the original schoolhouse for the ranch—two suites each with sitting room, Jacuzzi, private deck, and garden. Lush lawns, perfectly manicured gardens, towering trees, and secluded nooks provide a haven of beauty and tranquility. A swimming pool offers a refreshing interlude after a day of visiting the nearby Sonoma vineyards. *Directions:* From Hwy 101 north take the Central Healdsburg exit, turn left at the second traffic light, and go under the freeway. You will be on Westside Road for a half a mile and will see the hotel entrance straight ahead as the road bends to the left.

MADRONA MANOR
Owners: Trudi & Bill Konrad
Manager: Joe Hadley
1001 Westside Road
Healdsburg, CA 95448, USA
Tel: (707) 433-4231, Fax: (707) 433-0703
Toll Free: (800) 258-4003
22 Rooms, Double: $200–$650
Open: all year, Credit cards: MC, VS

The Hotel Les Mars is just off historic Healdsburg Plaza. From its limestone façade and exterior wrought ironwork to the 18th and 19th Century antique and authentic reproduction furnishings the entire experience speaks of uncompromised French elegance. A marble staircase with its iron balustrade sweeps up from the lobby to the first floor accommodations, eight rooms reminiscent of a fine Parisian Hotel. Canopied four-poster beds, modeled on those favored by 16th century European nobility. Fine Italian linens, massive antique armoires, grey and white marble and glass bathrooms and soaking tubs complete the picture. Eight rooms on the third floor are similarly equipped but also offer 20 ft high beamed ceilings, evoking images of country chateaux. A gourmet three course breakfast is served. Nightly wine and cheese tastings are presented in the library with its hand carved walnut paneling and leather bound books. Cyrus restaurant, serving exquisite contemporary fare, is handily located on the ground floor of the hotel. Advanced reservations are a must. A lovely swimming pool is found in a courtyard to the rear of the hotel. *Directions:* Leave Hwy 101 north at the Central Healdsburg exit. Drive down Healdsburg Avenue north and make a left on North Street. The hotel is on your right.

HOTEL LES MARS
Owners: Sarah & David Mars
Manager: Katie Ciocca
270 North Street
Healdsburg, CA 95448, USA
Tel: (707) 433-4211, Fax: (707) 433-4611
16 Rooms, Double: $575–$1050
Open: all year, Credit cards: all major
Relais & Châteaux

The Beach House at Hermosa Beach occupies a spectacular location on the beach just steps from the heart of this lively southern California town. Even if you have no desire to join in all the fun on the sand or roller-blade, bike, run, walk, or stroll the path that separates the beach from the inn, you will relish the people watching that this location affords. The rooms are referred to as "lofts" and all have a patio or balcony. Each loft is a tastefully decorated two-tiered suite (separate living room and bedroom areas) with a king-size bed and sleeper sofa. Designed with the guest's comfort in mind, every loft enjoys a wood-burning fireplace, wet bar, refrigerator, CD/stereo system, robes, and bathroom with deep tub. If you are traveling with children, ask about their family accommodation—two neighboring lofts that have an interconnecting door. Those on a budget might opt for a non-view room. The continental breakfast buffet of croissants, muffins, scones, and fruit is served either in the beachfront Strand Café or in the guestrooms. Room service is available from the adjacent Good Stuff restaurant. *Directions:* Going south on the 405, exit at Redondo Beach Blvd. Go right to the Pacific Coast Hwy, turn left, then right on Hermosa and left on 14th. Valet parking is $20 per day.

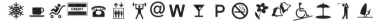

BEACH HOUSE
Manager: Kevin McCarthy
1300 The Strand
Hermosa Beach, CA 90254, USA
Tel: (310) 374-3001, Fax: (310) 372-2115
Toll Free: (888) 895-4559
96 Rooms, Double: $209–$459
Open: all year, Credit cards: all major

The Blackthorne Inn is the whimsical creation of Susan and Bill Wigert, a Hansel and Gretel house tucked among the treetops, with peaked roofs, dormer windows, turrets, bay windows, and an octagonal tower. Steps wind up through the trees to the main entry level which is wrapped by an enormous wooden deck. A dramatic floor-to-ceiling stone fireplace warms the soaring living room, its expansive windows looking out onto the trees. A full buffet breakfast is served here in the morning. Open-tread spiral staircases lead up and down to the rustically decorated bedrooms. The favorite choice of many is Eagle's Nest, located in the octagonal tower, where walls of glass give the impression that you are sleeping under the stars, adding to the woodsy-outdoors experience, the bathroom is found across a wooden brige, adjacent to the hot tub. All of the rooms have lots of personality, whether it is with stained-glass windows, a private entrance, a separate sitting room, or a bay window looking out into the trees. The Wigerts also offer accommodation overlooking Point Reyes Seashore and the distant Tomales Bay at their home in nearby Point Reyes Station. *Directions:* Take Sir Francis Drake Boulevard off Hwy 1 to Olema. Turn right, go 2 miles, then turn left toward Inverness. Go 1 mile, then turn left on Vallejo Avenue (at the Bakery and Deli) for half a mile to the inn.

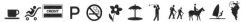

BLACKTHORNE INN
Owners: Susan & Bill Wigert
266 Vallejo Avenue
P.O. Box 712
Inverness, CA 94937, USA
Tel: (415) 663-8621, Fax: (415) 663-8635
5 Rooms, Double: $100–$250
Open: all year, Credit cards: MC, VS

Ten Inverness Way, a delightful shingled house built as a family home in 1904, sits in a quiet location at the center of Inverness, a very short walk from the shore of Tomales Bay. The heart of the house is the oh-so-spacious living room with comfortable sofas drawn round the large stone fireplace and little tables and chairs attractively set for breakfast. The adjacent sunroom is stacked with books and information on the area. Teri Mattson and Brett Poirier make guests feel really welcome. Teri and Brett are both passionate hikers, bicyclists, kayak paddlers, and readers happy to provide you with a picnic and give advice on where to go and what to see. For an additional fee, Brett will escort you on hikes and tours of the area. Accommodation is found upstairs in four very nice bedrooms, all freshly and prettily decorated. The most spacious and private quarters are offered by the ground-floor Suite with its meadow sitting room opening up to a private patio, its queen-sized bed set in an alcove decorated with a floral mural and a small kitchen nook. Settle in, relax, and make yourself at home—it's that kind of place—and don't forget to make a reservation for a private soak in the hot tub. Want to work while you are here—an office is available equipped with computer, fax an copy machine. *Directions:* Drive into Inverness on the main road, Sir Francis Drake Boulevard, and watch for the sign pointing to your left to Ten Inverness Way.

TEN INVERNESS WAY
Owner: Teri Mattson
Ten Inverness Way
P.O. Box 63
Inverness, CA 94937, USA
Tel: (415) 669-1648, Fax: (415) 669-7403
5 Rooms, Double: $165–$205
Open: all year, Credit cards: MC, VS

Built in 1859 and proudly claiming to be one of California's ten oldest hotels, the National Hotel is located on the main street of Jamestown, the gateway to the Gold Country. The first floor accommodates an acclaimed restaurant where an extravagant breakfast buffet and morning newspapers are set out for guests and where lunch, dinner, and a Sunday champagne brunch are available to guests and non-guests. The handsome old redwood bar in the Gold Rush Saloon offers refreshment, possible entertainment, and local gossip. A steep stairway just off the entry leads to the nine guestrooms on the second floor. Wonderful old brass-and-iron beds decked with regal comforters, handsome trunks, lovely old armoires, antique washbasins, and pull chain toilets in the bathroom dominate the decor, which is pleasing and reminiscent of the Gold Rush era—but with modern comforts including bathrobes. All guestrooms enjoy small private bathrooms and the hotel has a wonderful "soaking room" with an oversized claw-foot bathtub. This is available to all guests. The guestrooms are comfortable, air-conditioned, and all accessed off the one central hallway. The two front rooms overlook the balcony and the action of Main Street. *Directions:* Jamestown's Main Street intersects both Hwys 108 and 49 on the east and west ends of town.

1859 NATIONAL HOTEL
Owner: Stephen Willey
18183 Main Street
P.O. Box 502
Jamestown, CA 95327, USA
Tel: (209) 984-3446, Toll Free: (800) 894-3446
9 Rooms, Double: $140–$175
Open: all year, Credit cards: all major

Just a block off Main Street on a Julian hillside sits a special property which boasts a very loyal clientele. It is not surprising when you see the accommodation: guestrooms have elegant country furnishings complemented by beautiful coordinating fabrics. Cottage guestrooms, all with private entrances, are tucked in a garden setting along a wandering path. Cottage rooms have the comfort of a fireplace, and some have whirlpool tubs. At the top of the property, the handsome lodge offers smaller guestrooms. All rooms have a private bathroom which are modern and well appointed. The great room with its high vaulted ceiling and large river-stone fireplace welcomes all guests with its blend of comfort and elegant detail. A dining room and an upstairs common area equipped with a complimentary video library, sofa, computer and TV are other places to be enjoyed. Room prices include a full breakfast and afternoon hors d'oeuvres. Dinner is available on select evenings. *Directions:* Washington Street crosses Main Street at the north end of town.

ORCHARD HILL COUNTRY INN
Owners: Pat & Darrell Straube
2502 Washington Street
P.O. Box 2410
Julian, CA 92036-0425, USA
Tel: (760) 765-1700, Fax: (760) 765-0290
Toll Free: (800) 716-7242
22 Rooms, Double: $195–$450
Closed: Christmas, Credit cards: MC, VS
Select Registry

Looking for a place to stay with vineyard views, wine tasting, and comfortable accommodations all in one spot? Look no further. Landmark Vineyards owners Mary and Michael Colhoun offer a choice of two self-catering facilities. The Guest Suite, which is actually housed in a quiet wing of the main winery building, offers a large, elegantly decorated twin-bedded room with fireplace and high, beamed ceiling, and a modern bathroom. The view across its private patio and the vineyard beyond is dominated by Sugarloaf Ridge and Hood Mountain. Farther afield in the vineyard you find the white clapboard Guest Cottage. Delightfully modernized and decorated in bright blues and white, this one-bedroom cottage has a king-sized bed, a fully fitted kitchen, sitting room with comfortable sofa and chairs, bathroom, washer and dryer, and even its own wildflower garden with recliners on the lawn—everything you could need for a private getaway in the heart of Sonoma Valley. Select a favorite libation from the tasting room just a few steps away and take it back to sip on your patio while you drink in the views of vineyards and Sugarloaf Ridge. Breakfast muffins, tea, and coffee are provided on a hospitality tray in your room. *Directions:* From Sonoma, take Hwy 12 towards Santa Rosa. Landmark Vineyards is on your right after 15 miles.

LANDMARK
Owners: Mary & Michael Colhoun
101 Adobe Canyon Road
P.O. Box 340
Kenwood, CA 95452, USA
Tel: (707) 833-0053, Fax: (707) 833-1164
1 Room, Double: $200
1 Cottage: $150–$220 daily
Closed: Thanksgiving & Christmas, Credit cards: all major

Just a block from the ocean and the hustle and bustle of La Jolla village, The Bed & Breakfast Inn at La Jolla sits on a quiet, stylish suburban street. Originally built for George Kautz in 1913, the home's most famous occupant was the composer John Phillip Sousa, who lived here during the '20s. Behind its street-front façade you enter a grassy, flower-filled courtyard where the only sound is that of a tinkling fountain. Join fellow guests each morning in the dining room to share a candlelit gourmet breakfast and travel adventures. Bedrooms vary from snug upstairs rooms in the original house to a spacious suite with a sitting room offering distant views of the ocean horizon. Pacific View with its fireplace and ocean view is one of our favorites. Beautiful furnishings, lovely fabrics, and fabulous antiques have been carefully selected by the decorator, who also serves as the inn's PR person. It's an excellent location for walking to the beach, shops, and restaurants of La Jolla and it is just 200 yards from the Museum of Contemporary Art. I was pleased with the availability of on-street parking. *Directions:* Exit I-5 north at La Jolla Parkway (5 south at La Jolla Village), travel to Torrey Pines Road, and turn right on Prospect Street. Drive through downtown La Jolla, and opposite the Museum of Contemporary Art turn left on Draper Avenue—the inn is the second building on the left.

THE BED & BREAKFAST INN AT LA JOLLA
Managers: Margaret Fox & Patricia Thompson
7753 Draper Avenue
La Jolla, CA 92037, USA
Tel: (858) 456-2066, Fax: (858) 456-1510
Toll Free: (888) 988-8481
15 Rooms, Double: $210–$459
Open: all year, Credit cards: all major
Select Registry

Just steps away from the boutiques, bistros and beaches that comprise the essence of La Jolla the palm fronted, stone faced Hotel Parisi is a real find. A sweeping staircase leads up to the spacious reception area, accentuated by an Italianate column water feature. It's comfy seating and large fireplace with impressive carved-iron surround make this a perfect place to linger with coffee and newspapers on those rare cool southern California mornings. Continental breakfast is served in Piccolo Parisi Breakfast Room just off the lobby. The hotel occupies the entire second floor (an elevator takes you to and from private parking on the ground floor) and is comprised of twenty-one luxurious suites, all furnished on an almost minimalist modern theme and decorated in warm earthtones. King-and queen-size beds, sumptuous linens, immaculate marble and tile bathrooms and original artwork are complimented with a full range of modern creature comforts. Pamper yourself with a selection from the range of over 40 holistic spa treatments available in the privacy of your own room. Room service is available from Fresh Seafood Restaurant. *Directions:* Exit I-5 north at La Jolla Parkway (5 south at La Jolla Village), travel to Torrey Pines Road, and turn right on Prospect Street. Turn left on Herschel and immediate left into the hotel's parking garage.

HOTEL PARISI
Manager: Raven Warren
1111 Prospect
La Jolla, CA 92037, USA
Tel: (858) 454-1511, Fax: (858) 454-1531
Toll Free: (877) 472-7474
29 Rooms, Double: $245–$895
Open: all year, Credit cards: all major

The Scripps Inn enjoys an absolutely magnificent setting just steps away from the white sand of La Jolla's gorgeous cove and beach and expanse of sparkling blue water. You can walk or bike for miles along the pedestrian trail that contours along the bluff and it is also just a few short blocks up the hill to the heart of the village with its elegant shops and delightful restaurants. Two wings of guestrooms wrap around the central car park, with upstairs rooms accessed off a covered walkway. The rooms are fresh and pretty—light and airy in their decor with tans, creams, and beiges in the fabrics complementing the light woods of the furnishings. All of the rooms have glimpses of the ocean, though for view none can rival suite 14 where large sitting-room windows frame a 180-degree vista of La Jolla Cove. The two-bedroom suites and room 14 have a kitchenette and two rooms have fireplaces. In the evening it's a short walk into the village where you are spoilt for choice of restaurants. Muffins and pastries and a variety of juices (there are in-room coffee makers) are set out in the reception niche in the morning along with trays to take breakfast back to your room or to the lanai. *Directions:* Drive through downtown La Jolla on Prospect Street, and just after the Museum of Contemporary Art turn right on Cuvier, left on Coast, and immediately left into the inn's car park.

SCRIPPS INN
Manager: Elaine Akeroyd
555 Coast Boulevard South
La Jolla, CA 92037, USA
Tel: (858) 454-3391, Fax: (858) 456-0389
14 Rooms, Double: $185–$475
Open: all year, Credit cards: all major

Overlooking the Pacific, La Valencia with its pink adobe-like walls, Spanish-tiled roof, and tower domed with blue-and-gold mosaics has captivated guests since it opened in 1926. As you walk past the palm-shaded patio into the main lobby you are drawn into the living room with its dramatic wall of glass framing views of the Ocean. Exquisite Spanish mosaics, fresh flowers, hand-painted murals and ceiling set the tone. Guests gather in the Whaling Bar, with its collection of scrimshaw and murals, before dinner in La Rue Restaurant, or the 12-table Sky Room Restaurant, which sits atop the hotel with dramatic ocean views. While all 115 rooms are beautifully decorated, the most luxurious are those in the Ocean Villas that terrace down behind the hotel toward La Jolla Cove. In the main body of the hotel our favorite bedrooms have balconies just large enough for a couple of chairs—some have ocean views while others overlook the bustle of the village. An ocean view pool is set amidst perfectly tended gardens. The hotel offers exclusive privacy, many Hollywood stars retreat to La Valencia to escape stardom's spotlight. *Directions:* Exit I-5 north at La Jolla Parkway (5 south at La Jolla Village), travel to Torrey Pines Road, and turn right on Prospect Street. Pull up in front of the hotel and the valet will park your car.

LA VALENCIA HOTEL
Manager: David Friederich
1132 Prospect Street
La Jolla, CA 92037, USA
Tel: (858) 454-0771, Fax: (858) 456-3921
Toll Free: (800) 451-0772
113 Rooms, Double: $275–$2500*
*Breakfast not included: $17–$28
Open: all year, Credit cards: all major

Lake La Quinta Inn is a stunning, boutique-style inn: a two-story, creamy-beige stucco building that hints of the romance of a French château with its steeply pitched slate roof, whimsical chimneys, and jaunty dormer windows. The inn is in La Quinta, several miles from Palm Springs, an opulent town of gated communities catering to ardent golfers who come to play on some of the most outstanding courses in the world. As you step inside the inn, the tasteful, refined elegance give the feeling that you are a guest in a friend's home. The living room, with French doors opening onto the terrace overlooking the lake, has comfortable chairs and sofas cozily grouped around a fireplace. The splendid dining room also has views over the lake. There are only 13 guestrooms, varying in size from a standard room to a super-deluxe suite. Although each of the luxuriously appointed bedrooms has its own personality, they all are similar in mood with fireplaces, balconies or terraces facing the lake, splendid large bathrooms with double sinks, and top-quality linens. You might never want to leave the beautiful pool tucked in the garden, but if you are a golfer tee times can be arranged for you—there are over 100 golf courses to choose from. *Directions:* Take Interstate 10 to Washington and turn right. Drive 6 miles and turn left on Lake La Quinta drive after 47th Avenue.

LAKE LA QUINTA INN
Innkeeper: Julia Miskowicz
78-120 Caleo Bay
La Quinta, CA 92253, USA
Tel: (760) 564-7332, Fax: (760) 564-6356
Toll Free: (888) 226-4546
15 Rooms, Double: $109–$459
Open: all year, Credit cards: all major

Glendeven is a delightful New England-style farmhouse built in 1867 by Isaiah Stevens for his bride, Rebecca. Today, this beautiful clapboard home is absolutely decorator-perfect and continues to be one of our favorite places to stay. I'm certain you will echo our sentiments and whether you select a room in the main house or Stevenscroft, a stylish gabled annex in the garden, or choose the seclusion of the Carriage House suite behind the art gallery and Wine Bar[n], you will be as thrilled with the place as we are. Most rooms have superb, not-so-distant ocean views and fireplaces; all have immaculate decor and beautiful bathrooms. Breakfast is served in your room on a tray, or snugly in a picnic basket if you are away from the main house. We were reluctant to leave the confines of our room but just had to take the path across the highway that leads to the clifftops, to the beach of Van Damme State Park. There are other paths that go out the back through Glendeven's forest trail to the trails of Van Damme. Glendeven is a luxury farmstead with fresh eggs on-site, daily llama feedings, a green house and vegetable gardens. It is home to The Wine Bar[n] at Glendeven, a tasting room & wine bar on-site featuring local Mendecino wines. *Directions:* From San Francisco take Hwy 101 north, Hwy 128 west, then Hwy 1 north for just over 8 miles.

GLENDEVEN
Owners: John Dixon & Mike Roemmler
8205 North Hwy 1
P.O. Box 914
Little River, CA 95456, USA
Tel: (707) 937-0083, Toll Free: (800) 822-4536
10 Rooms, Double: $150–$330
1 Apartment: $260–$370 daily
Minimum Stay Required: 2 nights on weekends
Open: all year, Credit cards: all major
Select Registry

The Inn at Schoolhouse Creek offers a range of comfortable, charming, and eclectic accommodations. An assorted collection of century-old cottages, lodges, the historic Ledford family home (circa 1860), and two modern suites nestles in 8 private acres set back across Hwy 1 from the ocean. All are individually decorated in a casual country-cottage style, liberally sprinkled with family antiques and curiosities, and offer a choice of views and varying degrees of spaciousness. Each has a fireplace (some wood, some gas), full bath (many with spa tubs), and private deck or garden sitting area. Some have self-catering kitchens. The focal point is the comfortable old Ledford farmhouse, with its redwood ceilings and paneled walls. Curl up with a book or game by the fire, enjoy breakfast on the sun porch. Owners Maureen Gilbert and Steven Musser go out of their way to stress that this is a family destination—children and pets are welcome, and well catered for. Sample the delights of nearby Mendocino but return in time to soak in the hot tub and reflect on the day's activities while you watch the sun set over the Pacific. *Directions:* From San Francisco take Hwy 101 north, Hwy 128 west, then Hwy 1 north for 7 miles and you will see the inn on your right before you reach the Van Damme State Park.

INN AT SCHOOLHOUSE CREEK
Owners: Maureen Gilbert & Steven Musser
7051 North Hwy 1
Little River, CA 95456, USA
Tel: (707) 937-5525, Fax: (707) 937-2012
Toll Free: (800) 731-5525
11 Rooms, Double: $175–$399
12 Cottages: $175–$399 daily
Open: all year, Credit cards: all major

Surrounded by the foothills and vineyards of the Livermore Valley the Purple Orchid Inn offers a convenient and luxurious retreat for exploring the local wineries. A beautiful, sprawling log structure set against a backdrop of its own olive orchards, the inn is intended to be a destination in its own right. The inn is described as a place of wellness where guests can visit, relax, and make healthy life choices. Enjoy the expanded spa, whose staff is extensively trained in various massage methods, special body wraps, salt glows, and skin care. Definitely ask about the spa and golf packages. For dining, there are lots of restaurants a fifteen minute drive away. In the mornings enjoy breakfast in the dining room, in some bedrooms, or poolside—weather permitting. The guestrooms, all with fireplaces and Jacuzzi tubs (some for two) are individually themed. The two oh-so-spacious patio suites come equipped with refrigerator, microwave, and coffee maker. *Directions:* Exit Hwy 580 at Vasco Road to the south. At its end turn left on Tesla Road and then take a left on Cross Road to the inn.

PURPLE ORCHID INN
Managers: Bhervi & Kaushik Banerjee
4549 Cross Road
Livermore, CA 94550, USA
Tel: (925) 606-8855, Fax: (925) 606-8880
Toll Free: (800) 353-4549
10 Rooms, Double: $170–$380
Open: all year, Credit cards: MC, VS

Los Olivos was originally a stagecoach town; now its main street houses interesting stores, restaurants, and Fess Parker's inn and spa. (Hollywood aficionados will remember Fess playing Davy Crockett in the '50s.) Beautiful in decor and lavishly comfortable, this elegant inn is an excellent place to stay and sample the wines of the Santa Inez Valley—of course you must visit the Fess Parker Winery. Each of the guestrooms, whether upstairs in the main building or across the street, features wood moldings, brass fixtures, and French armoires, all of which combine to create a romantic, early-20th-century ambiance. Guestroom amenities include a mini refrigerator, television, fireplace, beds topped with plump down comforters, and, in several rooms, a Jacuzzi bathtub. The award-winning Vintage Room restaurant has an elegant, French-country ambiance and Le Saloon is an attractive full-service bar opening onto the sheltered patio. Summer travelers appreciate the lovely heated swimming pool and Jacuzzi. Pamper yourself with a massage or a treatment at Spa Vigne, located just up the road in a little cottage. *Directions:* From Los Angeles, take Hwy 101 north. Approximately 5 miles north of Buellton, exit onto Hwy 154. Proceed 2 miles and turn right on Grand.

FESS PARKER'S WINE COUNTRY INN & SPA
Manager: Cammy Pinoli
2860 Grand Avenue
P.O. Box 849
Los Olivos, CA 93441, USA
Tel: (805) 688-7788, Fax: (805) 688-1942
Toll Free: (800) 446-2455
20 Rooms, Double: $295–$545
Open: all year, Credit cards: all major

Behind Casa Malibu's bland '50s motel façade you find a simple, attractive entry, dressed with fresh flowers, opening onto the back central courtyard. The manicured back garden is beautifully landscaped and flows to a tiled patio, which extends out to a glass-enclosed bay-window alcove set with tables overlooking the ocean. A single-story wing of 8 lovely rooms sits right on the beach. These delightful high-ceilinged rooms are decorated in pale colors, furnished with wicker and open onto glass-walled decks. Several have Jacuzzi tubs, fireplaces and connecting doors. Other rooms are found in the building either on the first floor overlooking the lush interior courtyard or on the second floor enjoying views of the courtyard garden and glimpses of the distant blue water. Some rooms are equipped with kitchenettes, some with gas fireplaces, and others with a deck. Continental breakfast is offered each morning in the lobby and room service is available from local restaurants for lunch and dinner. Beach towels, umbrellas and chairs are on hand for you to take down to the beach which is freshly raked every morning. *Directions:* Located in the heart of Malibu 1/3 mile south of the pier.

CASA MALIBU
Owners: Joan & Richard Page
22752 Pacific Coast Hwy
Malibu, CA 90265, USA
Tel: (310) 456-2219, Fax: (310) 456-5418
Toll Free: (800) 831-0858
21 Rooms, Double: $179–$529
Open: all year, Credit cards: all major

The McCloud Hotel with its pretty yellow façade proudly dominates Main Street. Inside, the high, beamed ceiling and informal grouping of sofas and chairs set before a large fire give the feeling of a mountain lodge. Although the exterior of the hotel was in relatively good shape and required only cosmetic repairs, guestrooms benefit from the complete renovation and modernization of the interior. At the top of a wide, handsome staircase is an inviting parlor with access to the front expanse of porch. Standard rooms, facing onto Main Street, are a wonderful value, with a nice-size room, washbasin, toilet, and private bathroom. Deluxe rooms, at the back of the building, have four-poster queen beds and an additional sitting area. Three comfortable suites enjoy big Jacuzzi tubs, three of which are located in the room proper. The decor is similar in theme throughout, with the use of country patterns, old trunks, and special attention to detail. A full breakfast is served between 8 and 9:30 am. Meals are served on the garden terrace in warm weather, or in the dining room when the weather is inclement. *Directions:* From I-5 at Mt. Shasta City, take McCloud-Reno exit, drive east on Hwy 89 for 9 miles. Turn left on Colombero, cross tracks and turn right on Main Street.

MCCLOUD HOTEL
Owner: Lee Ogden
Manager: Carla Atwater
408 Main Street
P.O. Box 730
McCloud, CA 96057, USA
Tel: (530) 964-2822, Fax: (530) 964-2844
Toll Free: (800) 964-2823
15 Rooms, Double: $120–$235
Open: all year, Credit cards: all major

The Agate Cove Inn has a lovely location on a bluff above the Pacific Ocean. The view, looking out over brilliantly colored flowers to the sparkling blue sea framed by windswept cypress trees, is magical. The heart of the inn is a charming 1860s blue-trimmed, white clapboard farmhouse where you find the reception area and an appealing lounge with comfy chairs facing a brick fireplace where a cozy fire crackles on chilly days. Windows stretch across the entire west wall of the lounge, giving guests a spectacular view of the coast as they enjoy a scrumptious hot breakfast. Two of the bedrooms are attached to the main farmhouse with their own entrances, while the others are scattered about the property in little cottages painted a pretty country-blue with white trim. All but 1 of the rooms have a gas fireplace, a deck, and a view of the sea. Even the least expensive rooms, although smaller and simpler, are sweet and pretty. Laraine offers lots of nice touches: flowers in the room, maps of hiking trails, books, restaurant menus and an endless supply of tea, coffee, and biscotti. It's an easy walking distance to Mendocino Headland State park and a short drive into town. *Directions:* From Hwy 1 take Little Lake left (west), then Lansing right (north).

AGATE COVE INN
Owner: Laraine Galloway
11201 North Lansing Street
P.O. Box 1150
Mendocino, CA 95460, USA
Tel: (707) 937-0551, Fax: (707) 937-0550
Toll Free: (800) 527-3111
10 Rooms, Double: $159–$329
Open: all year, Credit cards: MC, VS

When Brewery Gulch Inn opened in 2001 it brought a new look to the area of mostly victorian style lodgings. Redwood logs, originally harvested in the 1800s and preserved, buried deep in the silt of the neighboring Big River before being "rescued", are a key ingredient in its construction. Set in 3 acres high on a bluff overlooking Smuggler's Cove, the architecturally distinctive, redwood-shake-covered inn contains ten guestrooms. The redwood is used throughout, blending with craftsman-style furnishings and colors selected to harmonize with the inn's natural setting. Each room has an ocean view and fireplace, most have their own private deck, and all are luxuriously equipped with every modern convenience to make your stay complete. The inn's resident chef prepares gourmet breakfasts, afternoon hors d'oeuvres, and special-event dinners with Brewery Gulch-grown organic products. Guests can sample local vintners' produce at the wine bar, warmed by the heat thrown from logs burning in an enormous, custom-built fireplace made of stainless steel and glass, the focal point of the living/dining room. *Directions:* Heading north on Hwy 1 you will see the Brewery Gulch Inn signpost to your right just before you get to Mendocino.

BREWERY GULCH INN
Owner: Guy Pacurar
Manager: Jo Ann Stickle
9401 North Hwy 1
Mendocino, CA 95460, USA
Tel: (707) 937-4752, Fax: (707) 937-1279
Toll Free: (800) 578-4454
10 Rooms, Double: $210–$465
Open: all year, Credit cards: all major

The John Dougherty House has a fabulous location, just steps from Mendocino's quaint shops and cute restaurants, yet only a few short blocks from the splendid headlands where you can stroll the bluffs with only the pounding of the surf, the cry of the seagulls, and the barking of the sea lions to disturb the silence. The heart of the inn is a beguiling blue cottage with perky white trim, dating back to 1867. Some of the guestrooms are in the main house, one in the adjacent wood-shingled water tower, another in the old carriage house, and others in cottages nestled in the beautifully kept garden. Décor is top of the line: crisp, modern and uncluttered. For the finest view, splurge on the Captain's Room, which has a spacious verandah looking out over the village to the bay. If this isn't available, choose either Raven or Osprey with their view balconies, king-sized four-poster beds, fireplaces, cable TVs, DVD players, and jet tubs. The cozy gathering room has a breakfast table at one end and comfortable chairs grouped before a brick fireplace where a fire blazes on chilly days. When the weather is warm, most guests choose to enjoy the hearty breakfast outside on the terrace overlooking the garden and the sea. *Directions:* Coming north on 101, take the first street into Mendocino. Turn right on Kasten, then left on Ukiah.

JOHN DOUGHERTY HOUSE
Owners: Andrew Hindman & Damien Wood
571 Ukiah Street
P.O. Box 817
Mendocino, CA 95460, USA
Tel: (707) 937-5266, Fax: (707) 937-1440
Toll Free: (800) 486-2104
8 Rooms, Double: $130–$275
Open: all year, Credit cards: MC, VS

The Joshua Grindle Inn, located just a short walk from the center of Mendocino, is surrounded by a 2-acre plot of land. A white picket fence encloses the front yard of this most attractive white clapboard farmhouse, which, although architecturally simple, has hints of the Victorian era in the fancy woodwork on the verandah. In the 1879 farmhouse you find the guest lounge, a sedate room with old paintings and portraits on the walls, a fireplace, white lace curtains, a trunk as a coffee table, and an antique pump organ. The light, airy guestrooms have a New England-country ambiance enhanced by early-American antiques and some have their own fireplace. Of the five bedrooms in the main building two overlook the town of Mendocino and the distant ocean. All of the bathrooms here have been remodeled with marble counters and whirlpool and deep soaking tubs. A natural-wood cottage, Saltbox Cottage, has two cozy bedrooms, each with custom pine cabinets and luxurious Jacuzzi tubs and showers. The most romantic rooms are those tucked into the age-weathered water tower in the rear garden. Especially attractive is Watertower II, a sunny, cozy room on the second floor with a glimpse of the ocean. *Directions:* Follow Hwy 1 north into Mendocino. After crossing the bridge into town, take the second left at the stoplight onto Little Lake Road.

JOSHUA GRINDLE INN
Owners: Cindy & Charles Reinhart
44800 Little Lake Road
P.O. Box 647
Mendocino, CA 95460, USA
Tel: (707) 937-4143, Toll Free: (800) 474-6353
12 Rooms, Double: $189–$389
1 Cottage: $279 daily
Open: all year, Credit cards: MC, VS
Select Registry

Set back in its own immaculately tended gardens with commanding views over the rocky coastline Sea Rock Inn is a collection of individual cottages and two, two story complexes of luxurious suites. Upscale country architecture blends original art, contemporary furnishings and knotty pine paneling with all the creature comforts demanded by the savvy traveler, fluffy robes, down comforters, TV/DVD's, WiFi and modern bathrooms (several have tubs for two with ocean views). Andy and Susie Plocher have lovingly rebuilt and upgraded the inn which started out in the late 1800's as a private residence and brewery, falling on hard times in the era of Prohibition. A generous buffet breakfast is served in a separate cottage within the sound of the breakers. Explore the beach, curl up by your own fireplace or relax on the deck at sunset with a bottle of wine, the choice is yours. Mendocino village with its galleries and restaurants is just up the road. The staff is particularly helpful and happy to make recommendations on hiking, what to see and where to go, suggest restaurants and make dinner reservations. *Directions:* From Highway 1 take Little Lake left (west), then Lansing right (north).

SEA ROCK INN
Owners: Susie & Andy Plocher
11101 Lansing Street
P.O. Box 906
Mendocino, CA 95460, USA
Tel: (707) 937-0926, Fax: (707) 676-9008
Toll Free: (800) 906-0926
14 Rooms, Double: $179–$385
Minimum Stay Required: 2 nights on weekends
Open: all year, Credit cards: all major
Select Registry

Joan and Jeff Stanford have created a sophisticated hotel in several attractive natural-wood buildings on 10 sheltered acres just to the south of Mendocino village. The personable staff are happy to offer advice on activities from special walks to DVD selection from the inn's vast library. Browse through the gift shop's selection of books (organic gardening, spirituality, dogs, vegetarian cooking and travel) and make yourself at home with the friendly resident cats in the expansive living room. Beyond the living room lies the Raven restaurant, which serves vegetarian fare featuring organic fare and offers a full bar serving organic liquors and wines. All rooms and suites have private decks with views across beautiful gardens and pastures where llamas graze. Paneled walls are hung with artwork and the fireplaces are supplied with plenty of wood to warm you on nippy nights. Everything is fresh and pretty and smart. A wonderful bonus is the greenhouse enclosed sauna and pool where guests can enjoy a swim, take a sauna, or soak in the spa even on blustery days. Enjoy a yoga class, massage in the forest or a workout in the exercise room. You are very welcome to bring your well-behaved dogs and children. Borrow mountain bikes and tour the town or explore the adjacent Big River by kayak or canoe. *Directions:* A quarter of a mile south of Mendocino village at the intersection of Hwy 1 and Comptche-Ukiah Road.

STANFORD INN BY THE SEA & SPA
Owners: Joan & Jeff Stanford
Hwy 1 & Comptche-Ukiah Road
Mendocino, CA 95460, USA
Tel: (707) 937-5615, Fax: (707) 937-0305
Toll Free: (800) 331-8884
41 Rooms, Double: $198–$478
Open: all year, Credit cards: all major

If you are looking for a place to stay in the heart of Mendocino that absolutely oozes decadent Victorian charm, then the Whitegate Inn is definitely for you. This clapboard home, built in 1883, is set off from the sidewalk by a white picket fence and, of course, a white gate. Inside, you step into an elegant home of the 19th century brimming with decorative Victorian antiques. To the right of the entry hall there is a parlor whose decor perfectly captures the Victorian era, with an Oriental carpet, crystal chandelier, elaborate furniture, gilt mirrors, ornate lamps, fancy drapes, bouquets of fresh flowers, and the owners' collection of silver, Staffordshire dogs and Victorian chintz china. The parlor opens to a formal dining room where a gourmet breakfast is presented each morning on a beautifully set table using fine china and silver. The guestrooms capture the same elegant Victorian mood with antique beds piled high with pillows and made with luxurious linens, featherbeds and down comforters on queen and king-sized beds. All rooms have a wood-burning or gas fireplaces, with snug en suite bathrooms (two with jet tubs), cable TV/DVD (complimentary library of movies) and wireless internet. Enjoy the peace and quiet of this location just a block away from the heart of town. *Directions:* From the junction with Hwy 128 drive 9 miles north on Hwy 1 to Mendocino. Turn west at the stoplight (Little Lake Road) then left on Howard Street for two blocks.

WHITEGATE INN
Owners: Susan & Richard Strom
499 Howard Street
Mendocino, CA 95460, USA
Tel: (707) 937-4892, Fax: (707) 937-1131
Toll Free: (800) 531-7282
7 Rooms, Double: $159–$319
Open: all year, Credit cards: all major

The historic English manor is a quintessential country inn. The Tudor-style home is beautiful—shaded by giant oak trees in an acre of wooded gardens full of colorful camellias, fuchsias, rhododendrons, and lush ferns all set in a quiet Monterey suburb. The inside of the house is an oasis of tranquility where everything is done with the comfort of the guest in mind—it's rather like a land bound cruise ship you never go hungry: cheese, yogurt, juice and sodas are always available in the guest fridge, fresh baked cookies and hot beverages are always available; wine and hors d' oeuvres are on hand in the early evening and truffles are a treat when you come in from dinner. All of the bedrooms in the main house, cottage, and carriage house have fireplaces, many have whirlpool tubs for two, and all are beautifully decorated and thoughtfully appointed. In the main house one of our favorite rooms is the Brightstone Suite with its bedroom, shower room and freestanding hydration tub for two sitting beside the fireplace in the sitting room. For complete privacy opt for the privacy of the Garden Cottage, with a separate sitting room, spa for two, and a skylight for gazing at the stars. Breakfast is posted the night before and can be served at the long mahogany table in the dining room at 9am or in the privacy of your bedroom. *Directions:* Exit Hwy 1 at Soledad/Munras, cross Munras, go right on Pacific and Martin Street is on the left in a ½ mile.

OLD MONTEREY INN
Owner: Patti Valletta
500 Martin Street
Monterey, CA 93940, USA
Tel: (831) 375-8284, Fax: (831) 375-6730
Toll Free: (800) 350-2344
9 Rooms, Double: $269–$379
1 Cottage: $449 daily
Minimum Stay Required: 2 nights on weekends
Open: all year, Credit cards: MC, VS
Select Registry

As an alternative to a bed and breakfast we recommend the Spindrift Inn, a lovely hotel with a great location overlooking Monterey Bay. Just down the street from the fabulous Monterey Bay Aquarium, its rooms overlook either the bustle of Cannery Row or the serenity of the bay. We stayed in a front room overlooking Cannery Row and were happy to find that the deep-set windows and heavy drapes blocked out the noise of late-night revelers. Guestrooms on the bay side enjoy wonderful water views and corner rooms are spacious and have a lovely window seat. Bedrooms are handsomely decorated with rich European fabrics and all have wood-burning fireplaces, beds topped with down comforters and feather beds, and bathrooms finished in marble and brass. The feeling is European and the amenities are first-class. A continental breakfast of fresh-baked breads and a selection of fruit is served on a silver tray in the room and in the evening a buffet of wine and cheese is set out in the front lobby. There is always someone at the front desk to assist with information or reservations. This is an efficient, attractive, and comfortable hotel with a premier location. *Directions:* Take the Pacific Grove/Del Monte exit off Hwy 1. Follow signs to Cannery Row and the Aquarium—the Spindrift is on the right-hand side on Cannery Row.

SPINDRIFT INN
Manager: Randy Venard
652 Cannery Row
Monterey, CA 93940, USA
Tel: (831) 646-8900, Fax: (831) 646-5342
Toll Free: (800) 841-1879
45 Rooms, Double: $199–$499
Open: all year, Credit cards: all major

Set amongst a meadow of wildflowers surrounded by windswept Cypress trees Seal Cove Inn looks out towards the distant ocean across the Fitzgerald Marine Reserve where you enjoy secluded beaches, explore tidepools, watch seals and follow woodland paths along the bluffs. Only the sound of the distant foghorn penetrates the quiet and it is hard to believe that you are just 20 miles south (a half hour drive) from San Francisco. A spacious entrance hall draws you into the most comfortable of living rooms where a large fireplace is centered between French doors. Adjoining the living room is a breakfast room where a hearty buffet breakfast is set out in a morning and wine and hors d'ouevres are served in an evening. Fresh baked cookies, coffee and tea are always on hand. A small conference room is available. Bedrooms are large enough to accommodate an oh-so-comfortable California-king bed and comfortable reading chairs by the log burning fireplace. All of the rooms have a view of the distant ocean (best from upstairs) and doors opening to either a private balcony or onto the terrace. Room refrigerators are stocked with complimentary beverages and the inn has a large selection of complimentary movies for you to borrow. A Four Sisters Inn. *Directions:* From San Francisco take Hwy 1 south to Moss Beach. Turn west on Cypress (at the Moss Beach Distillery sign). Seal Cove Inn is one block off the road on the right.

SEAL COVE INN
221 Cypress Avenue
Moss Beach, CA 94038, USA
Tel: (650) 728-4114, Fax: (650) 728-4116
Toll Free: (800) 995-9987
10 Rooms, Double: $225–$325
Open: all year, Credit cards: all major

The Pelican Inn is a wonderful re-creation of an English country pub, complete with old-world guestrooms tucked upstairs. The Public Bar serving draught beers, ales and stout, low, beamed ceilings hung with horse brasses, a giant inglenook fireplace with its secret priest hole, a cozy guest lounge and a dining room with trestle tables all contribute to the atmosphere. Next to the dining room, is the conservatory where breakfast is served and, in an evening, guests can dine by candlelight on linen-decked tables. Upstairs there are seven cozy bedrooms where the English theme is continued with draped half-tester and four-poster beds and little mullioned windows. We particularly liked room 1, the largest and airiest room overlooking the garden, and room 2, the smallest room with it's high queen bedded four poster bed tucked in a corner. There's often lots of revelry on weekend evenings (11pm closing) but know that you can always retreat from the hubbub to the guests private sitting room. The location is fabulous: a few minutes' drive from the giant redwood grove at Muir Woods and a five minute walk to the most beautiful of beaches. Reservations for summer weekends need to be made several months in advance. The restaurant is closed on Mondays from November to April. *Directions:* From Hwy 101 take the Stinson Beach/Hwy 1 turnoff. At the Arco station, go left for 5 miles on Hwy 1 to Muir Beach. Pelican Inn is on the left.

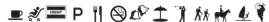

PELICAN INN
Owners: Susan & Ed Cunningham
Manager: Will Koza
10 Pacific Way
Muir Beach, CA 94965, USA
Tel: (415) 383-6000, Fax: (415) 393-3424
Toll Free: (866) 383-6000
7 Rooms, Double: $208–$292
Open: all year, Credit cards: MC, VS

After the 49er gold boom Murphys dozed quietly under its locust and elm trees until, more recently, tourists discovered its charms. Just off Main Street within easy walking distance to town Dunbar House, 1880 is a handsome Victorian with a wraparound porch where guests can sit and sip Gold Country wine or enjoy a refreshing glass of lemonade. Rich and Arline have lavished time and attention to ensure that every room in their home has as many amenities as possible, at the same time focusing on preserving the privacy of their clientele. Each guestroom has a gas log fireplace, a small refrigerator, water, a bottle of wine and an appetizer plate, instant hot water for making hot drinks, and a flat-screen direct TV/DVD player hidden away in an armoire. The Sequoia room has a king-size bed and a two-person whirlpool bath. The Cedar room, just off the downstairs parlor, has a small sitting room with a Jacuzzi tub and a private porch. Upstairs, the Ponderosa room has a king bed, large claw-foot tub and views of the garden, and Sugar Pine is a two-room suite with a private balcony. Up the steep attic stairs you find the spacious Blue Oak room with its sloping ceilings and a large sundeck. Breakfast is served in the Dining room or rose garden. The Cedar and Sequoia Rooms offer private in-room dining. *Directions:* From Angels Camp drive 9 miles east on Hwy 4. Turn left onto Main Street, go two blocks, and turn left, by the tall flagpole, into Dunbar House's driveway.

❄ ☕ 💳 ☎ @ W ⅄ P 🚭 🖼 🚶 🐎 ⚓ 🍷

DUNBAR HOUSE, 1880
Owners: Arline & Richard Taborek
271 Jones Street
Murphys, CA 95247, USA
Tel: (209) 728-2897, Fax: (209) 728-1451
Toll Free: (800) 692-6006
5 Rooms, Double: $190–$280
Open: all year, Credit cards: all major
Select Registry

Set back a few yards off bustling Main Street, The Victoria Inn is a few minutes walk from all of the attractions of Murphys, one of our favorite Gold Country towns. Owner Michael Ninos has created an oasis of elegant tranquility that unfolds as soon as you step into the shade of the wraparound porch and into the lobby. A cozy sitting area with club chairs is perfect for coffee, small talk and newspapers in the morning or aperitifs in the evening, beckons you into the intimate V Restaurant & Bar, which also does catering and receptions in a private garden. Select a bottle of wine from the cellar and, if the weather appeals, enjoy your meal outdoors on the porch. Guestroom décor is in earthtones with splashes of color, punctuated by a well-placed mix of reproduction and antique furniture. A combination of clawfoot tubs, fireplaces, pot-bellied stoves and private balconies ensures that one will fit your needs. All are equipped with invitingly comfortable beds and sparkling tile bathrooms, some with spa tubs, and topped off with the finest linens and towels. Number 6, the only theme room is modeled on a rustic cabin, replete with corrugated iron ceiling and open beams. For more space, three separate guest suites adjacent to the main building provide luxurious accommodations with more privacy. *Directions:* From Angels Camp drive 9 miles east on Hwy 4 to Murphys. Turn left onto Main Street and right into Victoria Inn's driveway.

THE VICTORIA INN
Owner: Michael Ninos
402-H Main Street
Murphys, CA 95247, USA
Tel: (209) 728-8933, Fax: (209) 728-8914
15 Rooms, Double: $125–$310
Open: all year, Credit cards: all major

Napa Blackbird Inn Map: 4

Sitting quietly on its corner lot on First Street for close to a hundred years and previously used as a family home and commercial offices, this fine old shingle-sided structure was carefully made over in readiness for its new life as the Blackbird Inn. Resplendently renovated with a new interior in the Greene and Greene style of Arts and Crafts architecture, it provides a haven of welcome and comfort just a few minutes' walk away from the delights of downtown Napa. The sitting room with its exquisite leaded stained-glass front door, large fieldstone fireplace, comfy sofas, stained-glass accents, soft-hued lighting, and gleaming mahogany woodwork sets the tone. The eight guestrooms, five up the imposing staircase, three on the main floor, are varied in size but similar in standard and amenities. Most have gas fireplaces, two have private, albeit small, decks, and half have jetted spa tubs. All are decorated in a pleasing Craftsman style—many pieces of furniture were handcrafted by the owner. Spend your days exploring the Napa Valley and return to the inn to relax with a glass of wine and hors d'oeuvres. A Four Sisters Inn. *Directions:* Take the downtown Napa exit from Hwy 29 and turn left on Jefferson. Blackbird Inn is located at the corner of two busy downtown streets First and Jefferson.

BLACKBIRD INN
Manager: Emily Deeter
1755 First Street
Napa, CA 94559, USA
Tel: (707) 226-2450, Fax: (707) 258-6391
Toll Free: (888) 567-9811
8 Rooms, Double: $160–$285
Open: all year, Credit cards: all major

176 *Places to Stay*

Nestled in two secluded acres next to Highway 29 between Napa and Yountville are eight brightly colored luxury cottages, a creation of owner Mike Smith. What was formerly a motor court (the oldest of the original cottages dates back to the 1920's) has been transformed into a garden court, with open space and mature trees. Opened in late 2005, individual accommodations vary in size from 450 to 600 square feet. Generally the larger the unit, the better it is equipped for self catering. The largest has a full kitchen. Furnishings and appointments are first class. King size beds (supplemented with queen sized folding beds for extra guests) vaulted ceilings with their signature cupola skylights, fireplaces, and wood floors are the order of the day. Modern bathrooms feature heated floors, with earth tone tiles and two-person soaking tubs. Every cottage has its own patio or porch and wood burning chimenea. Wine and cheese tastings are hosted on Friday evenings. Continental breakfast, is delivered to your room and features scrumptious pastries from nearby Bouchon Bakery. The concierge will be happy to help with custom wine tours, bicycle tours, dinner reservations and hot air ballooning. Too active for your taste? Relax with a massage in your room or in secluded privacy beneath the redwoods. *Directions:* From Yountville take Highway 29 south for 2 miles. Turn right on Darms Lane and The Cottages are immediately on the right.

THE COTTAGES OF NAPA VALLEY
Owner: Mike Smith
Manager: Mary E. Stevens
1012 Darms Lane
Napa, CA 94558, USA
Tel: (707) 252-7810, Fax: (707) 252-7825
Toll Free: (866) 900-7810
8 Cottages: $305–$525 daily
Open: all year, Credit cards: all major

Conveniently situated just north of Napa, Milliken Creek is nestled on 3 lushly wooded, secluded acres fronting a quiet stretch of the Napa River. Reputedly it was the first stagecoach stop on the Silverado Trail, constructed circa 1857. Bedrooms are in the Main and South Houses and the very private Cottage. All are luxuriously decorated in a contemporary style, and provide a mix of river views, fireplaces, private balconies, decks, and whirlpool tubs. A hot French country breakfast is served in your room each morning. In the afternoon a generous tasting of wine and cheese features some of the area's finest selections. Popular treatments at the spa include: the Couples Massage, a romantic side-by-side treatment; Soothing Stones; a Grapeseed Body Polish; and the Miliken Trio, a massage, reflexology and essential oils focused on the head, hands and feet. Relax and soak up the ambiance of the inn and sample the epicurean delights of nearby Napa Valley restaurants. *Directions:* Take the Trances exit from Hwy 29 in Napa, drive through the town, and, immediately after a left-hand turn for the Silverado Trail, bear right across the Milliken Creek Bridge (signposted Napa). Turn right at the stop sign (Silverado Trail southbound). Milliken Creek is on the right after a mile—its entrance is marked by a black sign with an "M."

MILLIKEN CREEK
Manager: Connie Gore
1815 Silverado Trail
Napa, CA 94558, USA
Tel: (707) 255-1197, Fax: (707) 255-3112
Toll Free: (800) 835 6112
12 Rooms, Double: $350–$725
Open: all year, Credit cards: MC, VS

Surrounded by 600 acres of vineyards, Oak Knoll Inn has an idyllic setting in the Napa Valley. You find the entry and prettily decorated front sitting room in the original stone farmhouse. Another building was added to each side to house guestrooms, each with a private entrance opening onto a wraparound deck overlooking the vineyards. Breakfast is a feast served on winter mornings in front of the stone fireplace, on warm mornings outside on the deck, or in the privacy of your room. Barbara, John and their staff are all especially knowledgeable and happy to plan personalized tours, recommend restaurants for dinner and lunch and make dining reservations. Whether it is your first, or your fiftieth time in the valley; whether overview tour of the wineries, or your passion is Pinots; they will plan a detailed trip for you. Guestrooms are especially large, magnified further by the high vaulted ceilings. Our favorites, number 6 and 1 both have arched windows that tower to the height of the ceiling and offer splendid views of the vineyards. Each luxurious bedroom enjoys a king-size bed, a sitting area before a fireplace, and a top of the line modern bathroom. After a busy day sightseeing relax poolside and enjoy the quiet and beauty of a backdrop of vineyards and the valley's rolling hills. *Directions:* Go north on Hwy 29 through Napa, then right on Oak Knoll Avenue, which has a left-right zigzag across Big Ranch Road. The inn is on the left.

OAK KNOLL INN
Owners: Barbara Passino & John Kuhlmann
2200 E. Oak Knoll Avenue
Napa, CA 94558, USA
Tel: (707) 255-2200, Fax: (707) 255-2296
4 Rooms, Double: $350–$750
Minimum Stay Required: 2 nights on weekends
Open: all year, Credit cards: MC, VS

Situated at the end of its private drive, high above the valley floor with commanding views across the local vineyards, the Poetry Inn evokes a plethora of superlatives. Spacious, luxurious, decadent, innovative, intimate. Suites range in size from 850 to 1,450 square feet. Sparkling white décor is offset by dark wood furnishings and splashes of earthtones. Modern marble and glass bathrooms share the common theme of (remarkably secluded) outdoor showers. All the rooms have large soaking tubs, indoor showers for the less adventurous, private patios and genuine wood burning fireplaces (a relative rarity in the wine country). The king sized four poster beds, large flat screen TV's, fine Italian linens, sumptuous towels, fluffy robes and stunning views make for utter self indulgence. Breakfast is served on the balcony overlooking the valley or for an additional charge, in the bedroom. With a little advance notice spa treatments and massage services can be provided in-house. The heated outdoor pool and hot tub are located a few steps away. Wine tasting, an essential part of the Napa valley experience, starts at the adjacent Cliff Lede Vineyards: enjoy a flute of Sauvignon Blanc in the garden or sit by the fire in the craftsmen-style tasting room with a glass of Cabernet. *Directions:* Take highway 29 north up the Napa valley, turn right on Yountville Cross Road and Poetry Inn faces you when you come to Silverado Trail.

POETRY INN
Owner: Cliff Lede
Managers: Lena Thompson & Chris Parkes
6380 Silverado Trail
Napa, CA 94558, USA
Tel: (707) 944-0646, Fax: (707) 944-9188
4 Rooms, Double: $685–$1400
Open: all year, Credit cards: all major

La Residence has grown around The Mansion—a beautiful Gothic-revival home built in the 1870s. In later years, additions more Victorian in style changed the appearance of the house. Now it houses 8 of the bedrooms decorated in period style and varying in size from cozy, top-floor rooms tucked under slanted ceilings to spacious and elegant accommodations with fireplaces on the first floor. Just across the way The French Barn, the heart of the inn, is, as its name suggests, French country in style and decor. All the bedrooms enjoy fireplaces, French doors opening onto a patio or balcony and pine antiques from France and England. Three king-bedded Cellar House suites overlook a small vineyard. For complete privacy opt for the Cottage Suite, a self-contained cottage. Fruit and a cooked breakfast is served at 9am. Tastings of local wines accompany hors d'oeuvres in an evening. Relax by the pool after a day of sightseeing. Guests often walk up the lane to Bistro Don Giovanni for dinner. The splash of large fountains and a substantial planting of trees shield you from road noise from the nearby highway. *Directions:* Travel north on Hwy 29 through Napa. Take the first right turn after the Salvador intersection onto Howard Lane that winds back south to the inn.

LA RESIDENCE
Owners: Kathryn & Craig Hall
4066 Howard Lane
Napa, CA 94558, USA
Tel: (707) 253-0337, Fax: (707) 253-0382
Toll Free: (800) 253-9203
31 Rooms, Double: $225–$600
Open: all year, Credit cards: all major

Heavy iron gates swing open magically, allowing you to enter a world far removed from the everyday activity of Oakhurst, a town just to the south of Yosemite National Park. You enter through the château's heavy doors, cross a cool, limestone flagged foyer, and step down into a stunning living room opening onto a circular tower room. A grand piano sits beneath a whimsically frescoed ceiling. Doors open to reveal a sunny breakfast room and a tiny chapel. A spiraling stone staircase leads up to the individually decorated bedrooms named for herbs and flowers: Saffron has an enormous ebony bed and black-marble fireplace; Lavender is sunny in colors of periwinkle blue and lavender; and Elderberry is cool in blue and white. Each of the splendid bedrooms has a wood-burning fireplace, goose-down duvet, hidden CD player, luxurious bathroom with a deep soaking tub (many large enough for two), the finest toiletries, thick towels, and the softest of robes. A beautiful villa offers two luxurious suites. Spend your days by the pool and indulging in treatments at the spa. In an evening walk across the garden to the restaurant which presents a spectacular fixed-price six-course dinner. *Directions:* From the center of Oakhurst take Hwy 41 toward Fresno. As the road climbs the hill, turn right at Victoria Lane and drive in through the wrought-iron gates.

CHATEAU DU SUREAU
Owner: Erna Kubin-Clanin
48688 Victoria Lane
P.O. Box 577
Oakhurst, CA 93644, USA
Tel: (559) 683-6860, Fax: (559) 683-0800
10 Rooms, Double: $385–$585*
1 Villa: $2950 daily*
*Service: 12%
Closed: first two weeks of Jan, Credit cards: all major
Relais & Châteaux

Occidental nestles between the rugged Sonoma coast and the vineyards of the Russian River valley. The Inn at Occidental, a block east of the Bohemian Highway, dates from 1877. From the wraparound porch you enter the living room whose elegant furnishings are set in front of an inviting fireplace. The dining room where breakfast is served is located in the wine cellar. Breakfast offerings include freshly baked pastries, seasonal fruit, homemade granola, and such tempting delights as orange pancakes. Beautiful fir floors accented with lovely Oriental carpets are found throughout the living room. Each guestroom's decor echoes the colors in the original art displayed in the room and feather beds topped with down comforters assure a wonderful night's sleep. The inn has 16 rooms with appealing amenities such as a romantic fireplace, a hot tub in a private garden oasis, or a luxurious spa tub. A neighboring cottage is perfect for a family or long-term stay. Conference facilities are available. Jerry, Tina and their staff make this inn very special. *Directions:* One hour north of San Francisco. Take Hwy 101 to Hwy 116 west to Sebastopol then take the Bodega Hwy west for 6 miles toward Bodega Bay to the Bohemian Hwy to Occidental.

INN AT OCCIDENTAL
Owners: Tina & Jerry Wolsborn
3657 Church Street, P.O. Box 857
Occidental, CA 95465, USA
Tel: (707) 874-1047, Fax: (707) 874-1078
Toll Free: (800) 522-6324
21 Rooms, Double: $209–$359
Open: all year, Credit cards: all major
Select Registry

Olema Druids Hall stands in its own grounds above the village, the initials UAOD on the front façade is evidence of its origins as the meeting place for that secretive society. It has been renovated in outstanding detail to provide two luxurious double bedrooms, an impressive suite and a deluxe self contained cottage. The spacious Olema Room is to be found downstairs off the main sitting room with its comfy seating, impressive open fireplace, antiques, and unique collections. Between the hours of 7:30pm and 10:30am the sitting room is reserved for the exclusive use of the Olema Room. The "Nest" on the second floor is a generously sized queen-bedded room which only appears snug when compared to the other accommodations. The Grand Suite has a fully equipped gourmet kitchen and sitting room. Expanded spa like bathrooms are spectacularly modern. Everything you need for an expanded continental breakfast: Organic local produce, breads, cheeses, coffee, tea, fruit and juice are provided in your own refrigerator. Fresh pastries and the daily newspaper are delivered to your door each morning. *Directions:* Exit Highway 101 at San Anselmo/Sir Francis Drake Blvd. Take Sir Francis Drake Blvd for 20 miles to Highway 1 (T junction at Olema). Turn left and the inn is signpost on your left after 1 block.

OLEMA DRUIDS HALL
Owner: Robert Cain
Manager: Victoria Swift
9870 Shoreline Hwy One, P.O. Box 96
Olema, CA 94950, USA
Tel: (415) 663-8727, Fax: (415) 663-1817
Toll Free: (866) 554-4255
39 Rooms, Double: $185–$435
1 Cottage: $355–$410 daily
Minimum Stay Required: 2 nights on weekends
Open: all year, Credit cards: MC, VS

The slogan of the Crystal Pier Hotel & Cottages, "Sleep over the Ocean," aptly expresses what is unique and special about this property. Charming white clapboard cottages trimmed in blue and dressed with windowboxes cover the length of both sides of this private/public pier in colorful Pacific Beach. When the tide is in, the surf washes beneath the cottages and wooden slats of the pier. Cottages all enjoy an expanse of deck and unobstructed views of ocean, surfers, and beachcombers. It is easy to get to know your neighbors while watching the sunset over the ocean as only low white picket fences divide each patio. The most private units are those towards the end of the pier for they are set at an angle and have private patios and the most spectacular ocean views. All the cottages enjoy a little kitchen and living room and are priced according to whether they are a spacious studio, one bedroom with bath, or two bedrooms with two baths. Although it is locked in the evening and has 24-hour security, the pier is open to the public by day. Be advised that the morning starts early on the pier with fishing at its end, the rumble of guests' cars on the wooden slats, and the arrival of beachcombers, lifeguards, and surfers on the beach below. *Directions:* Leave I-5 at Balboa/Garnet Ave. The pier is at the end of Garnet Avenue on Ocean Front Walk.

CRYSTAL PIER HOTEL & COTTAGES
Manager: Jim Bostian
4500 Ocean Boulevard in Pacific Beach
Pacific Beach, CA 92109, USA
Tel: (858) 483-6983, Fax: (858) 483-6811
Toll Free: (800) 748-5894
29 Cottages: $235–$500 daily
Open: all year, Credit cards: all major

Tucked between the busier resorts of Monterey and Carmel, Pacific Grove has managed to avoid much of their more touristy ambiance and retains the air of being an inviting Victorian summer retreat. The Gosby House Inn is a perfect place to retreat to, with certainly a lot more fun and frolic than in days gone by when it was the summer home of a stern Methodist family. While the decor is decidedly Victorian in flavor, it has an air of whimsy and fun that banishes all formal stuffiness: teddy bears are posed rakishly on each bed. The bedrooms are scattered upstairs and down, some have garden entrances and two deluxe rooms occupy an adjacent clapboard house tucked behind the pretty garden. Over half the bedrooms have fireplaces and all have well-designed and decorated bathrooms. Each room is appealingly decorated with flowery wallpapers and comforters and many benefit from the romantic touch of antique beds. Our particular favorites are 21, a garden cottage, and 22 and 23 in the Carriage House with spa tubs and large decks. Before you step out for dinner, enjoy hors d'oeuvres and wine in the living room. A full breakfast is set out downstairs between 8 and 10 every morning. It's a perfect location for visiting Carmel, exploring Carmel and visiting Big Sur. A Four Sisters Inn. *Directions:* Take Hwy 1 to Hwy 68 west to Pacific Grove. Continue on Forest Avenue to Lighthouse Avenue, turn left, and go three blocks.

GOSBY HOUSE INN
Manager: Sharon Carey
643 Lighthouse Avenue
Pacific Grove, CA 93950, USA
Tel: (831) 375-1287, Fax: (831) 655-9621
Toll Free: (800) 527-8828
22 Rooms, Double: $130–$250
Open: all year, Credit cards: all major

The Green Gables Inn is sensationally positioned overlooking Monterey Bay. This romantic, half-timbered, Queen Anne-style mansion with many interesting dormers is as inviting inside as out. The living room and dining room have comfortable arrangements of sofas and chairs placed to maximize your enjoyment of the view. Many of the upstairs bedrooms, set under steeply slanting beamed ceilings with romantic diamond-paned casement windows, offer ocean views. While the Garret room does not have an ocean view, it is the coziest of hideaways. All but two of the upstairs bedrooms share bathrooms. The elegant ground-floor suite has a sitting room and fireplace, while the rooms in the adjacent carriage house are all especially spacious, have fireplaces, sitting areas, and private bathrooms—some with Jacuzzi tubs. As a guest at the Green Gables Inn you will certainly not perish from hunger or thirst—beverages are available all day, goodies are readily at hand in the cookie jar, and wine and hors d'oeuvres appear in the evening. Breakfast, too, is no disappointment: it's a hearty buffet of fruit, homemade breads, and a hot egg dish. A Four Sisters Inn. *Directions:* From Hwy 1 take the Pacific Grove-Del Monte exit. As you go through the tunnel, Del Monte becomes Lighthouse Avenue, which you follow into Pacific Grove. Go right one block and you are on Ocean View Boulevard—the inn is on the corner at Fifth Street.

GREEN GABLES INN
Manager: Honey Spence
301 Ocean View Blvd.
Pacific Grove, CA 93950, USA
Tel: (831) 375-2095, Fax: (831) 375-5437
Toll Free: (800) 722-1774
11 Rooms, Double: $135–$300
Open: all year, Credit cards: all major

What sets Seven Gables Inn apart is that every one of the twenty five guestrooms has an ocean view. The beakfast and sitting rooms also capture wall-wide windows of vistas of Monterey Bay. Such is the draw of the ocean that guests often sit at breakfast studying the bay through binoculars. Bedrooms are found in seven sunny yellow buildings and range in size from Fairlawn—a cute cottage-like room built into the front of the main house to Jewell Cottage a two-bedroom house with its own dining and living room. I was particularly impressed with bedrooms in the Beach House and especially enjoyed Seal Rocks, a medium sized room that opens up to an expanse of window framing the bay and Lovers' Point. The ornate style of the main house, a grand 1886 Victorian mansion, sets the tone of the décor. Sitting rooms are furnished with ornate French antiques (lots of gilt and inlay) complemented by Oriental rugs, sparkling crystal chandeliers and intricate stained glass windows. The décor throughout is French elegant. Bed-linen and bathroom products are top of the line as is the hot buffet breakfast, served in the Beach House. The only television is found on the sun porch in the main house. *Directions:* Take Hwy 1 to Hwy 68 west to Pacific Grove. Continue on Forest Avenue to the ocean. Turn right and the inn is on the corner of Ocean View Boulevard and Fountain Street. Parking is in the inn's courtyard or on the street.

SEVEN GABLES INN
Owners: Susan & Ed Flatley
555 Ocean View Boulevard
Pacific Grove, CA 93950, USA
Tel: (831) 372-4341, Fax: (831) 372-0150
25 Rooms, Double: $200–$550
Open: all year, Credit cards: all major

The Andalusian Court is two minutes walk from the bustle of Palm Canyon Drive with its antique stores, restaurants and entertainment. Set beneath the towering wall of rock that guards the eastern perimeter of town its terra cotta roof tiles, inlaid ceramic tile, soft earth-tone decor and shady inner courtyards conjure vision of southern Spain. A series of mini villas, each behind its own private, gated wall. Private outdoor whirlpool tubs, fire pits, mountain views, the choice is yours, and everywhere the soothing sounds of the many water features found throughout the property. Artfully selected furnishings and décor reflect the 1920's Spanish Revival and Art and Crafts periods. All accommodations feature modern marble or stone enhanced bathrooms, dining and living areas, and fully equipped self catering kitchens. A full size swimming pool is tucked into one corner, perfect for escaping the heat of the day. Prepared breakfasts are delivered to your room until late in the morning. An excellent walk into town location. *Directions:* Turn west off Palm Canyon on Arenas and go four blocks—the hotel is on your right.

THE ANDALUSIAN COURT
Owner: Yuka Akimoto
458 West Arenas Road
Palm Springs, CA 92262, USA
Tel: (760) 323-9980, Fax: (760) 323-9280
Toll Free: (888) 947-6667
7 Rooms, Double: $170–$270
Open: all year, Credit cards: all major

Casa Cody is a moderately priced hotel in the heart of Palm Springs. Although quite simple it stands out like a gem. There is a nostalgic, old-fashioned comfort to these one-story, pink-stuccoed buildings with turquoise trim, the oldest continuously functioning hotel in Palm Springs. It had fallen into a state of hopeless disrepair until bought by Therese Hayes and Frank Tysen, who restored it with hard work, lots of imagination, and much love. The Casa Cody once again blossomed into an appealing small hotel with a nice choice of accommodations ranging from a standard double to a spacious two-bedroom, two-bath suite. Many of the rooms have the added bonuses of kitchenettes and fireplaces. The interior decor exudes a fresh, clean "Desert" look, with a southwest color scheme and handmade furniture. This friendly, comfortable inn is a remarkable value, especially the reasonably priced studio units such as 1, 2, 3, 4, 21, and 23, which have both fireplaces and well-equipped kitchens. We loved the 1920s doll-house-like, one-bedroom cottage tucked in under the trees in the corner of the property. Our favorite is the two-bedroom Old Adobe House, where Charlie Chaplin used to stay. *Directions:* Drive south through Palm Springs on Palm Canyon Drive. Turn right on Tahquitz-Canyon Way, then left on Cahuilla Road, and Casa Cody is half a block along on the right.

CASA CODY INN
Owners: Therese Hayes & Frank Tysen
Manager: Elissa Goforth
175 South Cahuilla Road
Palm Springs, CA 92262, USA
Tel: (760) 320-9346, Fax: (760) 323-4994
Toll Free: (800) 231-2639
28 Rooms, Double: $69–$229
Adobe House: $269–$369 (2 bed) daily
Winter House: $469–$669 (4 bed) daily
Open: all year, Credit cards: all major

The scent of flowers and a gentle, friendly ambiance permeates the air of the Desert Hills Hotel. The location is excellent—an easy walk to the historic heart of Old Palm Springs and a few blocks from shops, galleries and restaurants—snuggled up against the rugged San Jacinto Mountains. The hotel retains the aura of years past with rooms and suites reminiscent of the 1950s and 60s original desert decor. The rooms open to a central courtyard with a lush lawn and well-tended gardens surrounding a pretty pool. Ranging in size from snug, through spacious rooms with kitchenettes (the majority) to a two bedroom apartment with fireplace, all are kept in tiptop condition with excellent lighting, quality mattresses, and spotless bathrooms. From the outside the one-story Desert Hills looks like most of the other hotels of similar vintage—you only realize its uniqueness when you see that every detail shows loving care. The Desert Hills is not a flashy, trendy hotel, but rather a classic, tranquil oasis where you can settle in for an extended time, relaxing by the pool, hearing the wind whisper through the palm trees, and feeling like a friend of the family. Guests enjoy continental breakfast, outdoor kitchen with barbecues, a hot Jacuzzi, and vintage style bicycles. *Directions:* Turn west off Palm Canyon on Arenas and go six blocks—the hotel is on the northwest corner of Arenas.

DESERT HILLS HOTEL
Owners: Debbie & Bill Broughton
601 West Arenas Road
Palm Springs, CA 92262, USA
Tel: (760) 325-2777, Fax: (760) 325-6423
Toll Free: (800) 350-2527
14 Rooms, Double: $99–$350*
*Breakfast not included
Minimum Stay Required: 2 nights on weekends
Open: all year, Credit cards: all major

It's a long way from Tangiers, yet nestled in the heart of the Southern California desert, at the base of the San Jacinto Mountains lies an unmistakable southern Mediterranean experience Korakia Pensione. Desert living of "Old Palm Springs" is lovingly re-created at two adjacent historic villas: the Moroccan-style villa of painter Gordon Coutts and the Mediterranean-style villa of early screen star J. Carrol Naish. Whitewashed walls, Oriental carpets, handmade furniture, lovely natural fabrics, antiques, Moroccan fountains, fragrant fruit trees, torches blazing by the pools, and bougainvillea-draped archways create a stunning ambiance. Bedrooms, found around each of the villas swimming pools, are mostly ground floor and offer lots of privacy. For a treat, request one of our favorite rooms, the Nash House or the Artist Studio. Private dinners are available Thursday through Sunday nights, served either in the room or poolside. Enjoy Moroccan tea in an afternoon, old movies outdoors (most of the year), a relaxing massage, and a full breakfast served on the sun-drenched patio. *Directions:* Turn west off Palm Canyon on Arenas, go four blocks, and turn south on Patencio Road.

KORAKIA PENSIONE
Manager: Paulette Monarrez
257 South Patencio Road
Palm Springs, CA 92262, USA
Tel: (760) 864-6411, Fax: (760) 864-4147
28 Rooms, Double: $159–$789
Open: all year, Credit cards: all major

Once a sleepy desert town, Palm Springs was discovered in the 1920s by glamorous movie stars who made it their secret hideaway. This balmy paradise also captivated the heart of Samuel Untermyer, a New Yorker and famous antitrust lawyer of the time, who bought a beautiful estate, The Willows, snuggled next to the mountains just a few blocks from the center of town, where in winter he entertained many distinguished friends. The home remained a private residence until opening as a deluxe small hotel after a complete renovation that returned it to its former elegance and successfully captured the ambiance of the 1930s. The clay-colored building sitting on a rocky outcrop is almost hidden from view by a profusion of palm trees and colorful flowers. An inviting pool nestles on the lower garden area, the living room is of grand proportions while the glass wall of the adjacent breakfast room opens up to a flagstone terrace enclosed on one side by a wall of natural rock with a cascading waterfall. Every gorgeous guestroom has its own personality, with the price basically reflecting its size. You feel like a guest in a private home displaying the opulence of a bygone era. *Directions:* Located in the heart of Palm Springs. From either Palm Canyon Drive or Indian Canyon Drive, take Tahquitz Canyon Way west. In a few blocks the street dead-ends. The Willows is at the end of the road on your right.

❄ ☕ 🏊 CREDIT ☎ @ W Y P ≈ 🏌 🕴 👫

THE WILLOWS
Owner: Tracy Conrad
412 West Tahquitz Canyon Way
Palm Springs, CA 92262, USA
Tel: (760) 320-0771, Fax: (760) 320-0780
Toll Free: (800) 966-9597
8 Rooms, Double: $275–$595
Closed: mid-Jun to Labor Day, Credit cards: all major

Built in the 1880s, this lovely three-story home, with dormer windows and wraparound porch set on a lush lawn shaded by large trees is a delightful find. On one side of the entry is the cozy library looking out to the swimming pool; on the other side, through French doors, is the beautiful living room decorated with period antiques and sofas in front of the hand carved fireplace. The back of the fireplace opens up to the dining room where guests enjoy breakfast on delicate Limoge china (breakfast can also be served poolside or in your room). Peek into the butler's pantry just beyond the dining room: its tin roof is original to the home and its shelves display a collection of antique china. The spacious king-bedded Garden Room is located on the third floor with its jacuzzi tub overlooking the swimming pool. A little porch sitting area, unusual shower room and snug queen-bedded room give Victoria lots of appeal. Select English Holiday for its quintessential English country décor. Wine and dessert are served in the evening while cookies, fruit, tea and coffee are available round the clock. Stay at Bissell House for the annual New Year's Rose Bowl Parade, a prime location as guests walk to grandstand seating and enjoy the pre-parade festivities. *Directions:* From either the 134, 210, or 110 freeways, take the Orange Grove Avenue exit. The Bissell House is on Pasadena's historic Millionaires' Row on the southwest corner of Orange Grove and Columbia.

BISSELL HOUSE
Owner: Juli Hoyman
201 Orange Grove Avenue
Pasadena, CA 91030, USA
Tel: (626) 441-3535, Fax: (626) 441-3671
Toll Free: (800) 441-3530
5 Rooms, Double: $195–$350
Open: all year, Credit cards: all major

Justin Winery has a glorious setting, tucked in gently rolling hills 16 miles west of Paso Robles. The winery complex (consisting of the tasting room, reception, boutique, restaurant, and guestrooms) is beautiful and the setting is serene. The attractive wooden buildings are set off to perfection by lush lawns and well-tended gardens. The suites at the Just Inn combine the luxury and amenities of a five-star hotel with the friendliness of a family-run inn while looking out over the vineyards. The suites feature European antiques, fine fabrics, feather beds, down comforters, frescoed ceilings, flower-filled windowboxes, marble bathrooms with hydro spas, and wood-burning fireplaces. The Sussex suite (a little bit of the English countryside) opens onto the garden while the Provence and Tuscany suites have balconies where you can sip a glass of wine while looking over the vineyards. For the ultimate winery experience opt for the Bordeaux suite, a pied-a-terre, located several miles away from the inn at the winery proper. Guests also have the use of a pretty swimming pool tucked in the garden. Amazingly for such a small inn, there is a restaurant, Deborah's Room, which is open every night. In this cozy, elegantly decorated dining room a gourmet dinner is served nightly. *Directions:* From Hwy 101, at Paso Robles, exit at 24th Street. Go west (24th becomes Nacimiento Lake Road) for 8 miles and bear left onto Chimney Rock Road for another 8 miles.

❄ ☕ 🍽 ☕ 💳 ☎ @ W Ⓨ P 🍴 🚫 🌿 ≈ 🖼 ⚷ ⛵ 🎿 🏃 🚣 🍸

JUST INN
Owners: Deborah & Justin Baldwin
11680 Chimney Rock Road
Paso Robles, CA 93446, USA
Tel: (805) 238-6932 Ext. 300, Fax: (805) 237-4164
Toll Free: (800) 726-0049 Ext. 300
4 Rooms, Double: $375–$395
Open: all year, Credit cards: all major

Deborah and Douglas Thomsen welcome their guests with genuine hospitality. Rooms are found across the garden in the Carriage House with its graciously furnished living room. The Fireside room has a country-English motif, four-poster bed, fireplace and a deck overlooking the vineyards and countryside. The Countryside room has soft linen floral fabrics with silk drapes and a deck with wonderful countryside views. Each room enjoys its own sitting area in addition to sharing the central living room. A third room, the Garden View, is located in the main house and has its own entrance and deck. It has a King feather bed, seating area and fireplace. Deborah not only serves a full breakfast each morning in the main house, but also delights in assisting her guests plan their sightseeing—she helped us with our wine itinerary of the Paso Robles area and has lots of great information on the nearby coastal region. Deborah was an interior designer before she and Doug left southern California to live in the country and build their dream home. *Directions:* From Hwy 101, at Paso Robles take Hwy 46 west for 8 miles. Turn right on Vineyard Drive for 2½ miles. The entrance is on your left.

ORCHARD HILL FARM
Owners: Deborah & Douglas Thomsen
5415 Vineyard Drive
Paso Robles, CA 93446, USA
Tel: (805) 239-9680, Fax: (805) 239-9684
3 Rooms, Double: $230–$285
Open: all year, Credit cards: all major

The Summerwood Inn, with its nostalgic charm of a lovely country English-style home, makes an ideal choice if you want to stop en route between San Francisco and Southern California. Its setting is superb—nestled in a spectacularly beautiful area of gently rolling hills, either covered with vineyards or dotted with oak trees. You enter the long, low, white frame home with its old-fashioned wraparound porch and overhanging roof through large double doors into a spacious entry hall. To the left is a formal dining room, to the right is a sun-filled living room—bright and cheerful with sofas and chairs covered in colorful English-style fabrics. In the morning guests can choose from five items on the breakfast menu. Wine and cheese are served in the afternoon, coffee or tea and a dessert at night. The guestrooms, all large and individually decorated, have a mood of comfortable elegance. Each bedroom has either a private terrace or balcony that looks out over the Summerwood vineyards (my personal favorites are the rooms in the rear that have the most expansive views) and a beautifully appointed bathroom. All of the rooms have their own gas log fireplaces. The adjacent Summerwood Winery has a gift shop and offers wine tasting. The inn makes a good base for visiting Hearst Castle, which is just a short drive away by a scenic road. *Directions:* From Hwy 101, at Paso Robles take Hwy 46 west for 1¼ miles. Summerwood Inn is on your right.

SUMMERWOOD INN
Manager: Andrea Boatman
2130 Arbor Road
Paso Robles, CA 93446, USA
Tel: (805) 227-1111, Fax: (805) 227-1112
9 Rooms, Double: $239–$529
Open: all year, Credit cards: all major

People simply driving by the Inn at Playa del Rey would probably not be drawn inside by the inn's exterior and location on a busy road. However, this newly constructed Cape Cod-style inn, just three blocks from the beach, backs onto the Ballona Wetlands, a 350-acre bird sanctuary, and was beautifully designed to complement rather than compete with the setting and natural surroundings. Large picture windows frame a panorama of a grassy expanse of wetlands and distant marina. A narrow channel banded by an inviting bike path weaves through the wetlands, often navigated by tall-masted boats charting a course to the ocean. The decor is light and airy, with pine furnishings matched with lovely fabrics and attractive wallpapers. The spacious guestrooms are each individual in style and floor plan, and maximize any opportunity to incorporate views. The choice rooms are, of course, those at the back of the inn with unobstructed views of the wetlands. Rooms at the front are less expensive and enjoy the morning light while dual-glazed and shuttered windows minimize the noise of traffic. Public areas include an outdoor courtyard and a lovely breakfast room and living room running the length of the back of the building, banked by French doors. *Directions:* Exit the San Diego Freeway (405) onto the Marina Freeway (90) and travel west toward Marina del Rey. The freeway ends at a stoplight at Culver Blvd. Turn left and drive west for 2 miles to the inn.

INN AT PLAYA DEL REY
Owner: Susan Zolla
Manager: Liz Hall
435 Culver Boulevard
Playa del Rey, CA 90293, USA
Tel: (310) 574-1920, Fax: (310) 574-9920
21 Rooms, Double: $195–$450
Open: all year, Credit cards: all major

The known history of the Rancho Santa Fe property dates back to 1845 when an 8,842-acre land grant was given to Juan Maria Osuna. In 1906 the Santa Fe Railroad purchased the land grant, changed the name to Rancho Santa Fe, and planted millions of eucalyptus seedlings with the idea of growing wood for railroad ties. The project failed, so the railroad decided instead to develop a planned community and built a lovely Spanish-style guesthouse for prospective homebuyers. This became the nucleus for what is now the Inn at Rancho Santa Fe and houses the lounge, dining rooms, offices, and a few guestrooms. The lounge is extremely appealing, like a beautiful living room in a private home, with a large fireplace, comfortable seating, impressive floral arrangements, and a roaring fire. The dining rooms have a cozy atmosphere. The grounds are lovely, filled with flowers and shaded by fragrant eucalyptus trees. Here you find our favorite rooms tucked away in cottages, ranging in size from a snug queen-bedded room with private patio (a standard room) to a luxurious three-bedroom house. We especially loved the rooms with a private patio and fireplace, though have to admit we were smitten by room 133, a tiny little cottage. Slip away to the inn's beach house in nearby Del Mar or enjoy the pool and tennis courts on the property. *Directions:* From San Diego go north for 25 miles on I-5, take the Lomas Santa Fe Drive turnoff east, and travel 4 miles to the inn.

INN AT RANCHO SANTA FE
Manager: Kerman Beriker
5951 Linea del Cielo at Paseo Delicia
P.O. Box 869
Rancho Santa Fe, CA 92067, USA
Tel: (858) 756-1131, Fax: (858) 759-1604
Toll Free: (800) 843-4661
87 Rooms, Double: $249–$1500*
*Breakfast not included: $12–$20
Open: all year, Credit cards: all major

Rancho Valencia is a luxurious Relais & Châteaux hotel tucked away in the hills above Rancho Santa Fe minutes from the picturesque seaside town of Del Mar. This secluded hideaway offers privacy, relaxation, and recreation on a very intimate scale. Sports enthusiasts love it here, for the resort has 18 tennis courts and privileges at exclusive private golf clubs. Spa enthusiasts adore the new spa which offers an expansive choice of skin care, facials and sensual couples treatments. Garden paths bordered by an abundance of flowers wind through the grounds to the 26 casitas scattered throughout the property. One is a luxurious three-bedroom home while the rest are either spacious studios or suites. All have cathedral ceilings with exposed beams, lovely fireplaces, plantation-shuttered windows, and French doors leading to private garden patios. The heart of the property is the clubhouse with its central courtyard patios overflowing with flowering plants. Rancho Valencia's signature restaurant offers casual, elegant dining inside and alfresco dining on the tiered terrace overlooking the tennis courts and the valley. *Directions:* From I-5 in Del Mar, take the Via de la Valle Road east to El Camino Real to San Dieguito Road east and follow signs to Rancho Valencia.

RANCHO VALENCIA
General Manager: David Friederich
5921 Valencia Circle
P.O. Box 9126
Rancho Santa Fe, CA 92067, USA
Tel: (858) 756-1123, Fax: (858) 756-0165
Toll Free: (800) 548-3664
49 Rooms, Double: $495–$1800*
*Breakfast not included: $15–$30
Open: all year, Credit cards: all major
Relais & Châteaux

High on a hillside above the Silverado Trail, with magnificent views south along the Napa Valley, Auberge du Soleil sets the standard for luxurious self-indulgence. The bedrooms are housed in cottages nestled amidst manicured slopes of olive trees and are decorated in Mediterranean style—cool earth tones are the backdrop for splashes of color from large modern artwork to brilliant persimmon and vermilion soft furnishings. Beautifully appointed, oversized bathrooms are equipped with large tubs, walk-in showers, and an abundant supply of fluffy white towels and luxurious robes. After a hard day of shopping, lunching, or touring the nearby vineyards, settle down to savor the sunset on your private trellis-covered patio. Stroll the trail of modern sculptures, swim in the beautiful pool, or let the specialists at the spa soothe and pamper you. Sample the gastronomic delights of the restaurant with its sensational view matched only by the cuisine. Featuring a full range of regional delicacies, a most impressive wine list, and attentive staff, dinner is an integral part of the Auberge du Soleil experience. For those with smaller appetites the bar offers lighter fare in a cozy atmosphere or outside on the wraparound deck. *Directions:* From Napa go north on Hwy 29 towards Calistoga. At Rutherford turn right on Rutherford Crossroad, cross the Silverado Trail on a left-right jog, and take Rutherford Hill Road up the hill to the hotel.

AUBERGE DU SOLEIL
Manager: Bradley Reynolds
180 Rutherford Hill Road
Rutherford, CA 94573, USA
Tel: (707) 963-1211, Fax: (707) 963-8764
Toll Free: (800) 348-5406
52 Rooms, Double: $550–$4500*
*Breakfast not included: $18–$28
Open: all year, Credit cards: all major
Relais & Châteaux

Situated in a private 250-acre valley, Meadowood, an appealing complex of sand-gray gabled wooden buildings with crisp white trim, is a resort community in a secluded setting sheltered by towering Ponderosa pines and Douglas firs. Wooded areas open up to a nine-hole golf course, croquet lawns, tennis courts, and swimming pools. With accommodation spread out across the property (lots of privacy here), guests are often driven in golf carts to the centrally located clubhouse, a three-story structure overlooking the golf course. Here you find The Restaurant, featuring Napa Valley inspired cuisine in an elegant setting, The Grill, offering meals in a less formal setting, a golf shop, and conference facilities. There are 13 guestrooms in the Croquet Lodge, which overlooks the perfectly manicured croquet lawn. Other bedrooms are found in clusters of lodges scattered about the property. The atmosphere, relaxed, informal, and unpretentious, is accurately described as "California casual." The accommodations are expensive but lavishly appointed and attractively furnished, reflecting an incredible attention to every luxurious detail. Guests keep busy with a state-of-the-art health spa, hiking trails and bicycles. *Directions:* From Napa go north on Hwy 29 towards Calistoga. At Saint Helena turn right on Pope Street. Go left on the Silverado Trail, right on Meadowood Rd, which will merge onto Meadowood Lane.

※ ✕ ♨ ▭ ☎ 👤 @ W ⏶ P ⑪ 🚭 ♣ ≈ 🏃 ⚘ ⚕ 👤 🏃 🏇 🚣 🎿

MEADOWOOD NAPA VALLEY
Manager: Alain Nequeloua
900 Meadowood Lane
Saint Helena, CA 94574, USA
Tel: (707) 963-3646, Fax: (707) 963-3532
Toll Free: (800) 458-8080
120 Rooms, Double: $475–$8750*
*Breakfast not included: $20–$30
Open: all year, Credit cards: all major
Relais & Châteaux

Just off Hwy 29 at the corner of El Bonita, on the outskirts of Saint Helena, the Vineyard Country Inn backs onto an expanse of vineyards. Constructed to resemble a French country manor, the inn's attention to detail and the quality of appointments are impressive. Handsome slate roofs dotted by whimsical brick chimneys top the complex of buildings. A path winds from the main building, which houses the lobby and attractive breakfast room, past the enclosed pool and Jacuzzi, through patches of flowering garden to the guestrooms. Accommodations are all suites enjoying a sitting area in front of a wood-burning fireplace, and a bedroom furnished with either a king bed or two queen sleigh beds. The decor is clean and elegant in its simplicity. Bathrooms have lovely tile and wallpaper and are beautifully fresh and modern. Under beamed ceilings, the downstairs bedrooms (except for two) open onto patios; all the upstairs rooms open onto private decks. The Vineyard Country Inn's guestrooms are spacious and offer excellent value for money in comparison to other luxury accommodation in the valley. A bountiful breakfast buffet is served and trays are available so that you can take your repast back to the privacy of your room. *Directions:* From San Francisco take Hwy 101 north to Hwy 37 east, then Hwy 37 to Hwy 121/129. Located on Hwy 29 at El Bonita.

VINEYARD COUNTRY INN
Owners: Mary Ann & Michael Pietro
Managers: Patricia & Ortwin Krueger
201 Main Street
Saint Helena, CA 94574, USA
Tel: (707) 963-1000, Fax: (707) 963-1794
20 Rooms, Double: $185–$325
Open: all year, Credit cards: all major

The Wine Country Inn is one of those delightful places that thumbs its nose at being minimalist, chic, and cozy—it delights in being spacious, comfortable, and courteous. Occupying a collection of wood and stone buildings set on a low hillside, surrounded by expansive vineyards, 3 acres of ground give a spacious feel to this quiet spot, which is central to everything in the Napa Valley. The spaciousness is echoed in the room sizes— there's not a snug room in the place. Relax, spread out, and enjoy the tranquil setting. Fourteen rooms are housed in the main building, six in the Brandy Barn, and four in the Hastings House. Many of the rooms have private outdoor hot tubs, patios, balconies, and fireplaces. The latest additions are five individual cottages set on the hillside and down overlooking the vineyards. Decor ranges from rustic barnwood to contemporary. Do not be concerned about staying in one of the older rooms for everything is pleasingly maintained. Relax by the lovely pool and take your wine and hors d'oeuvres (delicious homemade appetizers) onto the deck to soak up the view across the vineyards to distant hills. An excellent breakfast is served. *Directions:* Two miles north of Saint Helena on Hwy 29 turn right onto Lodi Lane. The Wine Country Inn is a quarter of a mile down on the left.

WINE COUNTRY INN
Owner: Jim Smith
Manager: Deniese Steelman
1152 Lodi Lane
Saint Helena, CA 94574, USA
Tel: (707) 963-7077, Fax: (707) 963-9018
Toll Free: (888) 465-4608
24 Rooms, Double: $220–$660
Open: all year, Credit cards: MC, VS
Select Registry

The Petite Auberge is a little bit of France in the heart of San Francisco. Its location on Bush Street, just steps from the theater district, shopping and restaurants, makes it ideal for exploring the city on foot—hop aboard a cable car two blocks away. The façade is most appealing—a slim, four-story building with a column of bay windows bordered by narrow windows decorated with flowerboxes. A collection of French dinner plates, a large art poster and teddy bears give a warm welcome to the lobby. The attractive bedrooms come in three sizes: cozy queen, very snug queen-bedded room; queen with fireplace, a larger queen-bedded room with a fireplace that face towards a central courtyard; deluxe queen, the largest queen-bedded rooms with fireplace, sofabed and a windowseat overlooking Bush Street. Downstairs is a most inviting king-bedded "honeymoon" suite with a fireplace, spa tub, and private outside entrance and deck. Wine, sherry, and hors d'oeuvres are available each evening for those guests who want a quiet moment after a busy day. A delicious breakfast is served buffet style in the delightful breakfast room with its French marketplace mural and French doors giving onto a pretty patio which is a most inviting place to enjoy breakfast on warm mornings. *Directions:* Take Van Ness Avenue north to Bush Street. Turn right on Bush and go about 1 mile. The inn is between Taylor and Mason Streets. Valet parking is available.

PETITE AUBERGE
General Manager: Eric Norman
863 Bush Street
San Francisco, CA 94108, USA
Tel: (415) 928-6000, Fax: (415) 673-7214
Toll Free: (800) 365-3004
26 Rooms, Double: $119–$309
Open: all year, Credit cards: all major

Union Street is always a favorite place to dine, shop, and play; and the several blocks stretching out at the foot of exclusive Pacific Heights offer charming restaurants and pretty boutiques in quaint Victorian houses. Right in the heart of this attractive area, in a pretty, light-yellow Victorian house with green trim, is the Union Street Inn. Steps on the left side of the building lead up to the front door, which opens into a small reception foyer. To the left is an old-fashioned sitting room all kitted out in period furniture. Doors from the parlor lead out to the most special feature of the inn—an exceptionally attractive, English-style garden where a brick path meanders through a medley of shrubs, flowers, and shade trees. At the end of the garden, behind a white picket fence, is an adorable cottage converted into a guest suite (The Carriage House). In the house itself are five more guestrooms, each individually decorated in a traditional style. We liked the quiet location of the English Garden Room, with its little deck overlooking the garden and enjoyed the spaciousness of the New Yorker which is large enough to accommodate both a queen and sofa bed and has a large bay window overlooking the activity of Union Street. Wine and hors d'oevres are set out for guests each afternoon, and in the morning a full breakfast is served either on the deck, in the parlor or in your room. *Directions:* The inn is between Fillmore and Steiner Streets. There is parking nearby.

UNION STREET INN
Owners: Jane Bertorelli & David Coyle
2229 Union Street
San Francisco, CA 94123, USA
Tel: (415) 346-0424, Fax: (415) 922-8046
6 Rooms, Double: $195–$335
Open: all year, Credit cards: all major

Facing historic Washington Square, The Washington Square Inn has a great location in North Beach with its wealth of wonderful little places to eat. Turn right out the door and walk up to admire the city and bay views from Coit Tower or turn left and stroll the few blocks to Chinatown. A two-minute walk finds you at the Mason cable car line which takes you to Pier 39 or Union Square. The inn is the quintessential "Karen Brown" property with a parade of delightful bedrooms decorated with predominantly French antiques and a welcoming staff that go the extra mile for guests. Because of its city location do not expect the majority of the rooms to be large in size. However room 8 with its window seat overlooking the park and cathedral and room 7 with its corner window looking towards Coit tower and the park are very spacious king-bedded rooms. Two very small rooms and two rooms with their dedicated bathroom across the hall are especially good value for money. A hearty breakfast is set out in the morning (breakfast can also be brought to your room), in the afternoon enjoy tea or wine and hors d'oeuvres in front of the fire, coffee and tea are always available. *Directions:* In North Beach, on Washington Square, between Union and Filbert Streets. Valet parking is available.

WASHINGTON SQUARE INN
Owners: Maria & Daniel Levin
1660 Stockton Street
San Francisco, CA 94133, USA
Tel: (415) 981-4220, Fax: (415) 397-7242
Toll Free: (800) 388-0220
15 Rooms, Double: $179–$329
Minimum Stay Required: 2 nights on weekends
Open: all year, Credit cards: all major
Select Registry

The White Swan Inn, a delightful boutique hotel with a British theme, has a splendid location just steps from a wide selection of excellent restaurants and a five-minute walk from San Francisco's Union Square shopping and theater district. You enter off the street to a reception area, but the heart of the inn is down a flight of stairs where a spacious lounge awaits, with one section set up with tables and chairs for a full buffet breakfast —coffee and tea are always available. Beyond the eating area is a delightful sitting room with a fireplace and comfortable chairs where wine, sherry and hors d'oeuvres are set out each evening. Next door is the library where rather than books on the shelves there are detailed models of British cathedrals made from wooden matches. French doors into a small conference room (seats 14) which leads to a broad expanse of deck. However, what impresses us most about this hotel are the spaciousness of its bedrooms—considering its central city location. Even the smallest room has ample space for two small armchairs by the fireplace. Rooms at the back of the hotel are especially quiet and overlook a large tree. All the rooms have fireplace, small refrigerator stocked with complimentary drinks, coffee makers, direct-dial phone and TV. The Ashleigh Suite is ideal for families as the sitting room has a sofa bed, can accommodate a rollaway and has an additional bathroom. *Directions:* The inn is between Taylor and Mason.

WHITE SWAN INN
General Manager: Eric Norman
845 Bush Street
San Francisco, CA 94108, USA
Tel: (415) 775-1755, Fax: (415) 775-5717
Toll Free: (800) 999-9570
26 Rooms, Double: $159–$349
Open: all year, Credit cards: all major

The Gerstle Park Inn, a large, wood-shingled home on 2½ lovely acres that back onto a preserved woodland in a residential neighborhood of San Rafael. The inn carries an air of European sophistication complemented by a homey and welcoming ambiance. Just off the entry are the formal living room with its Asian-inspired decor and the enclosed wraparound porch, which serves as an intimate and elegant breakfast room where a full, cooked-to-order breakfast is served each morning. Upstairs, rooms range from the Redwood Suite, cozy and romantic with a pine-planked, low-angled ceiling and wooded views afforded by a row of windows at ceiling height; to the San Rafael Suite, spanning the length of one end of the building, with king bed and large deck facing the surrounding hills. The separate carriage house has two suites complete with well-stocked kitchens, breakfast nooks, living rooms, and private patios. Two stand-alone cottages have kitchens and provide complete privacy. All the rooms enjoy amenities and conveniences such as two-line telephones with voice mail, WiFi, televisions, VCR/DVDs, CD players, hairdryers, and robes. Owners Judy and Jim Dowling outline several daytrips from the inn to San Francisco, the Marin coast and the Napa and Sonoma wine valleys. *Directions:* Exit Hwy 101 at San Rafael Central exit. Go west on 3rd Street, then left on D Street, right on San Rafael Ave, and left on Grove Street.

GERSTLE PARK INN
Owners: Judy & Jim Dowling
Manager: Barbara Searles
34 Grove Street
San Rafael, CA 94901, USA
Tel: (415) 721-7611, Fax: (415) 721-7600
Toll Free: (800) 726-7611
12 Rooms, Double: $189–$265
Open: all year, Credit cards: all major
Select Registry

The Cheshire Cat is comprised of two lovely beige and white Victorians sitting side by side and connected by a tranquil flower-filled bricked patio (where breakfast is served), three private cottages, and a coach house. In the foyer of the main house a grouping of Alice in Wonderland figurines sets the whimsical theme of the inn. Each guestroom is unique in appeal although consistent in the Laura Ashley coordinated prints and wallpapers used in the decor; from sapphire blue in the Mock Turtle room to Burgundy, sage, and gold in the Cheshire Cat suite. Two spacious suites in the Coach House, Tweedledum and Tweedledee, enjoy their own entrance off the back of the garden. Tweedledum is especially appealing. In the bedroom along with its king-sized bed there is a Jacuzzi tub for two. It also has a cozy sitting room with fireplace, pine floor, wood beams, and oriental rugs. Three two-bedroom cottages, Woodford, Prestbury, and Mobberly, have a fully stocked kitchen, living room, fireplace, and a private redwood deck with a hot tub. *Directions:* Exit from Hwy 101 at Mission Street, go east on Mission for five blocks, go right on State Street for three blocks, and then turn right on Valerio.

CHESHIRE CAT
Owner: Christine Dunstan
Innkeeper: Jack Greenwald
36 West Valerio Street
Santa Barbara, CA 93101, USA
Tel: (805) 569-1610, Fax: (805) 682-1876
17 Rooms, Double: $159–$425
Minimum Stay Required: 2 nights on weekends
Open: all year, Credit cards: all major

Having always admired State Street for its whitewashed Spanish-style buildings, we were delighted to discover the Hotel Santa Barbara, situated in the heart of the plaza just one block from the town's open-air malls and quaint boutiques. There has been a hotel on this site since 1876, with the present structure being built in 1925 and recently restored and updated at a cost of $4 million. This family-managed hotel reminds you of the 1920s Hollywood movie era—in fact, it used to be a getaway for stars such as Clark Gable and Carole Lombard. With cool, tiled floors in the foyer and colors of sand and rust, the atmosphere is that of a Moroccan arched marketplace. There are comfy pillow-filled sofas and café-style seating in the area where your continental breakfast is served. This is a four-storied, mission-style building with the guestrooms, some with Juliet balconies, facing onto a U-shaped courtyard. Rooms, all air-conditioned, are furnished in bold colors of blues and yellows and have elegant, stark-white bathrooms. The large, well-appointed suites are extremely comfortable. There is some street noise, so request a room away from the activity. Valet parking is available. Children under 16 stay free with a parent. *Directions:* From Hwy 101 exit at Carrillo, drive for several blocks, then turn right on Chapala. Turn left on Cota—the hotel is on the right, half a block down at the corner of Cota and State Streets.

HOTEL SANTA BARBARA
Manager: Tamara Erickson
533 State Street
Santa Barbara, CA 93101, USA
Tel: (805) 957-9300, Fax: (805) 962-2412
Toll Free: (888) 259-7700
75 Rooms, Double: $169–$289
Minimum Stay Required: 2 nights on weekends
Open: all year, Credit cards: all major

The Simpson House Inn, a handsome, rosy-beige Victorian landmark with white and smoke-blue trim, is located on a quiet residential street only a five-minute walk from the historic downtown shopping and attractions of State Street. The lush surrounding gardens of the inn include an acre of lawn banded by beautiful flowerbeds and mature shade trees. An irresistible feature of the inn is a cheerful back porch under an arbor of draping wisteria with white wicker chairs and comfy pillows: a perfect niche to enjoy the garden. In the main house the sitting room and dining room are quite formal. However, the formality disappears upstairs in the charming guest chambers, each individually decorated with hand-printed Victorian wallpapers to suit different tastes—from feminine to a more tailored look. Four cottages in the back garden are beautifully decorated in rich fabrics and intimate with a Jacuzzi tub nestled right into a bay window. The barn also offers spacious accommodations, light and airy, with pine furnishings perfect against the exposed beams of the original barn. Each room enjoys niceties such as robes, fresh flowers, and bottled water. In the evenings sherry and local wine are offered with an extensive Mediterranean hors d'oeuvres buffet. Enjoy breakfast delivered to your room or on the verandah. *Directions:* From downtown take Santa Barbara Street northeast toward Mission, then turn left onto Arrellaga.

SIMPSON HOUSE INN
Manager: Nick Davaz
121 East Arrellaga Street
Santa Barbara, CA 93101, USA
Tel: (805) 963-7067, Fax: (805) 564-4811
Toll Free: (800) 676-1280
11 Rooms, Double: $255–$610
Open: all year, Credit cards: all major
Select Registry

The foundations of The Babbling Brook Inn date back to the 1790s when padres from the Santa Cruz Mission built a grist mill on the property, taking advantage of the small stream to grind corn. In the late 19th century a tannery powered by a huge water wheel was constructed. Beside the historic wheel a rustic log cabin stands as the "heart" of the inn with a homey living room where guests congregate around a roaring fire with tea, coffee and homemade cookies and enjoy a tempting breakfast buffet (trays are provided so that you can take your morning repast back to your room). Here you find my favorite room, Artists, with its outdoor tub recessed into its private deck, which looks out over the entire property. Most of the other bedrooms are found in shingled houses nestled in the garden surrounded by pines and redwoods and overlooking the idyllic little meandering brook. Each house has one room on the ground floor and one above and is decorated in French-country style with pretty fabrics and colors, and enjoys lots of amenities including a fireplace. Most rooms have a private deck and some even have soaking jet bathtubs for two. *Directions:* From San Jose or San Francisco take Hwy 17 to Santa Cruz. Turn north on Hwy 1, which becomes Mission Street, then left on Laurel for one and a half blocks to the inn, which is on the right-hand side.

BABBLING BROOK INN
Manager: Tom Col
1025 Laurel Street
Santa Cruz, CA 95060, USA
Tel: (831) 427-2437, Fax: (831) 427-2457
Toll Free: (800) 433-4732
13 Rooms, Double: $179–$289
Open: all year, Credit cards: all major

Frederick Sedgewick Lynch spent money he made during the California gold rush building this Grand Italianate home, the Santa Cruz Beach Boardwalk and the pier beside the broad sweep of white sand that fronts the bay. Meticulously renovated to highlight the home's architectural features, the inn is decorated with in a crisp, contemporary blue and white palette. King-sized beds with pillow-top mattresses, marble tile bathrooms (some with jetted spa tubs), fireplaces, artwork by local artists, furniture designed in Santa Cruz, and ocean views are the order of the day. For those who need to remain connected to the everyday world, WiFi, iPod player, DVD and TV are available. A second-floor room (without an ocean view) has a private, outdoor jetted hot tub. Under the eaves, two spacious suites (perfect for families) have separate sitting areas and oversized bathrooms. Room 3 with its large bay window overlooking the beach is a special favorite. In early evening, enjoy wine and hors d'oeuvres on the porch or in the sitting room. The beach is one block away; downtown Santa Cruz is a short drive. It's a perfect location for exploring this lovely section of the Pacific coast. A Four Sisters Inn. *Directions:* Arriving in Santa Cruz follow signs for The Boardwalk. When you reach the ocean (the pier is in front of you) turn right up the hill, for one block, and continue straight into the West Cliffs driveway (do not turn left on West Cliff Drive).

WEST CLIFF INN
Manager: Michael Hoppe
174 West Cliff Drive
Santa Cruz, CA 95060, USA
Tel: (831) 457-2200, Fax: (831) 457-2221
Toll Free: (800) 979-0910
9 Rooms, Double: $195–$400
Open: all year, Credit cards: MC, VS

The Channel Road Inn dates back to 1910 when Thomas McCall built an elaborate wood-shingled home for his large family. A third story was later added, giving plenty of space for the 15 guestrooms it now offers. The house has an interesting location: just on the fringe of Pacific Palisades yet on a busy street that leads through a somewhat eclectic neighborhood to the wonderful playground of a beach. The downstairs living room, library and dining areas of the inn are sedately decorated, beautifully in keeping with the style of the home. The guestrooms, tucked throughout the house, are all individually decorated and each has its own delightful personality. My favorite room was number 1, one of the less expensive rooms but delightful with a fresh white-and-blue color scheme and sharing a large, quiet rooftop terrace with the adjacent room 5. When making reservations, keep in mind that the rooms vary in size and decide whether you want a patio, soaking tub, or the relative quiet of an inside-facing room. A ground-floor handicap room has a children's sleeping alcove. Bikes are available for excursions along the strand. Recover from your exertions with a soak in the hot tub. A Four Sister's Inn. *Directions:* From Hwy 405 take 10 west, then Pacific Coast Hwy (Route 1) north for 2 miles. Make a hard right on West Channel Road, continue one block, and the inn is on the left.

CHANNEL ROAD INN
Manager: Heather Suskin
219 West Channel Road
Santa Monica, CA 90402, USA
Tel: (310) 459-1920, Fax: (310) 454-9920
17 Rooms, Double: $195–$500
Open: all year, Credit cards: all major

Shutters on the Beach is a stunning, deluxe, hotel fronting directly onto the superb Santa Monica beach and, although it is of new construction, the hotel has a delightfully nostalgic mood. The elegant, Cape Cod-like, whisper-gray, wood-shingled building is enhanced by white gingerbread trim. I am not sure how it is accomplished, but there is an engaging, homelike ambiance throughout—perhaps it is the wood-beam ceiling or the cozy groupings of plump, comfy sofas, or the fireplaces. The designer's goal was to create a hotel where guests would feel that they were staying at a friend's beach house rather than a commercial hotel: that goal has certainly been achieved. A garden terrace (where white lounge chairs are grouped around an attractive swimming pool) spans a small street to connect the beach house with a more traditional-looking hotel section. All of the guestrooms are attractive: nautical blues and aquas accent a predominantly white color scheme. An uncluttered, simple, yet elegant mood prevails, enhanced by Italian linens and furniture of excellent quality. Every room has heavy, wooden, white louvered shutters, which give the hotel its name. *Directions:* Go west on Hwy 10 (Santa Monica Expressway) to Santa Monica. Take the 4th Street exit south (right) onto Pico Boulevard. Shutters on the Beach sits where Pico Boulevard meets the beach.

SHUTTERS ON THE BEACH
Manager: Gregory Day
One Pico Boulevard
Santa Monica, CA 90405, USA
Tel: (310) 458-0030, Fax: (310) 458-4589
Toll Free: (800) 334-9000
198 Rooms, Double: $545–$5000*
*Breakfast not included: $20–$30
Open: all year, Credit cards: all major

The Vintners Inn is a natural choice for those who want to stay in a secluded hotel that has a close-to-everything location, perfect for visiting the Napa, Sonoma, or Russian River areas. Just off the 101 highway, the Mediterranean-style buildings are set amid 90 acres of vineyards (be sure to request a room that faces these) and I was astonished to find that I could not hear any freeway noise. The spacious guestrooms are housed in three buildings that encircle a fountain in the bricked courtyard. The rooms are decked out in restful tones of beige in a French-country decor, and all offer oversized tubs, small refrigerators, robes, televisions, data ports, and patios or balconies. Rooms are priced according to size, with spacious patio and balcony rooms being the least expensive and extra-large junior suites with sitting areas, fireplaces, and luxurious bathrooms (Jacuzzi tub and shower) being the most expensive. In the morning a complimentary continental breakfast buffet is set in the Provence Room: you can enjoy it here or on the patio, or take a tray to your room. On the edge of the vineyards is a Jacuzzi tub and those who must can work out in the gym. For dinner walk the few yards to the restaurant John Ash & Co. *Directions:* From San Francisco travel Hwy 101 north to Santa Rosa. Exit at River Road, turn left over the freeway, and take the first left onto Barnes Road. Turn left into the first driveway.

VINTNERS INN
Owners: Rhonda & Don Carano
Manager: Percy Brandon
4350 Barnes Road
Santa Rosa, CA 95403, USA
Tel: (707) 575-7350, Fax: (707) 575-1426
Toll Free: (800) 421-2584
44 Rooms, Double: $250–$505
Open: all year, Credit cards: all major

The Inn Above Tide is tucked away in bayfront oasis a few steps Sausalito's shopping and restaurants, just thirty minutes by ferry from San Francisco. The twenty nine rooms have expansive, unimpeded, views across the Bay to Angel Island, Alcatraz and the City's famous skyline. All except five have their own secluded waterfront terraces with floor to ceiling glass doors and windows which enhance the sensation of being right on the water. Binoculars are provided to bring you even closer to the ever changing array of waterbirds, boaters and marine activity dotting the bay. The two suites are both spectacular. Our favorite is the Penthouse Suite with its glass enclosed whirlpool tub and magnificent views of the city, pure decadence. Most of the rooms have gas or wood burning fireplaces, all are furnished in a comfortable contemporary style, decorated in beiges and earth tones, accentuated with vivid touches of burnt orange. Model yachts and porthole windows in the large, nicely appointed tile, marble and chrome bathrooms provide a nautical undertone. Soft robes, fine linens and fluffy towels abound. The buffet in the drawing room is set in the evenings with a selection of wine and cheese, in the mornings with a continental breakfast (trays or room service are available). *Directions:* From San Francisco cross the Golden Gate Bridge and take the Sausalito exit, follow your nose downtown and turn left off Bridgeway towards the water on El Portal.

THE INN ABOVE TIDE
Manager: Mark Flaherty
30 El Portal
Sausalito, CA 94965, USA
Tel: (415) 332-9535, Fax: (415) 332-6714
Toll Free: (800) 893-8433
29 Rooms, Double: $305–$1100
Open: all year, Credit cards: all major

The Hotel Sausalito boasts a colorful past. Its early days saw activity as a bordello and as a speakeasy during Prohibition—with its location next to the docks, liquor from the trucks that rumbled past its doors conveniently ended up in its parlor. It is now home to the Purdies, a delightful Scottish family whose brogue will charm you, but who will impress you most with their warm, professional approach to innkeeping. A steep flight of stairs (there is an elevator) leads up to guestrooms from the small street-side entry. With a backdrop of walls washed in warm pastel tones, the furnishings are custom-designed and handcrafted by local artisans and have been selected to enhance the individuality of each guestroom. The size, outlook, and bathroom appointments determine the room tariff. We enjoyed one of the larger rooms overlooking Sausalito's main street, buffered from the noise by well-insulated windows. Regardless of the guestroom's location or size all have most attractive furnishings, art, and linens as well as the convenience of internet access and cable television. A little rooftop patio is a tranquil place to relax. For breakfast you are given coffee and pastry coupons for the adjacent Café Tutti. *Directions:* Refer to directions for the Inn Above Tide—they are neighboring hotels. Parking is in the city lot across the square.

HOTEL SAUSALITO
Owners: Josephine & Billy Purdie
16 El Portal (at Bridgeway)
Sausalito, CA 94965, USA
Tel: (415) 332-0700, Fax: (415) 332-8788
Toll Free: (888) 442-0700
16 Rooms, Double: $155–$285
Minimum Stay Required: 2 nights on weekends
Open: all year, Credit cards: all major

We have quickly fallen in love with the quiet pace, beautiful vistas, and fabulous food and wine of the Sonoma Valley. Conveniently located just two blocks from the historic Sonoma Plaza, The Inn at Sonoma's casual décor extends to 19 well-appointed rooms, connected to the underground parking by elevator. Common features include fireplaces, 10-foot-high ceilings, private (albeit small) patios or balconies (for all but three rooms), and nicely appointed bathrooms. Our favorite rooms are those facing Broadway. We especially liked rooms 11 and 10 with their larger decks. An ample outdoor sundeck complete with huge hot tub and limited views of the surrounding hills completes the picture. Before you step out for dinner, enjoy hors d'oeuvres and wine before the fireplace in the living room or outside on the deck. After breakfast borrow one of the inn's bicycles to tour the town or walk to the shops and restaurants. The more adventurous can try a hot-air balloon or glider ride. A year-round temperate climate makes this a wonderful destination. A Four Sisters Inn. *Directions:* Hwy 12 becomes Broadway as it heads north into Sonoma. The Inn at Sonoma is on your right two blocks before you arrive at the square.

INN AT SONOMA
Manager: Rachel Retterer
630 Broadway
Sonoma, CA 95476, USA
Tel: (707) 939-1340, Fax: (707) 939-8834
Toll Free: (888) 568-9818
19 Rooms, Double: $165–$350
Open: all year, Credit cards: all major

Situated on Sonoma's historic Plaza the Ledson Hotel, with its impressive wrought ironwork and stone facade is at first sight a wonderful restoration of its former self. Not so. The building, designed from scratch and completed in 2003 occupies what was until then a disused downtown lot. Exacting attention to detail has produced six luxurious rooms replete with spectacular architectural highlights balancing antique grandeur with every amenity expected by the sophisticated traveler. Hand tooled hardwood flooring, intricately carved moldings, king sized beds, marble and glass bathrooms, in-room whirlpool tubs, fireplaces and balconies, all rooms are similar but every one is unique. Surround sound television and broadband internet access have been provided for those who simply must remain attached to the work-a-day world. Three rooms overlook the Plaza with its fountain and rose garden. Downstairs, the stylish Harmony restaurant is the private reserve of hotel guests for breakfast but opens to the public for lunch and dinner. Enjoy the chef's international cuisine, try his tasting menu complete with wine pairings or simply indulge in a little people watching from the marble sidewalk tables. *Directions:* Hotel Ledson is on the east side of Sonoma's town square adjacent to the Sebastiani Theater. Overnight parking available to the rear.

HOTEL LEDSON
Owner: Michelle Ledson
480 First Street
Sonoma, CA 95476, USA
Tel & Fax: (707) 996-9779
6 Rooms, Double: $350–$395
Minimum Stay Required: 2 nights on weekends
Closed: Christmas, Credit cards: all major

Just a four-block walk from Sonoma's historic plaza, MacArthur Place offers luxurious accommodation in a complex of Victorian buildings in 7 acres of manicured grounds with lawns trimmed by box hedges, flourishing rose gardens, majestic trees, ponds, fountains, and gardens decorated with modern sculpture. The original manor house has lots of appeal but our favorite rooms are in the cottages. The Caretaker's Cottage, a spacious suite, enjoys a Jacuzzi tub and a lovely private porch. Two new garden spa suites feature a wood-burning fireplace, jet hydrotherapy tub and private garden with outdoor shower and teak soaking tub for two, housed in a Japanese teahouse. All rooms have splendid garden views, modern bathrooms with oversized showers, walk-in closets, down comforters, monogrammed robes, DVD and CD players, and dual-line telephones with data port and voice mail. The Garden Spa at MacArthur Place offers body treatments, massages, and facials. An outdoor swimming pool and whirlpool are located next to the spa. Continental breakfast is served on the verandah in the gardens. Guests often dine at Saddles Restaurant, a delightfully casual steakhouse in the restored barn. *Directions:* Hwy 12 becomes Broadway as it heads north into Sonoma. MacArthur Place is on your right four blocks before you arrive at the square, on the corner of Broadway and MacArthur.

MACARTHUR PLACE
Owner: Suzanne Brangham
Manager: Bill Blum
29 E. MacArthur Street
Sonoma, CA 95476, USA
Tel: (707) 938-2929, Fax: (707) 933-9833
Toll Free: (800) 722-1866
64 Rooms, Double: $349–$699
Open: all year, Credit cards: all major

Barretta Gardens Inn is an elegantly restored 1904 Victorian farmhouse, fully air conditioned and well know for its warm atmosphere and Gold Country views. It's a 10 minute walk to downtown restaurants and antique shops. A splendid mansion from days gone by. Barretta Gardens benefits from the enthusiasm of its owners, Astrid Wasserman and Daniel Stone. On one side of the first parlor is the dining room whose chandelier is original to the home. During the summer months breakfast is served on the porch overlooking the gardens. Guestrooms are named after locally grown grape varietals. The Cabernet Sauvignon room enjoys 10-foot-high ceilings, Italian antique furniture and a living room (or second bedroom) with a fire stove and private entrance. The attached bathroom with whirlpool spa for two has lace-covered windows overlooking the rose garden and foothills. Decked out with lace curtains and dark red carpeting the Tempranillo's wall of windows look out to the Sonora hills. Downstairs, San Giovese, a two bedroom suite, has a fireplace in its living room, a walk in shower and soaking tub for two. Upstairs, the Zinfandel room is pretty in a wash of rose, while the Barbara room has a brass king-size bed. A parlor sits between the Barbara and Syrah, which together can be rented as a two-room suite or as a one-room suite with just the Syrah. *Directions:* Take Hwy 108 to Washington. Make a right on Restano Way, a right at Mono Way, and a left on Barretta.

BARRETTA GARDENS INN
Owners: Astrid Wasserman & Daniel Stone
700 South Barretta Street
Sonora, CA 95370, USA
Tel: (209) 532-6039, Fax: (209) 532-8257
Toll Free: (800) 206-3333
10 Rooms, Double: $140–$250
Minimum Stay Required
Open: all year, Credit cards: all major

Sutter Creek is a charming Gold Country town whose main street is bordered at either end by New England-style residences with their green lawns and neatly clipped hedges. One of these attractive homes is the Foxes, an idyllic hideaway where every spacious guestroom is decorated with great flair and offers the maximum amount of privacy for guests. The symbol of the inn is a fox and the perky fellow appealingly pops up in several places. We especially love the Victorian and Anniversary rooms, found upstairs in the main house, with their luxurious tiled bathrooms, walk-in showers, and antique claw-foot tubs. Another especially attractive room is the spacious Honeymoon Suite, a most elegant bedchamber where a large brick fireplace overlooks a magnificent bed and an antique armoire. Sparkling crystal chandeliers light the large bathroom. Most of the rooms have fireplaces, TVs, VCRs, and all have refrigerators placed in antique armoires. Each room has a sitting area with a table for breakfast, which is cooked to order and brought to your room with silver service accompanied by a large pot of coffee or tea. Monique, Mike and Morgan definitely pamper their guests. *Directions:* When coming from Sacramento (Hwy 16) take a left onto Old Hwy 49, or take a right onto Old Hwy 49 (Main Street) when coming from Hwy 88.

FOXES INN OF SUTTER CREEK
Owners: Monique, Mike & Morgan Graziadei
77 Main Street
P.O. Box 159
Sutter Creek, CA 95685, USA
Tel: (209) 267-5882, Fax: (209) 267-0712
Toll Free: (800) 987-3344
7 Rooms, Double: $160–$325
Open: all year, Credit cards: all major

Grey Gables Inn is a pretty, soft-gray-blue house detailed with white trim sitting appealingly behind an English boxwood hedge within easy walking distance of the wonderful array of shops and restaurants in Sutter Creek. A red-brick pathway winds to the front entrance and weaves its way through a lovely back garden with fountains, vine-covered arbors, and a patchwork of flowers. Inside, the inn's ambiance reflects the owners' heritage—the Garlicks hail originally from the Cotswolds, and they have brought a touch of the English countryside to the Mother Lode. All of the guestrooms are named for an English poet. Browning, Byron, Wordsworth, and Shelley are located on the main floor, just off the entry, while Keats, Brontë, and Tennyson are found on the lower garden level. Garden-level rooms have fewer windows. Secluded away on the top floor is the Rossetti Room. All the rooms are decorated with floral spreads in hues of greens, rose, and mauve. All rooms have fireplaces, wireless internet access, most have garden views, and some enjoy claw-foot tubs. Guests settle in the formal dining room and parlor to enjoy an informal afternoon tea with cake, wine and hors d'oeuvres in the evening, and a bountiful breakfast. *Directions:* When coming from Sacramento (Hwy 16) take a left onto Old Hwy 49, or take a right onto Old Hwy 49 (Main Street) when coming from Hwy 88. Grey Gables Inn is on the west side of Hwy 49, one block north of downtown.

GREY GABLES INN
Owners: Sue & Roger Garlick
161 Hanford Street
P.O. Box 1687
Sutter Creek, CA 95685, USA
Tel: (209) 267-1039, Fax: (209) 267-0998
Toll Free: (800) 473-9422
8 Rooms, Double: $115–$200
Open: all year, Credit cards: all major

The Cottage Inn, built as a resort in 1938, offers a number of storybook cottages nestled under the trees on the edge of Lake Tahoe. The lovely cottages, all with individual themes (Bird's Nest, Bit of Bavaria) capture the mountain-cabin atmosphere with their exposed knotty-pine walls, rich fabrics, pine furniture, and a variety of beds (brass, willow, or pine). We especially admired the 5 deluxe rooms in Bear Lodge appropriately adorned with life sized wooden carvings of bears. The Pomin House, the original home on the property, contains a reception area, a breakfast room, and a large sitting room with games, books, local restaurant menus, and a small sitting area where wine and cookies are set out in the afternoons before the blazing log fire. In summer you can happily while away the hours sunning yourself on the dock and swimming in Lake Tahoe's cool, clear waters—the inn has access to a private beach. The more energetic can take advantage of the lovely bicycle trail that passes in front of the inn and travels the lakeshore drive. Vikingsholm, Emerald Bay, and D. L. Bliss Park are a short car ride south. Ski resorts are between a five-minute and twenty-minute drive away. *Directions:* From Truckee take Hwy 89 to Tahoe City. Turn right at the traffic lights and follow the lakeshore south for 2 miles to the inn on your left.

COTTAGE INN
Owner: Susanne Muhr
1690 West Lake Boulevard
P.O. Box 66
Tahoe City, CA 96145, USA
Tel: (530) 581-4073, Fax: (530) 581-0226
Toll Free: (800) 581-4073
22 Rooms, Double: $150–$350
Open: all year, Credit cards: MC, VS

From the deck of this comfortable mountain lodge you can look over the crystal-clear blue waters of Lake Tahoe to pines and high mountains—an exquisite view at any time and magnificent when the mountains are capped with snow and pink and purple hues paint a spectacular sunset. Lake Tahoe has long been one of our favorite spots in California and since we found Sunnyside we have a base from which to go skiing in winter, water skiing, sailing, and hiking in the High Sierra in summer, and revel in the beauty of the area year round. A meal at Sunnyside is a real pleasure, for not only do the dining room and deck have magnificent lake views but the food is most enjoyable. It would be a shame to stay in such a lovely spot and not have a view of the lake, which Sunnyside's rooms offer you. Several bedrooms have wonderful river-stone fireplaces—what could be more romantic on a winter evening? Sunnyside has its own marina offering boat rentals and water skiing during the summer. In winter, discount tickets for nearby major ski resorts are available. If you are unable to bring your own mountain bike, you'll find no shortage of places to rent one. Nevada casinos with their gambling and super-star entertainment are less than an hour's drive away. *Directions:* From Truckee take Hwy 89 to Tahoe City. Turn right at the traffic lights and follow the lakeshore south for 2 miles to Sunnyside.

SUNNYSIDE RESTAURANT & LODGE
Manager: Don Edelstein
1850 West Lake Boulevard
P.O. Box 5969
Tahoe City, CA 96145, USA
Tel: (530) 583-7200, Fax: (530) 583-2551
Toll Free: (800) 822-2754
23 Rooms, Double: $155–$380
Open: all year, Credit cards: all major

Tiburon is an enchanting waterfront community with million-dollar views across the bay to San Francisco. It does not draw the huge crowds that its famous neighbor Sausalito does and that is part of its charm. Its little streets are home to some enticing shops, boutiques, restaurants, and a small theater. Sandwiched between two excellent restaurants, Sam's and Servinos, the hotel is located adjacent to the ferry dock (service to San Francisco and Angel Island) at the water's edge. Appropriately named, Waters Edge Hotel is a narrow, two-story building, two guestrooms wide, spanning the distance between Main Street and the dock. Rooms 220 and 221 are the prize accommodations, water front with unobstructed views across the yacht filled harbor. All the guests can enjoy this view from the large dock-front deck. Bedrooms all have fireplaces, small balconies, smart modern decor, beds topped with white feather duvets, soaking tubs in the bathrooms and comfortable seating by the windows. Wine and cheese is served in the lobby in an evening, continental breakfast is delivered to your room. *Directions:* Located to the north of San Francisco and the Golden Gate Bridge. From Hwy 101 north or south, take the Tiburon exit east. Follow it into town and take a right onto Main Street. The hotel is located on your left. Park outside to unload. Complementary parking in the Main Street garage is included in the tariff.

WATERS EDGE HOTEL
Manager: Justin Flake
25 Main Street
Tiburon, CA 94920, USA
Tel: (415) 789-5999, Fax: (415) 789-5888
Toll Free: (877) 789-5999
23 Rooms, Double: $169–$499
Open: all year, Credit cards: all major

The Lost Whale, a gray-wash Cape-Cod house with blue trim is set on over 9 acres of windswept Northern Californian coast. The mood is set by the living room with its wood floors warmed by throw rugs and comfortable sofas arranged to enjoy not only the fireplace but also the magnificent view across the garden, through the towering pine trees to the ocean. Four rooms capture this same glorious view while two overlook the northern gardens. Whichever room you select, you will find it decorated in a light, airy style. We particularly liked the ground floor room with its gossamer draped four poster bed set beneath a skylight. Several rooms have an extra bed to accommodate a child and two have a sleeping loft. Whereas most inns discourage children, at The Lost Whale they are made genuinely welcome. Relax in the hot tub, on the deck or on well-placed chairs in a quiet corner of the garden and listen to the crashing waves and the distant barking of sea lions. Stroll down the cliff path to the 2-mile private beach or pop into your car for the short drive up the road to Patrick's Point State Park with its miles of beaches, walking paths along rocky headlands, and the opportunity to explore a re-created Indian village. The Lost Whale is a homey inn in a spectacular setting. *Directions:* North from Trinidad, take the Seawood Drive exit, turn right on Patrick's Point Drive, and drive 5 miles north. South from Oregon, exit at Patrick's Point Drive and continue south 1 mile.

LOST WHALE
Owners: Guia & Gary Hiegert
3452 Patrick's Point Drive
Trinidad, CA 95570, USA
Tel: (707) 677-3425, Fax: (707) 677-0284
Toll Free: (800) 677-7859
7 Rooms, Double: $200–$325
Open: all year, Credit cards: all major

The McCaffrey House B&B Inn is a lovely country home nestled in a grove of giant oak, pine, and cedar trees. In 1996, Michael and Stephanie built this three-story house on the lot where Stephanie's family cabin sat for 35 years. The living room and other common areas are tastefully decorated and inviting for visiting with other guests or reading a book. You will also find over 500 videos for watching in your room. The warmth of the owners is apparent throughout the inn by the family photos hung on the walls and by their love of their pets. Because the McCaffreys designed the house as a bed and breakfast, its eight rooms are spacious, comfortable, and well appointed, each with an iron fire stove with a self-timer so that you can doze off in front of the fire, and a bathroom with tub and shower. A handmade Amish quilt sets the color scheme for each room, and robes and extra towels are provided. Most rooms have a balcony or patio, and some have views down to a creek. The McCaffreys serve a complete breakfast at 9, but are happy to accommodate schedules by serving earlier. Thoughtful appointments, charming owners, and a picturesque setting make this four diamond rated property a winner. *Directions:* From San Francisco take Hwy 580 east to 205, go east to 120, then east to 108. When you reach Sonora, travel east for 11 miles, and ½ mile above the East Twain Harte exit, make a right turn just beyond the 4,000-feet elevation marker.

MCCAFFREY HOUSE B&B INN
Owners: Stephanie & Michael McCaffrey
23251 Highway 108
P.O. Box 67
Twain Harte, CA 95383, USA
Tel: (209) 586-0757, Toll Free: (888) 586-0757
7 Rooms, Double: $139–$200
1 Suite: $159–$200
Minimum Stay Required: 2 nights on weekends
Open: all year, Credit cards: all major
Select Registry

While the attractions of staying in Yosemite Valley cannot be denied, a more serene, country atmosphere pervades the Wawona Hotel, located within Yosemite Park about a 30-mile drive south of the valley. With its shaded verandahs overlooking broad, rolling lawns and a nine-hole golf course, the hotel presents a welcoming picture that invites one to while away the afternoon beside the pool, fondly referred to as the swimming tank. Bedrooms are in several scattered buildings and private bathrooms are at a premium. Hotel rooms without private baths have bathroom and shower facilities located at the end of each building's verandah. The Annex building was completely refurbished in 2003 as was the main dining room in a gracious turn-of-the-century style. This is the kind of wonderful old hotel that attracts lots of families. In the summer rangers give interpretive presentations on such topics as bears, climbing, and photography, and there are carriage rides, wonderful Sunday brunches, Saturday-night barbecues, and barn dances. Ask about the Wawona's "discounted lodging packages", which are very good value for money. Accommodation and golf packages are available in the spring and fall. *Directions:* Wawona is in Yosemite National Park, 30 miles south of Yosemite Valley on Hwy 41.

WAWONA HOTEL
Manager: Joe Alfano
Yosemite National Park
Wawona, CA 95389, USA
Tel: (209) 375-6556, Res: (801) 559-5000
104 Rooms, Double: $145–$217
Closed: early Jan to mid-Mar, Credit cards: all major

The Ahwahnee with its 123 bedrooms hardly qualifies for inclusion in a country inn guide. It is a large, bustling resort with a level of activity in its lobby that is comparable to that at many airports, yet it merits inclusion because it is the most individual of hotels, with all the sophistication of a grand European castle, surrounded by the awesome beauty of Yosemite Valley. The lofty vastness of the lounge dwarfs the sofas and chairs and its huge windows frame magnificent views of the outdoors. The dining room has to be the largest in the United States: it is gorgeous with its massive floor-to-ceiling windows framing towering granite walls, cascading waterfalls, and giant sugar pines. In contrast to the surrounding wilderness, the dining room wears an air of sophistication in the evening when guests dress for dinner and flickering candlelight casts its magical spell. Bedrooms are in the main building or in little cottages in a nearby woodland grove. There is a small swimming pool just off the back patio and it is not unusual to see deer grazing on the lawn. This is undeniably a grand old hotel but if the price tag is a little rich for your blood, less expensive accommodations in Yosemite Valley are briefly outlined in the itinerary section. *Directions:* The Ahwahnee is located in Yosemite Valley just east of Yosemite Village.

THE AHWAHNEE
Manager: Chance Jorgensen
Yosemite National Park
Yosemite Village, CA 95389, USA
Tel: (209) 372-1407, Res: (801) 559-5000
99 Rooms, Double: $439–$1015*
24 Cottages: $439 daily*
*Breakfast not included: $18
Open: all year, Credit cards: all major

Lavender is a simply delightful little inn with a superb location, just a short stroll to the boutiques and restaurants in the quaint town of Yountville. The house was built in the 1850s by the Grigsby family, early pioneers who came across the continent by covered wagon. The two-story, gray building, which exudes the flavor of a country farmhouse, is charming in its simplicity. The house was totally renovated and completely modernized inside, but great care was taken to retain the shell of the building, which still maintains its authentic historic character. On the old-fashioned verandah you will find an inviting porch swing where guests can sit back and relax. In the grounds are three cottages providing six very private guestrooms, all with fireplaces, deep soaking tubs, air conditioning, and custom-made "old-world" furniture. Our favorites are rooms 5 and 6. The vibrant colors used throughout are reminiscent of Provence, a theme enhanced by nearly 200 feet of fragrant lavender planted in the garden, forming a seasonal garland of purple around the inn. The room price includes a scrumptious full gourmet breakfast, afternoon tea, wine and hors d'oeuvres, and the use of the inn's bicycles to explore the surrounding countryside. A Four Sisters Inn. *Directions:* Coming north on Hwy 29, take the Yountville exit. Turn right at the bottom of the exit, sharp left on Washington, right on Webber. Lavender is on the corner of Webber and Jefferson, marked by a giant oak.

❄ ☕ ✄ 🖥 ☎ @ W P 🚫 ♿ 🎿 👫 🐎 🍇

LAVENDER
Manager: Gina Massolo
2020 Webber Avenue
Yountville, CA 94599, USA
Tel: (707) 944-1388, Fax: (707) 944-1579
Toll Free: (800) 522-4140
8 Rooms, Double: $250–$275
Open: all year, Credit cards: all major

The location of the Maison Fleurie is superb—a short walk from the heart of the quaint town of Yountville. The inn (with a look of the French countryside) is a cluster of thick stone and brick buildings, entrancingly draped with ivy. From the moment you enter, the mood is conducive to a carefree holiday. You come into a parlor-like foyer with a corner fireplace, sofa, and chairs. When you begin to wonder if this is a hotel, you notice a discreet reception desk in the room beyond. To the right, a few steps lead down to an inviting sitting room. The price of the bedrooms depends upon size. The most spacious rooms are found in the Bakery Building and feature king-sized beds, fireplaces, spa tubs, and DVD players. Rooms 8 and 9 enjoy French windows that open up to the garden and the pool. Carriage House, a delightful 2 bedroom cottage has room 13, overlooking the street, and room 12 bordering the pool. Maison Fleurie offers many extras: a hearty breakfast, wine and hors d'oeuvres in the late afternoon, cold and hot drinks and cookies all day. The morning paper, bathrobes, turn-down service, and the use of bicycles are additional amenities. Tucked into the courtyards behind the inn are a swimming pool and a hot tub. The Bouchon Bakery and Restaurant are just round the corner. A Four Sisters Inn. *Directions:* Coming north from Napa on Hwy 29, turn right into Yountville onto Washington Street, keep to the right onto Yount Street.

MAISON FLEURIE
Manager: Gina Massolo
6529 Yount Street
Yountville, CA 94599, USA
Tel: (707) 944-2056, Fax: (707) 944-9342
Toll Free: (800) 788-0369
13 Rooms, Double: $140–$285
Open: all year, Credit cards: all major

Index

KAREN BROWN wrote her first travel guide in 1976. Her personalized travel series has grown to 17 titles, which Karen and her small staff work diligently to keep updated. Karen, and her husband, Rick, live in a small town on the coast south of San Francisco.

CLARE BROWN was a travel consultant for many years, specializing in planning itineraries using charming small hotels in the countryside. Her expertise is now available to a larger audience—the readers of her daughter Karen's travel guides. When not traveling, Clare and her husband, Bill, divide their time between northern California, Colorado, and Mexico.

JUNE EVELEIGH BROWN hails from Sheffield, England and lived in Zambia and Canada before moving to northern California where she lives in San Mateo with her husband, Tony, and their German Shepherd.

VANESSA KALE, the talented artist who produced several of the illustrations for this guide, is a native of Bellingham, Washington. Vanessa spent her high school years in Sonoma California. After graduating in Art from U.C. Davis, Vanessa moved to southern California where she lives with her husband, Simon and son, Nigel. She works as a freelance artist. *www.vanessakale.com.*

BARBARA MACLURCAN TAPP drew many of the delightful hotel sketches and illustrations in this guide. Barbara was raised in Sydney, Australia, where she studied interior design. Although she continues with architectural rendering and watercolor painting, she devotes much of her time to illustrating the Karen Brown guides. Barbara lives in Kensington, California, with her husband, Richard, and is Mum to Jono, Alex and Georgia. For more information about her work visit *www.barbaratapp.com.*

JANN POLLARD, the artist of the all the beautiful cover paintings in the Karen Brown series, has studied art since childhood and is well known for her outstanding impressionistic-style watercolors. Jann has received numerous achievement awards and her works are in private and corporate collections internationally. She is also a popular workshop teacher in the United States, Mexico and Europe. *www.jannpollard.com.* Fine art giclée prints of her paintings are available at *www.karenbrown.com.*

Karen Brown's World of Travel

A FREE KAREN BROWN WEBSITE MEMBERSHIP
IS INCLUDED WITH THE PURCHASE OF THIS GUIDE

$20 Value – Equal to the cover price of this book!

In appreciation for purchasing our guide, we offer a free membership that includes:

- The ability to custom plan and build unlimited itineraries
- 15% discount on all purchases made in the Karen Brown website store
- One free downloadable Karen Brown Itinerary from over 100 choices
- Karen Brown's World of Travel Newsletter—includes special offers & updates
  Membership valid through December 31, 2010

To take advantage of this free offer go to the Karen Brown website shown below and create a login profile so we can recognize you as a Preferred Customer; then you can utilize the unrestricted trip planning and take advantage of the 15% store discount. Once you set up an account you will receive by email a coupon code to order the free itinerary.

Go to ***www.karenbrown.com/preferred.php*** to create your profile!

Karen Brown's
2010 Readers' Choice Awards

Most Romantic
Tickle Pink Inn
Carmel Highlands

Warmest Welcome

Chateau de Vie
Calistoga

Greatest Value
Squibb House
Cambria

Splendid Splurge

Auberge du Soleil
Rutherford

Be sure to vote for next year's winners by visiting
www.karenbrown.com